C000128192

Young, Gifted and Black

Student–teacher relations in the schooling of black youth

Máirtín Mac an Ghaill

Open University Press
Milton Keynes · Philadelphia

Open University Press
Open University Educational Enterprises Limited
12 Cofferidge Close
Stony Stratford
Milton Keynes MK11 1BY

and
242 Cherry Street
Philadelphia, PA 19106, USA

First Published 1988

Copyright © Máirtín Mac an Ghaill 1988

All rights reserved. No part of this publication may be
reproduced, stored in a retrieval system or transmitted in
any form or by any means, without written permission from the
publisher.

Title taken from record, *Young, Gifted and Black*, sung by Bob and Marcia

British Library Cataloguing in Publication Data

Mac an Ghaill, Máirtín
  Young, gifted and black: student-teacher
  relations in the schooling of black youth.
  1. Great Britain. Schools. Teachers.
  Interpersonal relationships with black
  students. Black students. Interpersonal
  relationships with teachers
  I. Title
  371.96′7

  ISBN 0–335–90508–9
  ISBN 0–335–09507–0 Pbk

Library of Congress Cataloging-in-Publication Data

Mac an Ghaill, Máirtín.
    Young, gifted, and Black : student-teacher relations in schooling
  of Black youth / Máirtín Mac an Ghaill.
      p.   cm.
    Bibliography: p.
    Includes index.
    1. Students, Black—Great Britain—Case studies. 2. Teacher-
  student relationships—Great Britain—Case studies. 3. Racism
  —Great Britain—Case studies. 4. Educational sociology—Great
  Britain—Case studies. I. Title.
  LC2806.G7M33 1988
  371.1′02—dc19   88–19523
                                                                        CIP

      ISBN 0–335–09508–9   ISBN 0–335–09507–0 (pbk.)

Typeset by Inforum Ltd, Portsmouth
Printed in Great Britain by Alden Press, Oxford

To my parents Eilís Ní Dáley agus Seosámh Mac an Ghaill agus don deichníur marbh

Contents

Preface

Racism is undoubtedly one of the most divisive and destructive features of modern society yet at the same time it is one of the least visible. In our modern democracies there are no formal structures of discrimination; no segregated buses and no laws against inter racial marriage. Yet the invisible forces of discrimination are real enough. They permeate the job market, they determine patterns of residence and they silently influence the working of all major state institutions from the health service to the police force.

The education system is particularly vulnerable to racism. It is, perhaps, at first sight, difficult to understand why this should be so. If education is about developing the abilities of individual children, increasing their knowledge and skills and enlarging their understanding of the world then surely this is one area of social life where racism can be confronted, understood and banished from the minds of young people. Unfortunately, life is not so simple. Schools are part of society and they reflect its structure.

Education, as described above, cannot develop because the space and energy it would require has been usurped by a vast competitive structure in which 'understanding' is seen as subversive if it interferes with achievement and examination success. Thus weakened, 'education' is unable to confront and challenge racism.

The struggle to redirect education to take up the problems that increasingly engulf our society and to help to equip young people with a new intelligence is an enormous task. It is easy to be pessimistic at the present time. The first stage in this process of re-equipping education is to make available analyses of major problems that are well written, accurately researched and yet challenging.

Máirtín Mac an Ghaill has provided us with such a study. *Young, Gifted and Black* is the result of two long participant observation studies, one in 'Kilby,' an all boys school and the other in 'Connolly', a 6th form college. It has been patiently and sympathetically researched to give a detailed picture of black youth/white teacher relationships in two fairly typical British schools. The book reveals that these relationships are shaped by a broader framework of powerful forces – a framework of racism. The importance of the book lies in the way Máirtín has reconstructed the perspectives of groups of teachers and black pupils so that the reader can understand their world view and empathise with their problems.

The selection of a black female group, the black sisters, gives the study great strength. Giving prominence to a group of academically successful black students challenges the stereotype of black underachievement and at the same time reveals the mechanisms that create it. These students are able to describe how classroom events and teacher attitudes affected them but they do so from the position of having overcome them. 'I stood up and said I want to see a filim and the whole class started laughing. I felt so bad inside . . . they were laughing at me . . . my parents . . . everything associated with Patois, with everything black'. The girls go on to explain how they cooperate and help each other to withstand the pressures to take up 'black, working-class female work'.

The accounts of racism as experienced by two black gangs, the Rasta Heads (Afro-Caribbean) and the Warriors (Asian) form the bulk of the study. The picture that emerges challenges explanations of black cultural responses in terms of individual psychological inadequacy or cultural deficiencies. In doing so the book exposes the contradictions inherent in white culturalist explanations. For example, the consistent picture that has emerged from studies of job opportunity (frequently carried out by white researchers) show that when qualifications are taken into account black youth are discriminated against. The extent of this discrimination is large. Clearly this structural feature of discrimination is experienced and observed by black youth who comment upon it and attempt to expose these injustices. It is these very comments and behavioural responses that are used by the white community, including teachers, to classify the complainers as 'having a chip on their shoulder' or lacking in perseverance. The study demonstrates quite brilliantly how cause and effect become intertwined to produce the destruction of relationships and a gulf of misunderstanding.

The message from this book will be interpreted in many ways. For me it contains both grounds for hope and deep misgivings about the effects of schooling on black youth. It is clear that schools cannot 'solve' the problem of racism in our society. But they should surely not contribute to it, to the extent that they do. There is no simple or doctrinaire solution to the problem but the teaching profession can make a much larger contribution than they do at present. This book contains much of the information and understanding that will enable them to do so.

Colin Lacey
University of Sussex

Acknowledgements

I am indebted to a number of people for their help, support and encouragement. Mark Duffield, Henry Miller and Andrew Pollard for their continual intellectual stimulation. Bob Burgess, Chris Griffin and Colin Lacey for their constructive comments on earlier drafts of this study. Shirley Wilkes, Margaret Rochford and Diane McCormark for their patience in typing the script. Naomi Roth, Debbie Lewis and Juliet Gladston at the Open University Press for their help. The staff at Connolly college and Kilby school for their cooperation. Finally, to the students who participated in this collaborative work for their time and comradeship. A special thanks to their parents and friends for their hospitality, and particularly to Lance Dunkley for his expert advice. The black community in Kilby and other parts of the country were my main source in coming to understand the students' experience of school and its relation to the wider society. I owe an enormous debt to them for developing my political consciousness.

Introduction

'Why do teachers hate black kids?' At the time that Paul, an Afro-Caribbean student, asked me this question I did not appreciate its significance. I wondered what made him so resentful of white people. Examining the encounter of white professionals and black working-class students[1]* of Afro-Caribbean and Asian parentage, enables us to see their views of each other and of school and their responses. For most white teachers the primary cause of black youths' 'problems' lies in the black community itself. So, the solution lies in black youth changing and adapting to the schools' demands. For the students, the primary problem is that of racism, including the teachers' racist practices, and the solution lies in the schools changing to meet their needs. Paul's question and my initial response arise out of these alternative explanations that are based on our experiences of 'different realities' (see Hall *et al.*, 1986). The main aim of this book is to look at what is going on here!

In order to describe the complexity of schooling, both from the teachers' and the students' points of view, I present four case studies. The first study looks at a group of black female students, of Afro-Caribbean and Asian parentage, called the Black Sisters, at an inner-city sixth form college in an English city, during 1983–5, who respond positively to education. The following three case studies look at the interaction of teachers and two groups of anti-school black male students at an inner-city comprehensive, in an area of black population in the same city, during 1980–2.[2]

Racism

Bringing these accounts together may serve to show the serious limitations of the dominant 'race-relations'[3] ethnic approach.[4] This culturalist perspective focuses upon the black students' distinctive cultural attributes and suggests

---

* Superscript numerals refer to numbered notes at the end of this book.

that social behaviour is primarily to be understood in terms of culture. The dominant social images constructed by this approach sees the black community as a problem. Ethnicity is assumed to act as a handicap of their assimilation or integration into British society, resulting in their relative social subordination. So, for example, the differences in the educational attainment of Asian and Afro-Caribbean students is frequently explained in terms of the pathological structure of the Afro-Caribbean family and kinship organization. This is often contrasted with the cultural unity and strength of the Asian extended family network, providing the necessary support for the 'second generation'[5] (Khan, 1979). As Khan demonstrates, some theorists working with this approach also point to the positive elements of ethnicity; thus Driver (1980) suggests that the improvement in the academic performance of Afro-Caribbean females results from the strengths of their ethnic structure, such as the strong matriarchal Afro-Caribbean family organization. However, it has been the negative aspect of ethnic differences that has been the major focus of 'race-relations' discourse. The assumptions of this culturalist perspective are shared by 'race-relations' theorists, policy-makers and welfare practitioners, including teachers and social workers, and the more repressive agents of social control, such as the courts.

Bourne and Sivanandan (1980) in their examination of 'race-relations' in Britain attack the 'ethnic school' with its emphasis on cultural relations, for detracting from the black community's real struggle against racism. They maintain that:

> Culturalism in practice leads to a cul-de-sac nationalism, defeatism, inward-looking, in-breeding incapable of changing the power relations in society . . . cultural pluralism, the framework, and multiculturalism, the solution deal with neither (institutional) racism, nor class questions. Reactive ethnicity or cultural resistance, can only be a resistance to racialism in British society. Racialism is not about power but about cultural superiority. Racism is not about cultural superiority but about power; and the resistance to racism must in the final analysis be political resistance, expressed perhaps in cultural forms (pp. 345–6).

Bourne and Sivanandan make a distinction between the experience of colour prejudice and the institutionalization of prejudice in the power structures of society, that is, a distinction between racialism and racism. They point out that the 'ethnic approach' is exclusively concerned with the former. Hall (1980, pp. 2–6) divides into two broad tendencies the work on the analysis of racially structured societies, that of the economic and the sociological.[6] Such work has argued that the study of 'race relations' cannot be reduced to models of pathology or subjective discrimination. It has contributed important insights to our understanding of the structural subordination of the black population in Britain. The economic tendency is so called because economic relations and structures are seen, in the final analysis, as having a determining effect on the nature of the social formation. The second perspective, the sociological tendency, is characterized by the analysis of 'race' within a framework capable of being defined by a number of social or cultural considerations depending on the specific context, the economy being only one of these considerations. In each of the major areas of concern in this book, these broad tendencies can be observed and will be used as a framework within which to address the primary questions of this research. Neither a sociological nor an economic analysis is adequate on its own to describe fully the schooling of black youth. The former approach in the sociology of education shows little concern for structural links and constraints and tends to concentrate on either the teachers' or the students' perspective. The economic approach leads to a similar distorted view of the schooling process with its over-emphasis on the social control function of school, with little account of the student forms of negotiation and resistance. Student–teacher interaction can be understood more fully if both levels of analysis are employed and schooling is viewed as a whole process linked to wider social processes.[7]

Let us locate the form of racism, historically and socially, that operates upon and within schools in the mid-1980s. As Gilroy (1981, p. 208) argues: 'different racisms are found in different social formations and historical circumstances'. The present-day racist ideologies and practices are examined here in terms of what Barker (1981) calls the 'new racism'. He defines the character of this as follows:

> It is a theory that I shall call biological or better pseudo-biological culturalism. Nations on this view are not built out of politics and economics, but out of human nature. It is our biology, our instincts to defend our way of life, traditions and customs against outsiders, not because they are inferior but because they are part of different cultures.

Barker is arguing that racism now tends to be rationalized in terms of cultural differences rather than cultural superiority. This notion of the new racism with its dominant conception of intrinsic cultural differences as primarily causal of social behaviour is pervasive because of its strong ideological 'common-sense' appeal within Britain. So, for example, whereas liberal policy-makers, researchers and teachers would reject the racial inferiority/ superiority couplet, they do operate with the culturalist model.[8]

The education system is part of a wider system of constraints which, often unwittingly, helps to maintain blacks in a position of structural subordination. The major problem in the schooling of black youth is not that of their culture but of racism.[9] The four case studies demonstrate that racism operates both through the existing institutional framework that discriminates against all working-class youth (see Williams, 1986) and through 'race'-specific mechanisms, such as the system of racist stereotyping, which are also gender-specific. There may be no conscious attempt to treat black youth in a different way to white youth, but the unintended teacher effects result in differential responses, which work against black youth. Different strategies, that are informed by class and gender, are adopted by different sections of the youth in their resistance to a racially structured society. These collective responses which are linked to the wider black community can be seen as legitimate strategies of survival.

Multicultural/anti-racist policy

The policy response of the culturalist analysis of conventional 'race-relations' research has been the suggested implementation of a multi-cultural curriculum. The dominant national educational policy response to the presence of black students in schools from the 1950s to the mid-1960s was that of assimilation. The concept was never clearly defined but its general meaning revolved around the idea that new immigrants would be absorbed into the existing structures of British society. The education system came to be seen as the central social mechanism for achieving this cultural absorption.[10] Williams (1967) found in the 1960s that teachers in Birmingham responded to the presence of black children by:

> Putting over a certain set of values (Christian), a code of behaviour (middle-class), a set of academic and job aspirations in which white-collar workers have higher prestige than manual, clean jobs than dirty (p. 237).

The shift in perspective to plural integration involved two stages, that of integration in the mid-1960s and an emphasis on cultural pluralism in the late 1970s. One of the earliest formulations of integration was made in 1966 by Roy Jenkins, then Home Secretary. He defined it as: 'Not a flattening process of assimilation but as an equal opportunity accompanied by cultural diversity, in an atmosphere of mutual tolerance.' It was the officially perceived problems of the 'second generation' that were now of central concern. Black youth were projected as social cripples who deserved special treatment (see Select Committee on Race Relations and Immigration, 1969, p. 31). When the Select Committee produced its next Report in 1973, they acknowledged that equality of opportunity was not being achieved and, consequently, as they had warned, the seeds of racial discord were now in operation (SCRRI, 1973). In response to the growing unrest among black youth and their parents, there was a shift in emphasis in the plural integrationist perspective. This new emphasis was that of cultural pluralism. Street-Porter (1978, p. 82) defines this concept in the following terms:

> Cultural pluralism insists that minority groups are accepted as being equal participants in society . . . where cultural pluralism is genuinely

recognised and practiced it would mean that in cases of conflict between minority groups and the indigenous population a genuine negotiation process will take place.

However, as Mullard (1980, p.17) argues, the conceptual shift from assimilation to plural integration did not mark a fundamental educational change but rather a question of means to achieve the same ends, that of the accommodation of black youth. The difference was that while the assimilationists believed that the maintenance of the 'majority culture' was dependent on the suppression of minority cultural differences, the integrationists maintained that in order to achieve this end, there must be a minimal acceptance within the curriculum of these cultural differences.

By the early 1980s the official definition of multiculturalism included a greater awareness of the effects of racism on black youth. However, as illustrated in the Swann Report (1985), the question of institutional racism was not seriously addressed.[11] Hence, it remains within the plural integrationist perspective. Solomos (1983, p. 4) points out that little progress was made with what became a catch-all phrase for describing all racially discriminatory practices. As he adds: '. . . researchers have tended to neglect the way in which institutional racist practices are maintained by relations of power that are logically prior to the decisions and non-decisions of specific state agencies'. This points to the need for the study of the power relations operating upon and within schools, if local education authorities' anti-racist initiatives (e.g. ILEA, 1983a, 1983b; Brent LEA, 1983), which see the schools rather than the black students themselves as the problem, are not to be reduced to arbitrary forms of tokenism, like many of the earlier multicultural responses. The Connolly college and Kilby school studies provide an example of such an approach.

The case studies

My concern with the study of racism in schools arose partly as a result of working with the careers teacher at Kilby school, who informed me of the high proportion of Afro-Caribbean students who were achieving poor examination results and of their resulting high level of unemployment. I decided to focus on their transition from school to work and to investigate the relationship between the Afro-Caribbean and the Asian male students' response to schooling and their future destiny in the labour market. As pointed out above, the dominant explanation of 'race-relations' research is to define the 'problem' of schooling black youth in terms of the characteristics of their communities. At this early stage of the study, I also shared the assumptions of this culturalist approach.

Using participant observation, while examining the Afro-Caribbean students' response to the school, I came to see the internal logic and legitimacy of their sub-cultural resistance to racism. This changed perception of these anti-school students led me to reformulate my research problem. Initially, I had not intended to study the teachers but, having decided to, I felt their inclusion ensured that it did not become merely an 'underdog' account.[12] Lacey (1976, p. 56) reminds ethnographers that rather than being over-concerned with the notion of objectivity, they should attempt to describe the social system from a number of participants' perspectives. I adopted this approach, with the student–teacher relations at Kilby school becoming the central concern of the study and, in so doing, developed my understanding of how their different perspectives intersected to produce a social system. Focusing on the student–teacher interaction revealed the complexity of institutional racism in a class society.

A major advantage of my research for student teachers is that it has been carried out by a practising teacher. Many probationary teachers complain that they are not adequately prepared for the reality of the classroom. They are informed by experienced teachers that educational theory is of little value to the day-to-day practice of teaching. This book pays due attention to the teachers' point of view. Their classroom practices take place within the context of an under-resourced social service, in which teachers experience low morale, low pay and decreasing professional status. It is against this background that teachers develop specific responses that act as coping strategies, faced with classes of disaffected youth, many of whom do not wish to be there. Inevitably, a critical analysis, such as is presented here, empha-sizes the teachers' negative responses. However, this book does not work with a 'blame the teachers' explanation. At Kilby school I found dedicated teachers, many of whom coped better than I with an extremely tough situation. In taking this approach, I hope that the book will help to lessen the gap between sociology and teachers, and that future teachers will see its value in helping to solve their classroom problems (see Woods and Pollard, 1988).

Llewellyn (1980, p. 42) writes of how much of the existing sociological literature on youth and education systematically neglects the question of gender, thus making it invisible. The Kilby school study as reported here appears to follow a similar approach of excluding half the population from sociological research. However, this does not reflect the reality of the ethnographic work. The black women's activities within the Kilby commun-ity, on the picket lines and on anti-racist demonstrations challenged any sexist stereotypes of them as simply the 'mothers' or the 'girlfriends' of the boys who were the main focus of this study. Furthermore, they contributed extensively to the research, providing fruitful insights into my understanding of the black community's experience of living in a racially and gender structured society. Nevertheless, the primary concern of the Kilby study was the student–teacher relations and, due to the all-male student population and the majority male staff there, this part of the book tends to focus on the position of boys and men and to neglect the position of women.

To redress this imbalance, concerning the position of black females within the school system, I carried out a second study, of a small group of young black women at a sixth form college. I had recently completed work on the anti-school black boys. I gave this study to the black female students in my A-level Sociology class. They, by and large, agreed with the accuracy of my description. This gave rise to a discussion of the boys' ways of resistance and to the different experience of and response to school by young women. This prompted me to do a detailed study of the young women's 2 years at Connolly college.

The study of black females by a white male researcher raises methodological and political questions. Meyenn (1979) found, in his study of white girls, that private areas of their lives were not discussed with him. More importantly, as Lawrence (1981, p. 9) points out, in the past researchers have failed to take into account how their relationship with black respondents may be informed by racism. It should be added that the interaction with black females may also be informed by sexism. I hope that by adopting a theoretical position that places racism and sexism as the major barriers to the schooling of black women, a position that was developed in the carrying out of this study, that I have become more sensitive to how social location in a stratified society influences one's perspective, and that this in turn informs this study.

There are obvious criticisms of the presentation of the material in this book, which results in a disproportionate amount of it being concerned with the male experience of school.[13] More specifically, why is there not a chapter on the Connolly college teachers' attitudes/strategies to the Black Sisters? And, why are the Afro-Caribbean and Asian women's experiences not reported separately as is the case with the boys? There are a number of points that I would like to make here. First, these studies set out to examine different aspects of young black students' experience of school and build on each other. So, for example, a separate chapter on the Kilby teachers was central to a detailed examination of how racist practices operate within schools. As indicated above, the Black Sisters acknowledged the accuracy of my description in relation to their own experience of school and the general explanation is applied to Connolly college. Secondly, the teachers' differential treatment of the Afro-Caribbean and Asian students in the Kilby school study emerged as a major theme. So, separate chapters on the Rasta Heads and the Warriors served to highlight that their different forms of response were underpinned by common strategies of resistance; thus, challenging the dominant teacher stereotypes of the 'troublesome' Afro-Caribbean and the 'passive, cooperative' Asian male student. Furthermore, the young women formed a single friendship group in contrast to the boys' separate sub-cultural groups. Thirdly, the Connolly college study set out to demonstrate that black youths adopt a variety of survival strategies. Having examined the differences in the Afro-Caribbean and Asian students' responses, I wanted here to emphasize their common experience of racism, that they see as overshadowing all other social determinants of their present and future lives. Lastly, the Black Sisters did not feel that the book's present organization marginalized them, though they did suggest that their study be placed before the Kilby study.

Fieldwork

Detailed notes were taken within the school and the college, that I wrote up each evening. In order to build up case histories of the students, I interviewed each of them individually and in groups. After about 9 months into each study, I began to interview the students' parents in their homes, some of whom I had met at anti-racist meetings and demonstrations, such as those in support of the Bradford Twelve (*Race Today*, 1982, p. 124) or on picket lines. Further interviews were carried out with representatives of the black community and the local authority. From data collected within the local community, I saw the students' resistance to racism within and outside of the school/college as linked to that of their parents' resistance.

Over the 4-year period of observation at the school and the college, I developed the participant-observer role. McCall and Simmons (1969, p. 1) clearly describe the variety of methods involved in this approach:

> . . . participant observation is not a single method but rather a charac-
> teristic style of research which makes use of a number of methods and
> techniques – observation, informant interviewing, document analysis,
> respondent interviewing and participation with self-analysis.

The degree of observation and participation with the students varied from almost complete observation in many school/college activities, such as interaction with teachers, to almost complete participation in leisure activities, including hanging around the park and cafes, playing football and cricket, listening to music, attending 'blues' parties or involved in 'just talk'.

Two personal details were unexpectedly of importance for my ethnographic fieldwork. First, the students identified with my Irish nationality. For example, on a number of occasions outside of school, when the Rasta Heads' or the Warriors' friends questioned or objected to my presence, the standard reply was that I was 'Irish not white', and this seemed to satisfy their objections. I had frequent conversations with the students on the effects of imperialism on our respective countries of origin, and they showed a broadly sympathetic understanding of the Irish political situation, as was particularly demonstrated on such occasions as the death of Bobby Sands, the Irish Republican hunger striker. This shared political consciousness was more explicitly developed with the Black Sisters. Secondly, the students' access to my house, which is in the Kilby area, provided a mutually relaxed atmosphere and undoubtedly contributed to the quality of the data collected. During the research period, it became a sort of local communal centre where local youth gathered. They were around most evenings and over the week-ends and vacation periods (see Everhart, 1983 and Weis, 1985).[14]

Outline of the book

In Chapters 1 to 4, I deal with the four case studies and here the results of my intensive participant observation and interviewing are reported. Chapter 1 examines the major concern of the Connolly college study, that of the schooling of black young women, of Afro-Caribbean and Asian origin. They discuss their specific response to school, that of resistance within accommodation. Chapter 2 looks at the Kilby school study's first major concern, that of the absence of teachers from conventional 'race-relations' research and answers the question of the white teachers' responses to the schooling of black boys. In Chapters 3 and 4, I deal with the second major concern of the Kilby school study, that of identifying and examining the anti-school male students' sub-cultures and answering the question of the meaning of the students' resistance to school. Chapter 3 examines the Afro-Caribbean Rasta Heads group. In Chapter 4, the 'invisibility' of a group of Asian anti-school male students, called the Warriors, is contrasted to the 'visibility' of the Rasta Heads. I discuss the relationship between class and the response to racism, both within the community and the school.

I brought together the young women and men with whom I collaborated in carrying out this research. They discussed what they were now doing, what they thought of the studies and how they saw their futures following the latest inner-city rebellions. This is presented in the postscript. The final chapter summarizes the main arguments of the book and formulates some implications for those who work with young black people. It is suggested that future policy should be informed by the students' understanding of what school means to them and the wider black community's perceptions of their own needs.

Relative to other areas of research, there has been little study of the location of young blacks, of Afro-Caribbean and Asian parentage, within the school system. This paucity of information is all the more serious, given the fact that increasing numbers of them are seen to be 'failing' at school (Tomlinson, 1981). An examination of the student–teacher relations at Kilby school and the young women's response at Connolly college provides some understanding of the dynamics of the subordinate position that these students occupy within schools. These studies are particularly urgent at a time when one of the major functions of schools, that of the preparation of youth for the labour market, is called into question, as youth unemployment is no longer seen as a temporary phenomenon but a long-term structural problem.[15]

Finally, I hope that this book will help to develop the reader's 'sociological imagination' which 'enables us to grasp history and biography and the relations between the two within society' (Mills, 1970, p. 12). For Mills, a central task for sociology is the bringing together of 'private troubles' and 'public issues'. Such an approach, for example, enabled me to shift from seeing Paul's opening question in this book about teachers as simply a 'private trouble' to a 'public issue', involving wider historical socio-economic, political and other institutional dimensions. This approach underpins the studies reported here.

Chapter 1

The Black Sisters: Resistance within Accommodation

Introduction

Clarke and Willis (1984, p. 47), writing of the transition from school to work, maintain that there is no 'one' transition for all students but rather that a number of transitions are mapped out based on the social divisions of British society, those of class, gender and 'race'. This study is concerned with the academic success of a small number of black working-class young women of Asian and Afro-Caribbean parentage who formed a friendship group within a sixth form college. I called them the Black Sisters.[1] It focuses on their strategies of institutional survival, both at their secondary schools and at the college, that were developed in response to these social divisions that pervaded their schooling and that of their lives in the wider society.

As shown later in the book, the Rasta Heads and the Warriors adopted an anti-school stance that led them to reject formal education. The young women here demonstrate that different strategies, that are informed by class and gender, are adopted by different sections of black youth. Anyon (1983, pp. 19–23), writing of the American situation, argues that the interrelationship of accommodation and resistance is an element of the response of all oppressed groups and that such a process is 'manifest in the reactions of women and girls to the contradictory situations that they face'.[2] The Black Sisters, in responding to their schooling in terms of a strategy of resistance within accommodation,[3] provide evidence in the British context to support Anyon's insightful suggestion. On the one hand, they reject the racist curriculum; on the other, they value highly the acquisition of academic qualifications. Theirs is a strategy that is anti-school but pro-education.

The black sisters

Family and educational background

The nine young women involved in the main case study were all British-born. Four had Indian parents: Smita, Nihla, Chhaya and Minakshi; one had Pakistani parents: Hameeda; and four had Afro-Caribbean parentage: Wendy, Leonie, Joanne and Judith. They all lived in the inner-city. Two of the young women lived in mother-headed families; Minakshi's father had died and Judith's parents had separated when she was 6 years old. Four of the young women's mothers worked full-time and two had part-time jobs. They were from predominantly manual working-class backgrounds; all their parents were in manual jobs with the exception of Wendy, whose mother was a nurse. Two of the young women's fathers and one of their mothers had been made redundant during the last 2 years.

The Black Sisters came to Connolly sixth form college from three large local co-educational inner-city comprehensives. The three schools had black majority student populations and white male majority teaching staffs. At the time of their fifth year, the ethnic proportions were as follows. In the first school, which Joanne, Chhaya, Minakshi and Judith attended, about 40 per cent were of Afro-Caribbean origin, 30 per cent Asian and 30 per cent white. In the second school, which Hameeda, Wendy and Leonie attended, 40 per cent were of Afro-Caribbean origin, 25 per cent Asian and 35 per cent white. In the third school, which Smita and Nihla attended, about 60 per cent were of Asian origin, 10 per cent Afro-Caribbean and 30 per cent white. In the two former schools there was a balance between the numbers of males and females, and in the latter school, a male majority. All three schools operated a system of streaming.

Connolly sixth form college

Connolly sixth form college is an open-access co-educational institution, providing 16-plus education for students of all abilities. It has a good reputation for academic achievement, with students travelling to it from all over the city. It is situated in an English city, in a working-class residential area. The college provides courses leading to advanced and ordinary levels of the General Certificate of Education, two courses in secretarial studies and a 1-year Certificate in Pre-vocational Education course. At the beginning of the period of study there were 342 students in the college and of these 198 were female and 144 male. Twelve per cent of the students on roll were of Afro-Caribbean parentage and 21 per cent were of Asian origin. It has a white male majority teaching staff.

Research methods[4]

Much of the material for the study was collected from observation, informal conversations with the Black Sisters, their teachers at their secondary schools and at Connolly college and with six of the young women's parents, and from recorded, semi-structured interviews. Comparative material was gained from shorter interviews with a small group of black middle-class young women and white young women. This material is not fully reported here but informed the carrying out of the study. This was supplemented by two questionnaires that were given to the Black Sisters at the beginning and towards the end of their 2-year course. In addition, they kept diaries for a week, again at the beginning and at the end of the period.

This study is not simply another presentation of participants' accounts of schooling, though with the limited number of studies of black young women, this would be sufficient reason to carry out such work.[5] The young women's involvement in the production of the study was not only at the level of content but, more importantly, we collaborated in the construction of its form. Being equipped with some sociological theory and concepts, which the sociology students shared with the other young women, they were involved in the selection of the study's theoretical position and with the attempt to ground the theory in the data collected (Glaser and Strauss, 1967). So, for example, there was constant reference to the material on the white young women, in order to examine the question of the specific significance of 'race' in the schooling of working-class women, and reference to comparative material on black middle-class young women, to test the significance of class divisions. The Kilby school study of the black boys' response to schooling formed the major comparative source to test the significance of gender. There was a continuing discussion of the descriptions and interpretations of the data.

The A-level sociology students informed me that my anti-racist stance within the college was of primary significance in their deciding to participate in the study. They had experienced little contact with white adults, outside the context of the welfare professions, of whom they were generally critical. They claimed that I was not like a 'real' teacher. My visiting their homes and accompanying them to such places as the cinema, theatre, Asian restaurants and anti-racist meetings enabled us to break down the normal hierarchically structured relationship between teachers and students. However, I was not seen merely as a kind of community worker, I also functioned pragmatically as a teacher in preparing them for their examinations. So, for example, our discussion of black writers, such as Alice Walker, Farrukh Dhondy, Linton Kewsi Johnson and Tariq Mehmood enabled the young women taking A-level arts and social science subjects both to experience work other than that of white male authors which dominated the college curriculum, and at the same time to use these texts as a source to develop their study skills and improve their examination technique. Initially, the young women that I did not teach were apprehensive about cooperating with the study. However, those that I did teach helped to persuade them, arguing that black women were largely absent from sociological research and that this would give them an opportunity 'to tell it from the black point of view' (see Pollard, 1985, for an account of his collaboration with primary school students).

The peer-group network

The Black Sisters did not form a traditional school sub-culture, based on specific shared values and attitudes, style, argot, dress and common leisure activities, as the much-researched white working-class male peer groups suggest is a dominant response among youth.[6] Lambart's (1976) study of the 'sisterhood', a group of grammar school girls and, more particularly Fuller's (1980) study of black girls of Afro-Caribbean origin, more accurately reflect the distinctive response of resistance within accommodation of the young women in this study (see Chigwada, 1987). However, they did not display the inter-ethnic divisions that were reported in Fuller's study. On the other hand, it was significant that the group did not include middle-class black young women nor white female students.

They came together in the first term of their college course because of shared attitudes to school as black working-class young women. This loosely formed peer group acted as a resource base for the development of their strategies of survival. They did not think of themselves as a specific sub-cultural group, but they displayed a strong sense of friendship and loyalty to each other. They made frequent contact during the day, including sitting together in lessons, spending breaks and lunch-times together, helping one another with homework and generally conversing during the day. Outside of college, they made frequent visits to each other's homes and socialized in other leisure activities. Partly as a result of this close contact, their college teachers saw them as an identifiable group.

Schooling: 'race', gender and class

In terms of the power relations operating within British society, black working-class women are located at the base of the social structure. They experience a triple subordination on the basis of their 'race', gender and class. I am not primarily concerned here with a theoretical discussion of how these three dimensions are interrelated – such work is found elsewhere (see Parmar, 1982 and Brah and Minhas, 1985).[7] However, the study is informed by this debate. For the young women in this study, racism was the primary determinant of their lifestyles outside the domestic situation, though the interaction of gender and class with racism was acknowledged.

MM: You don't seem to take class and sexism as seriously as racism. Can you talk about it like this? Do class and sexism affect your life to the same extent as racism?

Hameeda: Well, yeah, of course, you can't really escape from any of them. You can see it with the middle-class Asians here. But

the first thing that people notice immediately, I don't think
that they are going to think, a woman. They're going to
think a black and then they're going to think a woman.

MM: But what about at the staff cricket match? There it was the
young women not the blacks making the sandwiches.

Hameeda: Yeah, there the sexist stereotype was on top, but the racist
stereotypes nearly always come on top.

Smita: The sexist part and class are hidden beneath the racism.
They're always looked at secondly.

Judith: And also, you can change your class position, and if you
got a sexist husband, you can change him or leave him. But
if yer black, you can't change. But for us, I agree with you
there, we get all the three sets of stereotypes which puts us
at the bottom of society.

Racism and secondary schooling

The Black Sisters claimed that racism pervaded the three schools that they
attended. For them, the stratified streaming system was the most visible
element of the racist processes in operation within their secondary schools. In
the two schools with an Afro-Caribbean majority student population, Afro-
Caribbean students were concentrated in the lower streams and remedial
departments. The division between the 'high-achieving' Asian and white
students and the 'low-achieving' Afro-Caribbeans was further reinforced by
the process of demotions to lower streams, with the latter group being
disproportionately selected. Both the Afro-Caribbean and Asian young
women recalled many Afro-Caribbeans of high ability who were demoted
during their secondary schooling. This process of demotion is discussed
further in the next chapter.

Chhaya: There was a large percentage of blacks there [at her
secondary school] . . . that was the first thing that we
noticed.

MM: What about the whites?

Joanne: Lots of whites, but then again, you've got this streaming
haven't you? The majority of whites were in the top stream
and the majority of blacks were in the bottom streams.

Minakshi: The divisions really began in the second year, right from
the beginning.

Joanne: Yeah.

Leonie: It was the same with us. In the first year they put us in
classes and there was about ten West Indians with me in
the top stream. By the fifth year, there was two of us, girls.

Hameeda: There was a lot of West Indians with us, with just as much
intelligence but they just put them in the lower class. Like

Denton and Diane, they were the cleverest in the first year
but they ended up at the bottom.

Leonie: A teacher actually admitted to me, some of my friends
were really good but they just did not like their attitude to
them, so they put them down. They didn't even try to
understand.

In the third secondary school, with a majority Asian population, white
students were over-represented in the top streams and Asian girls were
concentrated in the lower streams.

The Black Sisters maintained that a system of racial stereotyping informed
the racist processes in operation within these schools. At one level, the white
students were seen to be treated differently, in terms of more respect and
higher expectations being made of them than black students. The young
women interpreted this as resulting from the teachers' ethnic identification
with students of the same colour. At another level, the teachers were seen to
differentiate between the Asian and the Afro-Caribbean students, with the
former tending to be perceived as of high ability, hard-working and cooperative, compared to the Afro-Caribbeans, who were seen as low-ability,
troublesome students. Both the Asian and the Afro-Caribbean young women
reported that this hierarchical system of stereotyping operated within their
schools, which had majority Afro-Caribbean student populations. In the
third school, which had a majority Asian student population, Nihla and
Smita pointed out that their teachers worked with negative stereotypes of the
Asian community. This was expressed in terms of the teachers assuming that
there were intrinsic cultural differences between Asians and whites, with the
former negatively caricatured as alien, sly and over-ambitious. This is further
evidence of what is reported in the Kilby study, that the system of racist
stereotyping in operation in schools consists of both positive and negative
elements (see Notes, Chapter 2, no. 3, p. 161).

During the research period the young women frequently returned to the
question of racist stereotypes, their origin and the power of whites to
implement them within particular social practices:

Nihla: I think that all the teachers had these stereotypes. Like they'll
say for the blacks, yes they're stupid, for the Asians, yes
they're sly and the women have to stay in the house all day
and do the housework, and yes, they have to get married
when they're sixteen and yes they have to have all these kids.
And there are no stereotypes for white people.

Wendy: No stated ones.

Judith: There are stereotypes, but it's unstated, in a sense it's not
what you say but what you don't say. You can have good positive stereotypes, that's them for whites, superior compared to
us. They measure us against what they assume they are.

Nihla: Ye don't find blacks making up stereotypes about white people.

Wendy: They haven't got the power really. Even if they do, they can't make them stick, make them affect whites.

Judith: I don't know how all these stereotypes came about but I remember reading, right, that racism. It really surprised me, you know like it surprised me to find out cancer was just cells growing too much. Well, it surprised me that racism really started because the Europeans, with all their humanitarian business, wanted to justify slavery and indentured labour. How could they justify dealing with another set of human beings in this way? By saying that they weren't human and emphasizing all these negative aspects of it, and that's how it grew up to the extent it is now. Europeans always want to justify their actions somehow, with ethics an' all that sort of thing.

Smita: And now they use different stereotypes to justify how they treat blacks in school. And they use different ones to divide Asian and West Indian kids in different streams.

As Smita indicates, the young women were aware of the operation of the system of racist stereotypes and its material consequences for black students. However, they did not overtly challenge them as they claimed the anti-school students did. Rather, here we see an example of their mode of resistance within accommodation.

Chhaya: Act typical and yer alright, do what they expect. Don't show what you really feel.

Judith: As long as you fulfil these stereotypes teachers have. I mean ye know like teachers said to us act yer age, and when ye think about it, they mean act it. They don't mean be yerself. They're always on about act this, act that. Act like white people, like us.

Minakshi: The difference between us and the anti-school ones was that we acted.

Chhaya: It's all an act, isn't it?

Judith: Well, I'm giving them that act, their act, but underneath we know really.

Racism and Connolly college

The Black Sisters maintained that racism also structurally pervaded the sixth form college. They argued that it was present at all times but became most explicit on certain public occasions, such as college assemblies, which were predominantly monocultural like most of the curriculum, with its European,

Christian focus. The young women recalled many incidents of racist practices. For example, when Judith came to the college to be interviewed for
admission she was advised to take two A-levels and an O-level rather than
three A-levels as she wished. Judith had attained five O-level equivalent
passes, four of which were grade 1 CSEs. Therefore, according to the college's
requirements, she was technically qualified to take the course. Furthermore,
she was better qualified than other white middle-class students who were
allowed to follow the course. Judith declined the advice and after much
discussion she was eventually permitted to take three A-levels.

Mrs Williams, the teacher who carried out the interview, could not recall
the particular details concerning her assessment of Judith, but she maintained
that:

> If you look at the profiles of the West Indians who come here, you will
> see what I mean. They have exaggerated expectations of their own
> abilities. There are some strong candidates but most of them come with
> a couple of CSEs under their belts and expect to take traditional A-level
> courses. The coloured girls are the worst. One told me that she didn't
> want office work. They have no idea of our standards and the work
> involved.

Here we see the teacher's assumptions that inform her differential response to
black young women. Employing explicit racial and gender stereotypes, she
generalizes from particular black student's behaviour that she has known to
the social group as a whole.

There is evidence here of how 'race'-specific mechanisms operate against
the black young women. Equally important is the way in which racism
operates through the existing institutional ideologies and practices that tend
to work against all working-class youth, albeit, taking different forms. This
can be seen, for example, in relation to the differential evaluation of the
different types of examinations and its social and material consequences.
Although CSE grade 1 is officially accepted as equivalent to a GCE grade C
pass, most of the college teachers did not in practice operate with this
interpretation. Mrs Williams informed me that in deciding that Judith was
not a strong A-level candidate, she had taken into consideration the fact that
she had taken mainly CSEs rather than GCEs. Here we see that the teacher's
differential classification of students is not overtly informed by class or racist
discriminatory stereotypes. Nevertheless, given that working-class youth in
general and black students in particular are over-represented on these low
status examinations (Rex and Tomlinson, 1979), the teachers' response in
practice serves to discriminate negatively against these subordinated groups.

During the research period, I found a number of such mechanisms involving decision-making processes that on the surface appeared to operate on the
basis of objective, value-free, technical criteria, but that in practice were
informed by subjective 'common-sense' value judgements that tended to

work against the black working-class young women's interests.[8] A further example of the subjective criteria that most teachers implemented in the placement on courses of new students, was the crude assessment of type of secondary school they had attended. Students from grammar, private and outer surburban schools were assumed to have greater academic potential than those from inner-city schools, even in the case such as Judith, who had according to the official college criteria, demonstrated that she was a 'high-achiever'. An examination of the Black Sisters' interviews to the college confirmed the operation of this differential judgement. Only one of them, Wendy, was positively assessed as a 'strong academic candidate', even though objectively they could all be so classified, as they had attained four or more grade 1 CSEs. White and black middle-class students from high-status secondary schools, who had less qualifications were assessed as of greater academic potential. It may be added that these subjective value-judgements continued to inform the teachers' differential classification and response to the Black Sisters throughout their 2 years at the college, with significant implications for the next stage of their education. In turn these negative images would form the basis on which the teachers would assess the young women for places in higher education.

Complex processes are at work here, involving the interaction of white middle-class professionals and black working-class young women who are located at the base of the social structure. Further research in this area may reveal in more detail the dynamics in operation, involving the intersection of 'race', class and gender messages, in the material and social preparation of students for adult and family life and the labour market. However, we do know that these material and social mechanisms that serve to marginalize black working-class youth are only partially successful. So, for example, in the above case, Judith, who was an outstanding student, vindicated her own high assessment of herself by attaining two grade Bs and a C in her A-level subjects, thus gaining a university place and, in so doing, overcoming and subverting the college's expectations.

Racism and cultural reproduction

Much of the literature on black youth's assumed identity problems have systematically neglected gender, thus making it 'invisible'.[9] In contrast to the social scientists' simplistic models, the Black Sisters' descriptions reveal the complex nature of cultural reproduction in a racist society. They acknowledge the specificity of their situation as English-born black young women. On the one hand, they have experienced different influences in their primary and secondary socialization to that of their parents. On the other hand, they identify strongly with their parents' culture and share with them the dominant white society's perception of them as black immigrants, with the accompanying racist response. All of the young women spoke at length of how racist definitions, with their emphasis on skin colour, determined their status as English-born blacks and its implications for their present and future lifestyles.

Leonie: When I say back home, like if I was in France and I say back home, I don't mean England [said contemptuously]. I mean Jamaica. Well, down, if you want to go to the very extreme, Africa is the home of all black people.

MM: But do you really feel that yourself?

Leonie: What do you mean, do we really? Of course. Ye have to, ye only have to look at yerself and ye have to feel it. I mean no matter where ye go, no matter what country you're in, right, the colour of yer skin's gonna tell you where you really belong is Africa in the end. Whites can't understand. I mean all, I think that's what unites all black people. Maybe some want to deny it. I mean you can go and get yerself qualifications, marry some white man and all, be middle-class, have yer little semi-detached, a posh job and all that business. Ye know, won't be doing the traditional black jobs. But when ye come down to it, ye see that black skin and there's no way that you can deny it.

MM: Can a black person do that, be successful in that way, and stay black as far as you are concerned? Does it have to be a sell-out?

Leonie: No. All I am saying is that whatever you do with yerself, right, ye just have to be part of that bond between all black people. Like you, the Irish might have a different nationality and culture to the British but yer got the same colour skin and in time you can blend in, merge all the way down and lose yer Irish nationality.

MM: If you want to.

Leonie: Yeah, if you want to but what I'm saying is that if yer black ye can't. There's no choice.

MM: Would you want to?

Leonie: Want to what?

MM: Merge in an' forget.

Leonie: Of course not. Guess there might be some people. Yer treated bad, really bad as a black person but look, like you say, look what whites have done everywhere. All that oppression. It's still good, better to be black.

Like Leonie, the other young women inverted the dominant white racist definitions of black culture, seeing it as superior to white culture.

The Black Sisters rejected the concept of themselves as being 'caught between two cultures', as 'race-relations' experts suggest, that necessarily leads to psychological problems or the need to choose between their parents' culture or that of their country of birth.[10] As they point out, culture is not a static phenomenon, made up of a deposit of ethnicity that is handed on from one generation to the next. They also challenged 'race-relations' researchers' juxtaposition of an historically unchanging traditional rural Asian and Afro-Caribbean parent culture with that of their own experience of a modern urban Western culture. Such research also assumes that their parents, particularly Asian females, are uninfluenced by the latter culture. The young women offer a more sophisticated analysis, identifying positively with black culture, they present an empathetic assessment of their parents' demands upon them.

Hameeda:	They want ye to keep their values as well as yer own, though these are not always different. They know that you are not going to live their life and they know that they can't force you to. So they let you live yer life but the thing is that when they see you going too much away from their way, they put their feet down.
MM:	What are they objecting to?
Chhaya:	Well they can't be afraid of Westernized life because they've become a part of it as much as everyone else, probably, self-respect, self-respect towards society. They care a lot about what other Indians will say. I don't agree, but I understand. It's difficult to keep yer culture and live here, but I tell them ye can't hang onto the past. India's changing. We all say this when we go back, it's not like our parents say. What you call the immigrants dreaming because of what they suffer here. I understand.
Judith:	It's the same with me. My mom romanticizes about Jamaica. She knows nothing about what the Americans are doing. It's hard for them. If yer got horrible work to do all yer life and no respect from that society, you dream. Like Marx said about religion, it's an opium. You dream about the past and things, not like my mom's friend, she talks about smashing up all the racism. I've learnt a lot from her. She knows what it's like over there and here.

An interesting development that occurred during the research was the breakdown of the Asian and Afro-Caribbean young women's culturist assumptions concerning each other and the resulting racial stereotyping. Joanne, in the following extract, describes her changing perception of Asian young women:

Joanne:	I was surprised when I saw the Asian girls outside the library in the town snogging, I mean.
Nihla:	You had the image but we always told you it wasn't true.

> Joanne: I must have seen them before but I sort of never questioned what I thought before what you said. I was working with the stereotype image, because to tell you the truth, I thought, I wish I was Asian, they've got it made. They're hard workers, ye know, I believed all that. They really know where their head is an' all my friends giving up. But after we talked about all this, I thought, those Asians must have been away from school. And, of coure, here I can see Asians that are just as deviant as us.

Joanne highlights the pervasiveness of racial ideology, which as she indicates here, partially informed the young women's 'common-sense' view of each other's social group.

'Race', gender and class

The Black Sisters claimed that at their secondary schools, the 'visibility' of their being black could be contrasted with the 'invisibility' of their being female. They were aware of the sexist ideologies and practices that structure these institutions and they offered an analysis of their experience of being black working-class females within them.[11] The distinctiveness of their situation was pointed to by contrasting their position with that of white females. The contrast with white middle-class females was of particular significance for the Afro-Caribbean young women, as the Afro-Caribbean middle-class are under-represented in Britain at the present time. The return to their secondary school of these high-achieving students and the advice on summer vacation work that they received highlighted for them the pervasiveness of the gender messages that structure black female experience of school.

> Smita: There's sexist stereotypes for all women but there are different ones for white and black women.
>
> Nihla: Yeah. Even if, there's some for all working-class girls but then again there are special ones for blacks, even for, even different ones for West Indians and Asians.
>
> Smita: There's different sexist jibes made up, white women to black women. Like you say, cleaning is associated with the black woman or the white working-class woman. It is not for the middle-class white. I mean you're not going to think that they will do your cleaning.
>
> Judith: It's especially for black women. Teachers have expectations that you will do what they think are black jobs. They think yer grandmother did this for us in our countries, yer mothers are doing it now, keeping the hospitals going and you will do it next. That's what yer here for. And in South Africa, in their own country, in their own country, black

women do it there. So they think that's all black women have ever done, all through history.

Chhaya: It's like them telling us to get into cleaning jobs.

Minakshi: Yeah, we went back to our old school, our old teachers got us all planned out for cleaning.

Chhaya: Yeah, they even told us where to go to, posh areas.

Minakshi: Yeah, to clean.

Joanne: Posh areas like Hamstead [middle-class residential area]. Don't go round here, Get yer best gear on and go down there.

MM: When was she telling you this?

Joanne: Just last holidays. We just said we couldn't find any work anywhere and she said, Oh! cleaning you'll be able to do that and it will be good experience for the future. Facety, really facety [insulting].

Minakshi: That's what they mean by work experience, for blacks. An' they even said if they had the money, they'd pay us to do their houses.

Judith: Interview techniques as well, you know, dress up nice, speak nice, go round to the posh white areas and ask for a cleaning job. I mean women, black women, slaves. Nothing has changed.

Minakshi: No wonder they taught us like they did. Great expectations!

The diaries of the young women kept while at Connolly college indicated that traditional 'female work' such as child care, office studies and banking, were still recommended to them. One of the college teachers spoke of the difficulty of advising black girls on careers and of finding appropriate work experience for them. She claimed that they had 'a chip on their shoulder' concerning low skilled work.[12] Although the Black Sisters were academic high-achievers, such expectations were extended by the white staff to them.

The Asian young women claimed that at important points in their school careers – for example, choosing subject options for examinations and in career advice – their teachers, working with racist stereotypes that were 'gender-specific'[13] advised and encouraged Asian boys to choose high-status science subjects and displayed high expectations of their academic success in higher education. In contrast, they were offered low-status subjects, often of a practical nature, and it was assumed by teachers that they would complete their schooling at 16. The young women were critical of the liberal multicultural teachers, who rather than challenging these 'race'- and gender-based divisions, responded by implementing an 'ethnic' dimension to the curriculum. So, for example, Asian girls, though not the boys, were encouraged to make Asian food in home economics lessons. They felt that the teachers considered an academic course wasted on them. For the Asian young women, the dominant image that the teachers worked with was that of them awaiting arranged marriages.

They were not agreed on how many Asian young women would in the future have arranged marriages, but they all criticized the limitations of the teachers' generalizations, which were applied to all of them. They maintained that the situation was changing with regards to the question of the amount of choice one had in an arranged marriage, and varied greatly among different Asian communities and from one family to another (Amos and Parmar, 1981). They objected to what they saw as the school's over-concern with selected aspects of their culture, such as marriage arrangements and religious practices. They argued that the teachers' tokenism led to Asians being caricatured as 'aliens from a backward country'. Furthermore, they felt that although the boys, particularly Sikhs who wore turbans, were seen as essentially different, it was especially the girls who were treated as 'immigrants'. The response of white male and female teachers, who were both seen to work with these images were, however, described differently:

> Smita: I think Indian, well Asian girls are at the bottom. I mean we are the strangest for teachers. They of course have a lot in common with whites. Then West Indians, well they don't like them but they think, even if she is black she is a Christian, talks English and all of that. But us, I always think of all the films they are making about India and the film 'Aliens' and think that you could combine them and that would be a film of how they see us. I used to think the men, the male teachers, were afraid of us.
>
> Hameeda: That's true, the women teachers they kind of patronize ye, sort of tapped ye on the head and coped that way. But the men which most of them were in our last school, they had, they thought they had nothing in common with us, like aliens really. You were the first teacher that treated us as normal. Do they get on with white girls? I never really thought about that.

Much of the conventional 'race-relations' discourse, working within a culturalist perspective, has focused on the ethnicity of black females, reinforcing these racist 'common-sense' images. A major limitation of this approach is that it makes inferences on the basis of one dimension, in this case that of 'race', without reference to other important explanatory social dimensions, such as class and gender.[14] For example, in the discussion of Asian arranged marriages, there is an implicit comparison with white young women's marital arrangements. There is an assumed continuum of choice of partners, with white young women at one end with total freedom and Asian young women at the other end forced into unwanted marriages. However, white working-class academically-orientated young women at the college challenged this assumption of a homogenized situation for all white girls. For them, academic qualifications were seen as important as a means of escaping what they saw as the inevitable 'early marriage to someone who ye had met at the disco'. Amos and Parmar (1981, p. 141), discussing the 'myth of arranged marriages', present a similar argument. They conclude that:

> ... 'choice', 'arrangement', and 'freedom' are all relative concepts and often it's people's class which determines who they meet and whom they marry, more than any romantic or idealistic notions of falling in love with 'Mr Right' who happens to fatefully cross your path. For Asian girls the amount of choice they have over whom they marry varies a lot from one Asian community to another, and from one Asian family to another. Some parents are more strict than others, just like some white English parents exercise more control over their children than others.

Two of the Black Sisters, Nihla and Chhaya, were to have their marriages arranged, but they were to be included in the selection of partners. The young women's main argument was that it was a caricatured version of their community's social arrangements that informed the teachers' racist and sexist discriminatory response to them.[15] Furthermore, this was not simply a question of teacher attitude, which they tended not to place great value on, but as pointed out above, had significant material effects, such as their placement in low-status subjects and low streams resulting in low-status examinations. These in turn were seen as preparing them for the lower sector of the labour market that their mothers presently occupied and which they hoped to avoid.

Studies in the 1970s of Afro-Caribbean males who were influenced by the ideology of Rastafarianism, emphasized the frequent references they made to 'returning to Africa'.[16] This did not necessary involve their physical movement but should be primarily understood as a central element in the process of Africanization that informed their collective resistance to racism, as is illustrated by the Rasta Heads in Chapter 3. It can be read as Sivanandan (1985b) and Hall (1987) suggest as part of the wider black community's social construction during this period of black as a 'political colour', that was established through united black resistance, involving Asians and Afro-Caribbeans, young and old, both as a community and a class. It also forms a part of the rhetoric of all migrant labour, both black and white, that is transmitted to their children, that one day they will return to their country of origin.[17]

In contrast to the Rasta Heads, the Black Sisters have a less optimistic and a more critical cultural nationalist view. This is partly explained by the decreasing overt influence of Rastafari on black youth in the region by the mid-1980s. This does not mean that this ideology is no longer of importance but may suggest, as Leonie indicates below, that its positive contribution in challenging the dominant white definitions of blacks as culturally inferior, has become part of Afro-Caribbean youths' conception of themselves. Of particular significance to the Rasta Heads' and the Black Sisters' different evaluation of 'returning' to their countries of origin was the way in which gender informed the latter's position. The young women appear to show a more sophisticated approach. For the Afro-Caribbean and the Asian young women living in Africa, the Caribbean or Asia was seen in terms of what it would mean for them as females. They acknowledged that both in Britain and their countries of origin, women experience systematic discrimination but that it takes different forms.

> Nihla: Women are exploited wherever they are. In India the sexist stereotypes are more influenced by the traditional way of life but for black women here, they have the racist stereotypes as well that they have to deal with.
>
> Smita: I think a lot of women would prefer to be back in India. Over there they think that it is better here 'coz of the higher standard of living. But once yer over here, you really see. I think that it's better for us here 'coz it provides more opportunities. In a way it is a more open society, if yer prepared to fight what they try to force on you.
>
> Wendy: In traditional societies it's hard for women but for our mothers working there may be better than the hard work here for low wages. And they miss their families, their way of life. Either way they are oppressed. I would like to go back to Jamaica but with qualifications, with a job.

The Black Sisters' response: resistance within accommodation

The young women were aware of how the discriminatory practices on the basis of 'race', gender and class operated against them within their secondary schools and at Connolly college, they nevertheless demonstrate that this does not deterministically lead to a monolithic student response of educational rejection and hence 'academic failure'. It might be predicted that such structural barriers, which result in the young women being located at the bottom of the power structure within the school, reflecting that of the wider society, would produce an anti-school perspective. There is evidence of this, in their lack of identity with their schools, but they did not exhibit the behaviour of traditional anti-school students. Their specific mode of resistance within accommodation which involved a pro-education/anti-school stance, will be examined in terms of four interconnected elements of their perception and response to schooling.

First, they adopted subtle forms of resisting the institutional demands that schooling made on them. Their teachers at the secondary schools recalled that they were both diffident and devious. Teachers at two of the Black Sisters' schools emphasized their membership of peer groups as indicative of their anti-school approach. As with the black boys at Kilby school, I found that teachers tended to perceive a group of black youth as much more of a disciplinary threat than that of white students. In both these schools the term 'gang' was derogatively applied with the accompanying implications of a criminal sub-culture.

Their resistance, which was rarely overt, included such behaviour as coming together late to lessons, completing homework late, refusing to partake in group discussion, and chatting together in their own languages and other such behaviour that challenged the schools' and the college's daily routine and rules.

The Black Sisters defied the teachers' usual classification of students. Though they rarely directly confronted the school authorities, they were perceived by their teachers as a constant potential danger to classroom management. On the one hand, their teachers at Connolly college were critical of them for 'sticking together' as a group, for 'having a chip on their shoulder' and for not communicating with them in the manner that high-achieving students normally did. On the other hand, the young women had a good attendance record, worked consistently hard, completed homework and appeared 'bright'.

Unlike traditional anti-school students, such as the Warriors and the Rasta Heads, the Black Sisters' values were not necessarily in opposition to those of the school. So, for example, Chhaya and Minakshi, shared the school's evaluation of physics as a high-status subject; what they objected to was the attempt to exclude them from following the O-level physics course which they were told was over-subscribed. They were also advised that girls normally chose biology as a science option. Without the necessary power or support to challenge this decision, they were forced to take biology. Similarly, at Connolly college, although more liberal social relations appear to be in operation, the young women sharing the teachers' high value that they placed upon A-level courses, found mechanisms of exclusion informed by racist and sexist typifications operating against them.[18]

The teachers' difficulties in assessing these students' response to schooling is related to the institutional mechanisms of control that have been developed to deal with traditional forms of deviancy. Schools have a whole range of disciplinary measures at their disposal, including corporal punishment and transferral at secondary schools, the use of sarcasm and threats, writing letters of complaint to parents, suspension, exclusion from examinations and expulsion, to deal with those who directly confront the school authorities. The following extracts highlight the teachers' dilemma and the effectiveness of the students' strategy of resistance within accommodation.

Mr Richards: They [Judith, Smita, Wendy and Minakshi] are very strange. I didn't, I mean at first I didn't think that they were as clever as they undoubtedly are. Their written work is very good, at times excellent, especially Judith. But they have a strange attitude, I mean not the usual attitude for clever kids. They sit there huddled together in the class, chatting away, never directly interrupting but not fully co-operating either, if ye know what I mean. If it was the normal case of being directly cheeky or whatever, you could handle it in the usual way but what do you do with the likes of them. I don't know what makes them tick. Give me a cheeky lad any day.

Without understanding the young women's strategies of survival, their teachers nevertheless sense their institutional resistance.

Discussing the Black Sisters' general attitude to lessons, Judith and Chhaya explained their perception of and response to their history lessons, which was informed by their strategy of resistance within accommodation.

Judith:　With me like I go into school and I listen to the teacher and I put down just what they want. Christopher Colombus discovered America, I'll put it down, right. Cecil Rhodes, ye know that great imperialist, he was a great man, I'll put it down. We did about the Elizabethans, how great they were. More European stuff; France, equality, liberty and fraternity, we'll put it all down. At that time they had colonies, enslaving people. I'll put down that it was the mark of a new age, the Age of Enlightenment. It wasn't, but I'll put it down for them, so that we can tell them that black people are not stupid. In their terms we can tell them that we can get on. In their terms I come from one of the worst backgrounds but I am just saying to them, I can do it right, and shove your stereotypes up your anus.[19]

Chhaya:　They don't think that we have any nice history like them, winning all those battles, and we write it down. They don't think all those battles, conquering all those people, they're our people.

Judith:　And they're still at it. Look at America in the Caribbean and Central America. They're so proud of all their killing.

MM:　But you wouldn't be proud of British history?

Judith:　We're not proud but they are. You only have to look at what happened with the Malvinas to see how proud they are of being conquerors and all that. A few months ago we were doing imperialism, you could sort of sense it flowing out of them, this pride.

With the Rasta Heads, I found that they perceived the school's official language as a major instrument of their own deculturization. In response they refused to adopt a standard dialect and spoke Creole within the classroom, thereby using language as a mechanism of white exclusion. The Afro-Caribbean young women in this study were similarly aware of the cultural significance of the college's dominant form of language. However, in their response, as Leonie explains below, they implemented their strategy of resistance within accommodation.

Leonie: Talking of language, people don't really seem to think West Indians have a problem. They think, they speak bad English basically. It's not true. I found the language a problem and I don't mean like learning French. It's the fact that they made you reject yer own way of talking. That really got me. It was rejecting another part of you, being black you know, being part of you. Like the teacher at junior school got mad when I said, wha instead of pardon and all that and I found out that if you did not want to be laughed at, the best way to keep in the background was to try and speak the best English I could. So, I learnt to stop saying things like filim and all that business, coz when I was in junior school and the teacher asked, what did you do at the week-end? I stood up and said, well, I went to see a filim and the whole class started laughing. I felt so bad inside, you can't understand. I mean the teacher laughing as well. I mean they're laughing at me, they're laughing at my parents, they're laughing at everything associated with Patois, with everything black. Well, I took a different attitude to most of my friends. They just stood by it and talked Patois even more.

MM: You changed your style and they didn't?

Leonie: I changed my style on appearance but deep down I kept it. I've still kept that feeling. I told my friends and some like agreed, the best thing to do was to pretend to change an' to get on. Then they couldn't look down on us, but still keep yer language.

Hameeda: That's what we all do really, most of the time, in different ways.

Although at a manifest level their practices appeared to be those of isolated individuals, they were in fact supported and worked out by the peer group network, which was not simply a school-based group but related to the wider black community. The latter point will be further developed below.

Smita: I couldn't have stayed here without them [the Black Sisters]. It's like you say when oppressed people get together, like the

> miners, like in South Africa, well in our way we feel some-
> thing deep together.
>
> Joanne: Yeah, all the black women together.
>
> Judith: We always talk about things. Help each other with home-
> work and general problems. We don't consciously act a
> certain way, I mean plan it like the Rasta Heads in your study,
> but we feel we know that we have each other's support and
> help. We have a togetherness. We all want to succeed but at
> the same time not lose where we've come from, roots and all
> that. We support each other in the way that we do things here.
> It's natural really 'coz we all belong to the same community,
> the black community.

The second element of their specific mode of resistance within accommodation concerned their relationship to other students. Much of the
literature on school sub-cultures suggests that the two main dichotomous
groups, that is, the anti-school and pro-school students, perceive each other
in negative terms.[20] The Black Sisters, who adopted a pro-education position,
might have been expected similarly to reject the anti-school students. However, this was not the case. They were critical of those who overtly resisted
education but primarily from a tactical point of view, concerning the question
of its effectiveness. Significantly, they did not dissociate their own strategies
of survival from those who adopted a different route, within the context of a
racially structured institution. This was a very sympathetic evaluation of the
behaviour of those students who were highly critical of the young women for
their apparent 'conformist' approach.

> Leonie: Everyone says that the blacks, the Caribbeans are aggres-
> sive at school but I can understand. In this country you feel
> isolated. I don't blame them but they are forced into a too
> negative view to school. Let's put it like this. We were, the
> black people from Africa right, it's the first time that a
> large mass of the population was taken away from their
> country and planted somewhere to work for someone else
> under those conditions, slavery. You know, just you
> imagine it, if the Africans dominated the world and took
> the Europeans and plonked them in Africa. Told them they
> had to work, forced them to leave their homes and fami-
> lies, everything, and then put negative stereotypes on
> them. Just you imagine if all the Europeans were forced to
> be like that. What a massive change it would be and
> wouldn't they feel a large resentment to the Africans,
> wouldn't they? I mean people say black people are aggres-
> sive and there this and that but to tell you the truth I think
> they have every right to be, especially when nothing has
> really changed.

MM: But even all of that doesn't necessarily lead to rejecting education does it?

Leonie: No, that's the kind of attitude we've taken really. I think ours is a better way, maybe for us; but maybe for the whole of the black people, those who reject school completely will prove to be a better solution. Like you say about the white working-class and the grammar schools, does social mobility for individuals help the group as a whole. If we are successful, they can point to us and say, look it can't be the school that is failing the blacks, they got through. It's just that the rest of them are stupid and lazy. It partly depends on whether we stick with the black community after all this education, then individuals can help the group. I agree with you in a racist society we have few choices.

Minakshi: We were told by our friends not to take the academic view to education. They stopped talking to us, but we thought our way better; to show that we can be successful.

Joanne: I didn't get the full impact 'till third year. I noticed they didn't want to be near me. 'Coz they sort of associated getting on in school with what white people did and if you got on in school, you must be a choc-ice. I got to understand their resentment but I didn't agree with their way of giving into the school like that.[21]

The third element of the Black Sisters' response to schooling concerns their perceptions of teachers. Unlike many pro-school students, they did not see teachers as 'significant others' (Mead, 1934). On the other hand, unlike anti-school students, they did not simply reject them. Their response to them during their secondary schooling, which caused great confusion among their teachers, was quite instrumental. They provided the means to acquire academic qualifications but the teachers' assessment of them did not appear to affect them greatly. Two black female teachers were seen as an exception to this general functional response. For the Black Sisters, these two teachers were caught between the frequent rejection of black students for failing to identify with them against the white teachers and not being fully accepted professionally by the latter. The young women, particularly Wendy and Hameeda, who wished to be teachers, could see this as a possible major problem in their own future working situations. Their more general response to teachers continued at Connolly college, with neither teacher criticism or praise appearing to enter into their criteria of judging their own achievement.

The fourth element of the Black Sisters' pro-education/anti-school position is highlighted in their evaluation of academic qualifications. In a questionnaire concerned with what they saw as most important in school, all the young women in the main case study put qualifications in first place. In interviews with them, they indicated that their assessment of the value of high-status academic qualifications involved a number of dimensions which can be seen to be related to their social location as black working-class females in an institution and wider society, stratified on the basis of 'race', gender and class.

Like the young women in Fuller's study (1980), in contrast to the teachers' view of them, to which they were largely indifferent, academic qualifications were seen as a more neutral and objective evaluation of themselves. High-status qualifications served to publicly confirm their own high assessment of their own worth. They also served to indicate to others that black women can be successful in the mainstream areas of school knowledge that are the traditional preserve of white students. They further served to challenge racist and sexist assumptions about so-called 'black female skills' by refusing to be directed by teachers into marginalized sectors of the curriculum, such as home economics, music and sports.

Hameeda: I don't care what teachers think really. It's examinations that matter.

Nihla: Yeah. They're real proof that we are as good as anyone else. The teachers never thought much of us anyway, but we've proved them wrong by being successful, successful in the academic subjects, not just the practical subjects and their CSEs.

The Black Sisters were conscious of their own preparation for the important stage of the process of the transition from school to work. They were aware of the increasing competition for the scarce jobs in the local economy and of the disproportionate negative effects of the economic depression on their destination as black working-class females in the social division of labour. Hence, academic qualifications were also highly valued as a means of exchange in the labour market. They were seen as providing the opportunity to escape traditional 'black working-class female work' and avoiding the more recent development of the youth training scheme, which many of their brothers, sisters and friends had found disillusioning in not providing 'real' jobs. Most of the young women applied for higher education.

Joanne: Ye can't get anywhere without qualifications. We have to be better than the whites if we want to get away from the usual cleaning jobs an' shop work we're offered. I sometimes think that they built the hospitals, railways an' all that to keep us working.

The Afro-Caribbean young women maintained that their gaining academic qualifications and their exchange for 'good jobs' would provide an effective model for aspiring black youth. For them, the absence of Afro-Caribbeans from professional jobs served to deflate black youths' ambitions. Hence, qualifications were seen not only as a means of individual social mobility but also had intended implications for the wider black community. So, for example, Leonie, who got two Ds and an E at A-level, repeated a year in order to qualify for a university place. She explained that blacks were always pushed into an inferior position within the school, as she had experienced, having been entered for six CSEs at secondary school and attaining five at grade 1 and a grade 2. She argued that to accept a place at polytechnic would be to continue this historical process of accepting 'second best'.

Both the Afro-Caribbean and the Asian young women discussed their acquisition of qualifications in relation to black males. The Afro-Caribbean young women spoke of why black females appeared to be more successful than Afro-Caribbean males at school. They believed that the latter were more 'visible' to the teachers than other anti-school students in their mode of resistance. The Asian young women agreed that the Afro-Caribbean males were 'most likely to get picked on' because of the system of racist stereotyping in operation within schools, with Afro-Caribbean boys being perceived as the main troublemakers. Hameeda challenged the findings of the Rampton Report (1981), which argues that Asian students achieve higher academic examination results than Afro-Caribbeans. She maintained that the Report failed to take into account the class dimension and that Asian working-class males and females were also failing.[22] This question of Asian success and class is further explored in Chapter 4, on the Warriors.

> Hameeda: They don't look at the backgrounds, their social class. Lots of our friends are also failing. Those who are successful are middle-class ones who have financial backing. They have businesses behind them, but they don't look at this do they?

The Afro-Caribbean young women argued that many boys tended to inter-nalize the dominant racist image. Hence, they were successful in sport and music but fulfilled teachers' low expectations of their academic performance, resulting in a self-fulfilling prophecy.[23] The young women explained that they were less influenced than boys by their peer groups and so had greater freedom of choice in how they responded to school.

> Leonie: Without realizing it, I think they may start believing the stereotypes and I don't know. There's to tell you the truth, there's a saying that the blackman's ignorant and in a sense it's true.
> MM: What do you mean? Compared to black women?
> Leonie: Yeah. Oh! I don't mean stupid like the racists say, none of that. I mean not fully aware. I'll tell ye black men are not perfect. They're easily influenced to tell you the truth, they really are. I think women, all women are more independent,

> more strong minded. It's like those women ye told us about, they have to be strong just to survive. I think the boys, at our last school, had more pressure from each other.

However, as the young women pointed out, in their secondary schools and at Connolly college, academic success and failure cut across gender divisions.

There was disagreement among the Black Sisters concerning the value of the total rejection of school. As shown above, they tended to see their own strategy of survival as more effective. However, Leonie claimed that she could understand the response of overtly dissociating from a racist institution. She recalled that when she was starting secondary school Rastafarianism was an important influence, particularly on the boys. She emphasized the positive contribution of this influence at this period in attempting to establish the cultural superiority of the black community. She compared the political significance of Rastafarianism in the late 1970s in challenging the dominant white ideology, to the more recent development among black youth of what she saw as the cultural ghetto of black dancing, with their preoccupation with body-popping.

For all the Black Sisters', academic qualifications were seen to be important in relation to the domestic division of labour, in which they, like all females, experienced an unequal distribution of the housework. The Asian young women believed that academic success would strengthen their position in arguing that they were equal to their brothers and so should be given equal treatment. Furthermore, higher education would help them to establish their independence from their homes and to develop a new relationship with their parents that was less structured by traditional gender expectations.

Wendy: The woman has to do the housework. She is socialized from an early age to do it. You kind of learn that you are there to look after the men. Well yer supposed to. I never would.

MM: What about your brothers?

Joanne: They don't have to take part in the work really. But I think black women have more positive images of independence than white women. Just like my mom.

Minakshi: He's the boy. He doesn't do the work. You're the girl, you do the work.

MM: Do you think that it's any worse than in white families?

Smita: It's the same. The researchers on 'race' forget to mention it's just as bad for white women like the feminists say.

Chhaya: The general sexism is the same. The white girls on your questionnaire said it. But for Asians, well this is what we know from experience, they place greater, they've got greater respect for the boy. It comes from the property, the passing on of property. The male carries on the family

	tradition. They have always given greater respect to the boy. They always have done and they always will.
Smita:	Though the times have changed, they prefer the boy to the girl. But we hope that with good qualifications, we will be accepted as more equal.
Nihla:	Probably it will lead to that. In middle-class families the girls have more freedom. They're more liberal. Our parents won't change their ideas completely but they get used to ye giving more time to yer homework. Then when you get to university it may change and you will have greater freedom. And if the boys are at home while you're away, they will have to do their share. So, they will then all get used to it.

Conclusion

The Black Sisters' response to school and college appears to be highly instrumental, that is, knowledge is not valued for its own sake but as a means to an end, that of gaining qualifications. This response is not specific to academic orientated black females. On the contrary, traditional high-status knowledge as embodied in the A- and O-level GCE examinations has always been perceived as more vocationally orientated by both teachers and students than is officially stated.[24] However, a high evaluation of qualifications does not necessarily mean that all students share a similar assessment of their worth. A dominant theme within the sociology of education has been the metaphorical ladder of individual social mobility that school enables one to climb by exchanging a highly valued commodity – qualifications – for a 'good' job. This study indicates that the black working-class young women's motivation in working to be academically successful cannot be reduced to aspirations of individual social mobility.

In a socially divided society, in which the selection of knowledge, both in its form and in its content, tends to reflect the dominant groups' interests, it will inevitably offer little intrinsic value to such subordinated groups as the Black Sisters. Hence, their anti-school instrumental response to the official curriculum, which is a most effective strategy of survival in a racially and gender structured system that operates to exclude them. Equally significant is the fact that more than any other social group they do value knowledge not only as a means of economic survival but also as a means of social, psychological and political development. These Afro-Caribbean and Asian young women challenge any notions of conformity and passivity. They are proud to be black and female and are a central link in the black working-class community's struggles.

Finally, it is not suggested here that the Kilby school and Connolly college studies can be read as suggesting, as Driver (1980) argues, that the major determinant of black youths' educational achievement is that of gender response.[25] The Rasta Heads, the Warriors and the Black Sisters all identify racism as the major problem in their schooling and, as the Black Sisters point out, their different strategies of resistance to racism cut across gender divisions, with girls at their secondary schools totally rejecting school and boys sharing their pro-education/anti-school position. This needs to be kept in mind while reading the next three chapters, which examine the student–teacher interaction at Kilby school. I begin with the teachers' responses to the students.

Chapter 2

Teacher Ideologies and Practices

Introduction

This chapter examines the teachers' ideologies[1] and practices in operation at Kilby school and their effect on black male students of Afro-Caribbean and Asian origin. There are five broad areas of concern. First, an historical view of the development of the construction of the white staff's social images of the black community. Secondly, the identification of the different teacher ideologies and, thirdly, an examination of the relationship between these ideologies and the dominant monocultural educational perspective within the school.[2] The liberals' adoption of a multicultural approach is seen as a development of earlier educational reforms which were based on explanations of educational underachievement that focussed on working-class students' assumed cultural deprivations. Fourthly, an analysis of the teachers' racism with a particular focus on the process of racist stereotyping[3] and, fifthly, I shall examine the effects of this process of stereotyping in relation to the system of classification of students.

No simplistic division can be made between the Old Disciplinarians and New Realists, as representing a reactionary racist force in contrast to the liberals' progressive anti-racist ideology. Rather, it is shown that while the former groups tend to be overtly involved in racist practices, the main liberal position also serves to maintain a racially structured institution. The inconsistencies between the liberals' ideological position and their practices cannot simply be reduced to a question of the inevitable contradictions of adopting a subtler form of social control in a racially structured institution based on persuasion rather than coercion. The contradictions and limitations of the liberal educational ideology have a material base, an important element of which is the bureaucratic nature of the teachers' professional career structure (see Ball, 1987, p. 166, on 'politics of career').

There are important differences between the teacher ideologies which are explored in detail, but all these ideologies work from within a common educational paradigm, with a set of shared assumptions, from which emerge certain issues that are defined as problems.[4] Of primary significance is the teachers' shared perception of the black community itself as constituting the 'problem' in the schooling of black students. The ideological construction of this 'problem' by both the authoritarian and the majority of liberal teachers takes place within a culturalist perspective which assumes a class homogeneity of the black community and which operates with a differential response to students of Afro-Caribbean and Asian origin. Of central importance in defining this response is the relationship between the process of racist stereotyping and the system of classification in operation at Kilby school, which as part of a wider process of racism tends to structure social reality at the school. An examination of social background differences of the Afro-Caribbean and Asian students challenges the teachers' classification of them in ethnic terms. More particularly, such an examination will serve to demonstrate the racist nature of the teachers' ideological 'common-sense' division between the 'high-achieving' Asian student and the 'low-ability' Afro-Caribbean student. Before examining the areas of concern, I shall briefly describe the structure and location of Kilby school.

The school and the community

The school

Kilby school is an 11–16, four-form entry, boys only, comprehensive school situated on a single site. At the time of the research there were 580 students on roll, of whom 382 were of Asian origin 162 of Afro-Caribbean origin and 36 were white boys. There was a low staff turnover among the 33 full-time teachers and 3 part-time teachers. The senior management of the school consisted of head teacher, deputy head, head of upper school, head of lower school and two senior teachers. The school had a good reputation within the local community as a place that maintained high disciplinary standards and seemed to manifest little trouble. A further description of the school's structure and personnel will be examined later in the chapter in relation to teacher ideologies.

The community

Kilby school, which has Social Priority Status, is located within an inner-city suburb. In the early 1970s, Kilby was regarded as one of Britain's main black 'problem' areas. It was then described as a former prosperous residential area which had deteriorated into a typical decaying inner-city suburb with the usual multi-deprivation problems, characterized by lack of good employment opportunities, inadequate housing and social amenities and general disillusionment among the young. For the white population, this deteriorization was associated with the arrival of black immigrants. In the late 1970s other researchers challenged the popular image of the area as a black ghetto, pointing out that there were as many elderly white people as of black of all ages resident there. Its changing ethnic composition during the last 30 years may be summarized as follows: in 1951 it was a largely white working-class area, with a high proportion of Irish immigrants, by the early 1960s there was a significant number of Afro-Caribbeans who outnumbered Asians by three to one, while by 1971 it was the Afro-Caribbeans who were numerically marginally the minority. This trend has continued in the 1980s. Comparing the census figures for 1971 with those of 1981, reveals that the number of Caribbean-born residents in Kilby has continued to fall while the number of Asian-born residents has risen (Census, 1981).

Researchers in the late 1970s described the variety of different housing situations in Kilby, including owner-occupiers, private renters from private landlords, or housing associations and council tenants living mainly in old terrace dwellings or larger villa-type houses, some of which are multi-occupied by a number of families. A majority of the students lived in owner-occupied houses within the immediate vicinity of the school. In terms of housing, Kilby has a long history of development in contrast to the demolition of old houses and construction of high-rise dwellings in neighbouring areas. The students often spoke of council improvements to their homes and this undoubtedly contributed to their positive view of Kilby, although much of the housing still lacks amenities and looks in decay, as is true of the area's social amenities.

In terms of the industrial structure of the area, the metal industries – that is metal manufacturing, engineering and allied industries – play a dominant role in the economic life of the region. For black males, the metal industries represent typical forms of employment, especially the unskilled sector in foundry, forge and furnace work and other general labouring where they are over-represented. Similarly, the occupational structure for females shows that black women are over-represented in factory and hospital work. Much of this information is derived from published material on Kilby, but in order to maintain the area's anonymity, the names of the researchers will remain undisclosed. My own research into the occupations of the students' parents confirmed the above findings, with most of them involved, or formerly involved prior to redundancy, in these jobs and, for a significant proportion of them, their places of work were situated in neighbouring areas. The research was carried out at a time of growing mass unemployment, with over 2.5 million registered unemployed by July 1981, which has had a particularly harsh effect on the region.

Within Kilby the black community were disproportionately affected by unemployment because they were concentrated in declining industries. For black youth the situation was even worse, with almost a 50 per cent reduction from 40 per cent to 21 per cent in the total numbers entering employment within the region, during the period 1978–80, and within Kilby one out of every two white youths found work compared to less than one in three black school leavers. Furthermore, these figures underestimate the 'real' total. Examining information from Kilby's career service on the Kilby school leavers over the 5-year period 1978–82, revealed the limitations of the official statistics, with a number of students not registering and a disproportionately high number participating on the youth training schemes, which offer little hope of permanent employment (Cross and Smith, 1987). It is against this background of regional decline that I shall present a brief history of Kilby school.

History of teacher–student relations

National and local response

In order to understand more clearly the more specific history of the teacher–student relations at Kilby school, we need to examine the relationship between national and local developments in response to the schooling of black students. Kirp (1979) points out that Britain at a national level has adopted a policy of racial inexplicitness in education by subsuming the needs of 'ethnic minorities' under the more general categories of urban deprivation and educational disadvantage. This decentralized approach gave the Local Education Authorities a great deal of autonomy. However, many authorities have not taken the initiative to develop coherent strategies in the absence of an explicit national policy (see Dummett and McCrudden, 1982, Arnot, 1986 and Troyna and Williams, 1986 for discussion of policy).

The development of specific ideologies is an uneven process. So, while it is true that the dominant response of the white staff at Kilby school, including management, teachers, secretarial and domestic workers, to the black students was largely to reproduce the generally held racist stereotypes, developed in national policy, nevertheless, the local political circumstances determined the differential rate of appearance and development at this level. Three main stages can be identified in the historical development at Kilby school of the construction of the staff's social images of the black community that demonstrates the relationship between the national and local levels. The first stage was concerned with the initial interaction, with the black boys' arrival in the early 1960s, of the staff and the students. The second stage, which built on the earlier stereotypes, was in response to the growth in the early 1970s of a majority black student population. Thirdly, in the mid-1970s there was a shift away from an emphasis on cultural superiority to one of cultural differences.

Construction of staff's social images

First stage: initial interaction

Mrs Shepherd, a white domestic who had worked at Kilby school for 21 years, explained that when it opened there was among the predominantly white population high expectations of their new local secondary modern school. Her more recent negative perception of it is associated with the arrival into the area of the black community. Mrs Shepherd:

> It opened in 1959, we really looked forward to it, our own school. It was a beautiful school then. It was all white, now its all wrong. My two sons came here. It was still a good school then. The rabble have only come in the last ten years. First four came, then eight, then sixteen the next year, now it's over a hundred and a few whites, if you can get that. Mr Wilde [former headteacher] made the kids come in the back way. In those days there was no running around the school like there is now, everything's gone now. You were regarded as a snob if you lived in Kilby. Now if you say you work here, they regard you as riff-raff. Things have changed a lot since this lot took over. They should never have let so many of them come here should they? It's a wonder I haven't turned black I've been here so long.

It was during this early interaction between the white staff and black students that there emerged among the former group a social pathological view of the black community. Mr Willis, a former senior teacher at the school during this period, confirmed this view:

> Things were tough then, much tougher than now. I mean for individual teachers. In those days the first children who came to school were really a displaced generation. The families were broken up. There were lots of social problems, every type of problem, like culture shock, identity problems, a migrant population coming to terms with city life. It was very tough to have to cope with all this and try to teach.

Many of the teachers' social images of the black community in the 1960s emphasized the superiority of British culture. These crude racist images were historically linked to British imperialism. Mr Fleming, a former history teacher, remembered the arrival of the black students and offered an explanation of the 'problem black population' which, he claimed, had much popular support:

> They were seen as a threat really, a threat to the civilized standards of our society, of British society. They were seen as underdeveloped, backward, that is from backward countries, and from their rural

backgrounds they were unable to cope with the demands of a highly-advanced industrial society. They couldn't, especially the Indians. They had low standards at home, like their crowding, not because they had to, they preferred it. There was lots they couldn't cope with, like British toilets. The white workers were forced to ask for separate facilities; and the noise. The coloureds, the West Indians, had parties all the time.

These racist stereotypes were not simply locked away in individual teachers' heads. By the end of the 1960s they were translated into social and material responses. First, there developed among the staff a social acceptance of a high degree of overt racism. Mr Dempster, a senior teacher, described the situation during this period:

> People, teachers were much, were much more openly prejudiced. The West Indians were talked about as belonging to the jungle and all that sort of thing. Remember, it's often forgotten but in schools things like size are important. First years are easily, more easily controlled than fifth formers. Well, then teachers were confronted, it was always thought of as confrontation with big West Indians. They were challenged, so they resorted to derogative labelling. It was a kind of defence mechanism. And with Indian kids when they first arrived, there was a lot of talk about them being sly, pretending they couldn't understand you if they got in trouble.

Secondly, a more coercive disciplinary policy was adopted, including more frequent use of suspensions and corporal punishment. More significantly, this authoritarian strategy was backed up by an informal process of 'official bullying'. At this particular time there was much visible resistance among the students which often displayed itself in physical terms. In order to incorporate the boys into the school, the teachers met force with force. Mr Young (teachers' departments are not indicated in order to maintain anonymity) recalled these strategies:

> There's a lot of liberals here now compared to then. They were fascists – selected teachers, like the two PE blokes were used as a deterrent against the big West Indians, and if it broke down, they layed in against them.

These adopted strategies were the practical response to the assimilationist perspective with its attempt to absorb black students into British society.

Second stage: majority black student population

The second stage of the development of the teachers' negative racist stereotypes was in response to the growth of a majority black student population in the early 1970s. This was partly a result of the education authority that Kilby school is located in, which decided against the implementation of the policy of dispersal which was officially sanctioned in 1965 by the Department of Education and Science. As researchers have pointed out, the authority's decision was not based on the needs of the black community but was an attempt to contain assumed low academic standards spreading to every school in the city. Nevertheless, although at the local education authority level these crude mechanisms of control were rejected, individual schools responded differently to what they saw as a crisis of majority black schools.

The response at Kilby school demonstrates that the development of educational perspectives is an uneven process. Whereas the DES by the mid-1960s had incorporated an interventionist approach to multicultural education, it was not until the early 1970s that it was adopted at Kilby school. The policy-makers at the national level were responding to the black community's protest against racism within the schools. However, whereas black parent and student movements had successfully emerged in London, this organization was not as effective in Kilby. For example, the placement of Afro-Caribbean children in Educational Sub-Normal (ESN) schools was a central issue in other parts of the country but this issue was not at this time a major focus of local activity in Kilby's local authority (see Coard, 1971). This was partly as a consequence of an attempt by the local education authority to keep 'problem' students within the main schooling system. So, we can see that each local education authority has a certain autonomy and, in response to local conditions, it structures its own social reality at an institutional level and implements its own individual strategies within the schools.

What emerged at Kilby school from the earlier encounter during the 1960s of the white professionals and black students was the juxtaposition of the 'high-achieving conformist' Asian student and the 'low-ability, troublesome' Afro-Caribbean student. Whereas during this earlier period, it was believed that a 'colour blind' approach should operate, of treating all students the same, by the 1970s there had been a shift to a more interventionist strategy.

Partly in response to the frustration felt by many of the teachers against the local authority's refusal to 'disperse' black students, a highly stratified internalized system was adopted. The powerful caricatures of the Asian and Afro-Caribbean students which operated within the school informed the structuring of this approach. The abitrary selection mechanism for assigning students to different streams led to Afro-Caribbean students who were of 'higher ability' than their Asian or white peers being placed, on subjective behavioural grounds, into the lower streams.

Mr Johnson described the situation during this period:

> The coloured boys, there were a lot of them by the early 1970s. They were nearly all in the lower ability bands. We often didn't have a choice because we couldn't find special schools for all the troublemakers. Suspensions weren't really a deterrent. The authority were all for

keeping them within local schools but really they needed specialist help. Often much older boys were in the same classes with boys much younger than them. It was difficult to know their ages. They were, many of them, were so big. The coloured boys always ended up at the bottom. It was not always because they weren't bright. They were the worst behaved ones. It was their aggressive attitude. They went wild if you disciplined them. You couldn't reason with them. The problem was there was too many of them, too many problems.

What emerges from the relation between this stereotyping of Afro-Caribbean 'truculence' and Asian 'conformity' and the streaming process which discriminates against Afro-Caribbean students, is the way in which this racist practice at a local level served to reproduce these racist stereotypes that were already contained in national policy. The material response of implementing a tight stratification system at Kilby school demonstrates the streaming process's own dynamic in serving to reinforce the teachers' social definitions of the black students. There was now firmly established a strong differentiation among the perceived Asian students' 'technical problems' and Afro-Caribbean students' 'behavioural problems'.

Third stage: cultural superiority to cultural differences

During the mid-1970s there were significant structural changes at Kilby school. A new headteacher was appointed and the school officially became comprehensive. Also, at this time, there was the emergence of a group of teachers whose liberal educational ideology challenged the dominant authoritarian ethos of the school. The latter's perspective was considered to have failed and to have contributed to the hostitility between staff and students. The headteacher introduced a new radical pastoral system with the appointment of a new head of social studies, a head of upper and lower school and a tutorial system to operate in all years throughout the school. Corporal punishment was rarely used and its use restricted to the headteacher and deputy head.

It was during this period that there was an ideological move away from an emphasis on racial superiority to one of racial differences. In response to these perceived differences, a number of teachers attended multicultural courses to learn more about the students' home backgrounds. The religious education syllabus adopted a multi-faith approach and the English and History departments included multicultural material in their courses. These interventionist techniques were rationalized in terms of the specific cultural needs of the black students. Mr Harris explained this shift from assimilation to plural-integration and the perception of the special needs of the 'different ethnic groups':

It was thought that we could treat them all the same. The old assimilationist argument of creating a melting-pot, in fact in practice it means treating them all as white. Our idea, I mean the idea we worked with was to treat all cultures as equal and show them as equal inside the school. This will help create a multicultural society. But we were realistic, in fact, perhaps we weren't at first. We tried to balance out the negative images by concentrating on the positive ones but we began to see the effects of cultural differences. How could the West Indian kid from a one-parent family compete equally with a child from a good background? These kids have so many difficulties, social, educational, etcetera. I don't mean only the West Indian lads. The Asian kids often don't know whether they're coming or going between the two worlds they live in, and not belonging to either one really.

With the displacement of the earlier coercive disciplinary methods, psychology became of central significance. Educational psychology functioned, albeit unintentionally, to legitimate the racist classification of students. The over-representation of Afro-Caribbean students in the lowest streams of the school was justified in terms of 'common-sense' educational categories of ability, attitude, aptitude, etc. These ideologically constructed 'common-sense' concepts were still in use at Kilby school during the research period and will be examined critically later in this chapter.

Summary

A number of concepts of the black community have developed in the last 25 years which form the basis on which research workers and policy-makers have prescribed, and teachers have attempted to implement, proposed solutions. The above demonstrates how these three groups have each reproduced each other's social definitions. These early social images were further reinforced by the school authorities' material and social response to the schooling of black youth and their resistance. The history of Kilby school shows that the initial coercive policy that operated during the 1960s was challenged by a more liberally-inspired ideology of meeting the 'special needs' of black students by attempting to implement a multicultural curriculum. However, the growing contradictions of this attempt to attain educational equality of opportunity for black boys in a racist society led to a return to the adoption of a more authoritarian approach.

The conventional psychological and sociological concepts that are in use in the early 1980s to explain the 'educational failure' of black students were developed at an earlier period in response to the schooling of white working-class youth. However, the encounter of white professionals and black youth has its own particular significance. Racism as an ideology is mediated through the existing bureaucratic educational framework. The specific meanings and concrete practices that have developed in relation to this sector of the working-class is examined in the rest of the chapter.

Teacher typology and school ethos

Teacher typology

There were 36 teachers on the staff at Kilby school. They could be divided into three groups: the Old Disciplinarians, the Liberals and the New Realists.[6] An ideal type of each group would read as follows.

The Old Disciplinarians (OD)

A member of the National Association of Schoolmasters/Union of Women Teachers (NAS/UWT), common-sense ideological approach to learning, opposition to progressive development in educational theory, supported hierarchical nature of school administration and organization of curriculum in terms of streaming, subject-based, adopted an assimilationist perspective, pro-corporal punishment.

There are roughly 17 teachers who are termed Old Disciplinarians. A criterion for inclusion in this group was not that of middle-age, in fact many of these teachers were in the age-group 30–40. But the authority and main influence of this group lay with the six older teachers. Two of the four women members of staff belonged to this category. The interaction in the staffroom reflected the ideological divisions between the teachers. The Old Disciplinarians tended to sit together at one end of the staffroom and were criticized by the Liberals for their preoccupation with playing cards and dominoes during lunch-breaks instead of discussing educational matters (see Hargreaves and Woods, 1984).

The Liberals (L)

Late 1960s college-trained, member of the National Union of Teachers (NUT), often supporter of the Labour Party, theoretically-based pedagogy, applied new educational technology, strong bias to use of psychology, supported child-centred learning, emphasis on pastoral work, supported mixed-ability teaching groups, adopted a culturalist perspective, against corporal punishment.

There were 10 teachers who were classified as Liberals, including the two black members of staff. Their composition, which reflected that of the Labour Party in Britain, was very much an alliance of a broad church of active social democrats with the exception of a recent member of staff who was committed to revolutionary politics. The Liberals had regular school-based union meetings and a majority of them attended local branch meetings on a regular basis. Six of these teachers were in the age group 30–40, three were in the 25–30 age group and one was aged 50. A number of them had attended comprehensive schools and had been college trained, which they believed was largely determinant of their liberal ideological position. This group of teachers had close professional contact with an educational psychologist attached to the school, who visited regularly. They were responsible for the multicultural curricular changes within the school. In contrast to the assumed atheoretical position of the Old Disciplinarians and the New Realists, the Liberals were constantly updating their teaching practices with recent educational theory. It was here that they often found themselves in disagreement over the implementation of these new developments. For example, a minority of the Liberals were shifting to an anti-racist perspective, while the dominant view was that of plural culturalism. Their theoretical divisions contrasted with the apparent unity of the Old Disciplinarians and the New Realists.

The New Realists (NR)

Late 1970s graduate, often member of the Professional Association of Teachers (PAT), returned to common-sense educational ideology, acknowledgement of the failure of the 1960s educational reforms, accepted organizational structure of the school, tendency to authoritarianism, adopted assimilationist perspective, main concern insecurity of job.

There were five teachers who are termed New Realists. They were all recently qualified and products of the educational move to the Right. This was the first teaching post for three of them, while the other two had experienced supply teaching and were on 12-month contracts at Kilby school. They believed that teacher organizations should act as professional groups rather than adopt trade union tactics. Two of these teachers had left the NAS/UWT over the issue of the withdrawal of goodwill, concerning the carrying out of extra-curricular activities. They joined the PAT which is committed to a policy of non-striking. Although the New Realists are small in number, they were a significant group who tended to act in alliance with the Old Disciplinarians in creating the present general authoritarian ethos of the school.

The identification of these different ideologies enables us to see more clearly the internal power relations that operate at Kilby school. However, this overview may imply a number of unintended impressions. First, it is important to emphasize that this analysis of ideological conflict utilizes the analytical device of the Ideal Type and so, it follows from this, that these ideologies are not found empirically in pure form, nor is it possible to simplistically locate teachers within one category. The empirical world is more complex. However, these ideologies attempt to represent educational perspectives within which teachers at Kilby school tended to operate.

Secondly, it may seem that, during different periods in the history of the school, one ideology held exclusive control. This is not the case. What each of these periods represents is the relationship between competing ideologies in which a dominant position emerged. But it is this relationship and the various practices that the resulting power relations generates that is of primary concern. Of particular importance to this balance of power is the formation of alliances between the different groups. For example, this study was carried out at a time when a dominant authoritarian ideology had emerged at Kilby school as a result of an alliance between the Old Disciplinarians and the New Realists. However, this did not entail a simplistic return to the overt racism and practices of the early 1960s. The Liberals continued to challenge the practices of this alliance, as they operated their multiculturally informed pedagogy within their departments. Furthermore, there were important contradictory historical legacies that have remained in operation, for example the tight classification system and the pastoral system. This chapter examines the way in which the power relations in operation during this research period, structure the adoption of particular strategies and tactics in dealing with the black youth at Kilby school.

The Independents (I)

It is difficult to place in the adopted framework the four remaining teachers on the staff. They tended to support the dominant ideological perspective operating within the school at a particular period but generally their teaching practices were not easily identified with a particular group. For example, one teacher regarded his commitment to Christianity as the main determinant of his approach to teaching. He challenged the school's multi-faith religious education syllabus, he refused to teach about the theory of evolution, he would not join a teachers' union, but he was a strong supporter of the pastoral system.

The headteacher was also included among this group. Due to the strong hierarchical structure of the school, he was of central significance to its ethos (see Burgess, 1984). His arrival in the early 1970s, with the appointment of Liberal teachers, had challenged the dominant ideology of the Old Disciplinarians which had been based on disciplinary coercion and overt racism.

The newly-appointed senior teachers had been responsible for the attempted move from assimilation to plural culturalism. The latter perspective had never replaced the former position as a dominant approach throughout the school, but during the mid-1970s it had been seen by many teachers to be dominant as a result of the significant changes during the period. Finally, during the late 1970s, the Old Disciplinarians in alliance with the New Realists had implemented a more authoritarian approach which focussed on a return to more coercive sanctions, including more frequent use of corporal punishment, suspensions and transfers to Special Schools. Accompanying this, there had been a reorganization of the timetable which extended the streaming procedures and which excluded form periods in which pastoral work had been carried out. The New Realists had argued that basic literacy and numeracy must take priority over multicultural activities. Once again, the headteacher had been central to this shift in perspective as he had been to the earlier one. In particular, he had been responsible for creating a 'moral panic' concerning the growing resistance of the students to the demands of the school. The effects of these changes on the school ethos is now examined.

The school ethos

At the time of the research what might be called a 'new realism'[7] had emerged among the teachers at Kilby school. A number of factors were in operation at this time in the 1980s, which explained this new ethos. First, the effects of mass youth unemployment within the city were feeding back into the school. This expressed itself in terms of the increasing day-to-day dissatisfaction of the students. Secondly, there was low morale among the staff due to the fact that the education cuts imposed by central government had led to little promotion either within the school or, more importantly, to other schools. Also, new teachers' primary concern was their own permanent employment in a contracting labour market. This led to the Old Disciplinarian teachers in alliance with the New Realist teachers emerging as the dominant ideological force within the school. The liberal perspective which had been implemented in the mid-1970s with its emphasis on cooperation rather than coercion was dismissed as having failed and there was now a return to a more authoritarian disciplinary policy.

These material conditions were of importance in creating a numerical dominance of two to one in favour of the authoritarian perspective. Many of the Old Disciplinarian teachers who had been unsuccessful in gaining promotion to other schools had in the past been internally promoted. The Liberal teachers who now found it difficult to find promotion to other schools were thus also excluded from internal promotion. This had led to much despondency among them and, for some, a loss of their earlier enthusiasm for curriculum innovations. The ideology of most of the new teachers reflected the political move to the right in the wider society (Hall and Jacques 1983), which expressed itself in terms of their authoritarian approach. The teachers' career frustrations were compounded by their perception of the student population. In interviews many of them spoke of the pressures of dealing with the students' academic failure. Mr Hickey (L) believed that this perception of the students was of central importance in understanding the dominant ethos of the school:

> You must remember that the teachers here see themselves as having to deal with failures. This has a terrible effect on the place. Its like an old secondary mod really. The majority of kids are treated with contempt 'coz they're seen as thick an' if you're forced to stay here, you see yourself as part of the failure syndrome.

Mr Hickey considered that this represented the position of the authoritarian teachers. However, many of the Liberal teachers tended to share a common social perception of the students. Both authoritarian and Liberal teachers defined the problem of schooling black youth in terms of their academic failure and both groups offered explanations of this failure in terms of individual, intellectual and sociocultural deficiences.

> Mr Green: Nearly all these kids are bottom of the pile socially,
> (OD)   intellectually. They come from deprived backgrounds,
>   they're not motivated at home, broken families, fathers in
>   the West Indies, no English spoken at home and of course
>   there is no social mix here. They're all from around the
>   local area, it's just a bad catchment area.
> MM: Do you think that the school contributes to the failure?
> Mr Green: Well, even Basil Bernstein said that school cannot compen-
>   sate for the home and he wasn't even talking about the
>   kind of kids here.
> MM: I believe he said that it could not compensate for society.

Similarly, Mr Young (L) maintained that the low examination results were essentially determined by the assumed social pathology of the students' families.

> Yes you get depressed about the exam marks but you have to put them
> in context. A lot of our kids come from problem backgrounds, like the
> West Indian kids, a lot of them may be from one parent families. The
> Indian kids' parents, especially the mothers, may be finding it difficult
> to adjust so they are going to have other things on their minds apart
> from school work. So, these special or more specific problems must be
> taken in account, in fact they are of most importance.

Where the Liberal teachers differed from the authoritarian teachers was in their response to this commonly perceived problem. Mr Lynch (L), who was seen by the teachers to closely identify with the students, described the Liberals' interventionist approach:

> I have loads of kids thrown out of lessons and I have to investigate.
> When you hear what's going on in there you despair. I listen to both
> sides and I know that some of these lads are tough, a lot of them have a
> lot of social problems but that's the point isn't it? We have to treat these
> problems in a caring way. They're not just going to go away. That's
> where I blame the teachers who think that we can carry on without
> adjusting, without devising new strategies, special ways to deal with the
> special problems that our kids have here.

The general low morale of the staff expressed itself in a number of ways. First, there was much criticism of the school management. The headteacher was seen by the rest of the staff as having lost his early interest. It was assumed that he had served his time and was waiting for a move. The school management retained constitutional power but they did not operate as dynamic leaders. Mr Walker (OD) described the effect of this weak leadership on the staff:

> They are terrible for the place. I came keen as you do, but it's the whole place. It's a question of leadership. If the lot at the top are lazy bastards and are seen as such, then what can you expect from the rest of us? It works its way down doesn't it? No one gets promoted for being a good classroom teacher, it's a question of not disturbing them out there.

Secondly, there was a high rate of absenteeism among the staff. Frequently, there were several teachers absent and many of them took the maximum 3 days before a doctor's note was required. This of course meant that other teachers had to cover for them, and as a result, there was a great resentment at the loss of free periods. Thirdly, some teachers did little preparation and were frequently late for lessons. It is difficult to convey to people who have no experience of inner-city schools, the high degree of stress involved in under-resourced and overcrowded classrooms and the resulting teachers' perception of the legitimacy of these tactics. Mr Collins (L), who was very popular with the students, pointed out the difficulties of classroom interaction:

> It doesn't matter who you are, the hardest thing is in there, to be in there. Everyone is trying to get out, it's like, like thirty people stuck together in a room and no-one wants to be there, including the teacher, in fact in many cases, especially the teacher, and you can't blame him. It's really tough in there and there's no support, at the end of the day you're on your own. We have the autonomy to do what we want and for some it's the autonomy to go insane, quietly.

Fourthly, there was little social contact between staff and students outside of lessons. Three teachers were responsible for sport, but apart from this, there was little extra-curricular activities in the school. There was a sense in which the teachers could be described as being 'bussed' into and out of Kilby school with the least possible contact with the main population. Mr Raynor, who was highly critical of the staff's attitude to the students, claimed that you could phone up many of the teachers at home 30 minutes after school had finished. Finally, most of the teachers perceived their teaching role in terms of survival.[8] Mr Griffiths (I), who had been at the school for 6 years, described the strategies of survival that he had developed in the classroom.

> I have developed techniques to avoid confrontation. New teachers think that it's just a question of force, but of course it's much more complex. I think you learn to read the mood of certain classes, certain groups or even certain pupils. You ignore remarks maybe, don't

challenge everything that's going on, be selective. You have to, if you are going to survive the day, otherwise you just go mad.

Humour in the staffroom served as a means of defence against the harsh realities of the classroom.[9] Teachers joked with each other about the demands of the 'shop floor'. Selected 'problem' students were a source of severe ridicule. When a teacher informed the staff that she was leaving, it was suggested that tunnel four could now be filled in, as only one escaped from each exit. We may conclude from the above that the dominant ethos at the time of the research was that of the polarization of the predominantly white staff and the majority black student population. This polarization is now examined in more detail in terms of the ideological reproduction of the dominant culture of the wider society.[10]

Monoculturalism – multiculturalism

Although the composition of Kilby school consisted of a 93 per cent black male student population, structurally it remained a 'white' school. This monoculturalist perspective which pervaded all areas of school life is examined in terms of the ethnocentric nature of the content of the teaching materials and the school knowledge, and the implicit transmission of social and economic values, attitudes and dispositions, that is the 'hidden curriculum', which reflect the dominant culture. The Old Disciplinarians and the New Realists overtly maintained this monoculturalism; the Liberals, although theoretically committed to a multicultural approach, did, in practice, due to the internal limitations and contradictions of their ideology, serve to reproduce this cultural dominance.

Ethnocentric curriculum content

One of the main ideological divisions between the teachers at Kilby school concerned the question of the curricular content. The dominant perspective of the Old Disciplinarian and New Realist teachers at the school was that of assimilation. Most of the Liberal teachers pointed to the need for a plural culturalist perspective. The main argument of the former groups, working from within an ideology of 'common sense', was that they were preparing the students for a white society. Their position was summarized by Mr Gill, a senior careers officer in the area, who is a Punjabi:

What's culture? Most of the people in Kilby are from the Punjab, the most invaded area in the world. This is important, very important to remember, it affects how they react. They know all about foreign power. We have mainly the uneducated in this area. What are, is important to their children and so them? To be successful. And how is this to be achieved? By adapting to their new environment. It's a basic, fundamental law of nature, survival of the individual depends on adaptation. What's more important that these boys live in the past? What's important is that they learn English and take advantage of the opportunities that will then be open to them. I allowed my two sons to learn Punjabi. I mean the writing of it, after they had got their 'A' levels and places at university.

The Old Disciplinarian and the New Realist teachers claimed that they adopted a 'colour-blind' approach to the black students. They believed that this was the implementation of a non-racist curriculum. Mr Rogers (NR) believed that the Liberals' position was essentially concerned with social engineering, which he argued had never worked in the context of the British educational system:

> It seems to me that the safest principle is to treat all children regardless of colour as the same. If you take the multiculturalist position to its logical end, you see the dangers of this form of engineering change. It becomes a type of positive discrimination which can easily be seen as another type of racism. I don't think that you should interfere with the basic structure. If you want to help the children here, it must be all the children and so must be carried out by a neutral body, say like local authority aid to the inner-city. But change geared to one group, to one particular group of coloured children has never worked and it will not work if only a minority are to benefit.

One of the central assumptions of Mr Rogers' and of many other teachers at the school was that multicultural education was the exclusive concern of black youth. The Old Disciplinarian and the New Realist teachers defended their refusal to adopt a multicultural curriculum, as the following quotations show, in terms of conservative pedagogies, the external demands of the examination system and by reducing 'race' to class.

Mr Beckett: (OD)   I don't think that it's really to do with the question of being for or against a multiculturalist policy as I often argue. There are teachers who have taught their subjects for years in a certain way, a certain style. Why should they change? They have been teaching this way successfully to coloured and white kids.

Mr Tetley: (NR)   It's not as simple as wanting it or believing in it, not in the real world. We work with constraints. The exam system and before that the universities set a certain course and demand certain standards. Black Studies may be of some use but we have certain commitments. If you include all the cultural stuff then in fact you are discriminating against the black kids here as they are

| | competing with kids who only have to bother with passing exams. |
| Mrs Turner:
 (OD) | If you look at any society the ones at the bottom always do worse. If you are going to make the curriculum relevant for the coloured children, what about the white children who are under-achieving? White children from poor homes, from working class homes do just as badly. |

Teachers who have emerged from the working-class spoke of how they have had to adapt to the academic demands of the school in order to achieve social mobility. They found it difficult to understand how the black community can demand equality with white people and at the same time wish to create special recognition of black culture within the school. The following discussion took place at a meeting that Mr Parks was asked to attend, on the need to adopt a multicultural curriculum:

| Mr Parks:
 (OD) | I can't understand this lot. We all have to change. I was brought up in Lancashire. I'm glad I escaped going into the factory but I had to change at school. All this Black Studies I don't understand. It just divides kids. You can't ask to be treated equally and then ask for special treatment, you can't have it both ways. That lot this morning were so arrogant. Black culture, black culture. What the hell does it mean anyway? I've gotto get them through the exams. |

The Liberal teachers, who worked from within a plural culturalist perspective, argued that there must be an institutional acceptance of the black students' culture.

| Mr Young:
 (L) | It is essential if we are to overcome our problems that we take seriously the cultures of the pupils. The curriculum must reflect the multiracial society outside. We must play our part in making more equal the different cultures within the school. |

The Liberal teachers had attempted in their own respective subject areas to implement a multicultural curriculum. Also, a year after the research period began, Mr Raynor invited a multicultural unit into the school for a term to help to develop a multicultural curriculum. Most of the authoritarian teachers refused to cooperate. The Liberal teachers responded positively, and between them they developed multicultural material that they used in team teaching situations. What emerged from the seminars and the workshops was how little any of the white teachers at Kilby school, including the two teachers on multicultural courses, knew about the black community. One main project that was undertaken was the examination of racist stereotypes in the books used in the school. It was found that in the greatly under-stocked library that many of the old books either explicitly portrayed black people in a caricatured way which was mainly derogative or, implicitly assumed a white audience. It was concluded that most of the text books, scheme readers, and general reading material were culturally inappropriate for the black students at Kilby school.[11]

Against this background we can now examine how these different ideological meanings of the authoritarian and the Liberal teachers were translated into practices within the curriculum. In order to make clear this relationship between meanings and practices I looked at a major area of concern, that of the school's language policy.

Language policy

Hall *et al.* (1978, p. 341) have emphasized the importance of language as a vehicle of learning and have criticized schools' negative response to Creole. This view of Creole that Hall refers to, as a form of sub-standard speech, was shared by the authoritarian teachers at Kilby school. Informally, among themselves, they described the language of the black youth as aggressive, babbling, loud, meaningless, argumentative and jabbering. In interviews with these teachers they maintained the same derogative view of Creole. They labelled it as linguistically deficient, a more restricted code than non-standard white English, and as illogical. Mr Beckett (OD), who had taught at the school for 15 years, described this dominant view:

> Our job is impossible, the West Indians haven't got the basics, not really. They haven't access to English literature. I've spent years correcting the way they talk which is the way they write. Most of them can't even write in sentences or use plurals properly, the basics. Their main problem is their, I was going to say their language, but you can't call it language really. And this is what is written down, no sense of audience. You know how they all talk when they're ganged together. Sometimes I think they are doing it on purpose, like a mass refusal to accept standard English, but I suppose not, in my more rational moments. Call it a severe linguistic handicap if you like and I don't think that there is a cure for it, not in the school I mean. No, not until their parents are prepared to bring them up on a more standard diet of English.

The Liberal teachers challenged this negative evaluation of Creole. They had created a more positive language policy which involved the use of Creole in drama, mime, story-telling and writing. Mr Young had produced material making use of black writers, such as Selvon and Dhondy, for the CSE mode 3 English examination. The Liberal teachers had implemented ideas developed by the Inner London Education Authority (ILEA) and were in agreement with the ILEA English Inspectorate (1979) who argue that students' confidence in themselves is of critical importance to academic achievement:

> There can be little doubt that the greatest single factor contributing to pupils' achievement of mastery of the writing system is their confidence in their own ability to do it. . . . There is now a great deal of evidence to show that the teachers' expectations and attitudes play a very important part in the pupils' learning. If those attitudes include a view of the pupils' language which does less than justice to that language, then the result will be very damaging to the learning chances of the pupil (p. 6).

However, the Liberal teachers' response has contradictorily served to reinforce a negative evaluation of Creole. Their implementation of a pluralist approach had been uneven. It had been adopted in the lower streams of the school, while for the top stream standard English continued to be the accepted form. So, in practice, the use of Creole within an educational context was associated with the low status of the 'low-ability' students. If Creole is accepted as a different language with its own structure then its use within the classroom should be extended to all Afro-Caribbean students.

Recognition of the skill in the oral language of Afro-Caribbean students was found in their junior school reports (see Edwards, 1986). Their reports at Kilby school supported this view. Yet, this positive view of Afro-Caribbean students had not found expression in the mainstream curriculum. With few exceptions, the English syllabus reflected little of the recent research on 'language across the curriculum'. It was still grammar-based, and the writing mode which served as an effective means of class discipline excluded the spoken mode which many Afro-Caribbeans had shown to be competent in.

The question of Afro-Caribbean Creole was the Liberal teachers' predominant concern in reforming the school's language policy. They took for granted that the school had responded more positively to Asian languages, and pointed to the time-tabling of the English as a second language (E2L) classes that Asian students attended:

MM: What is the school's language policy as regards the Asian
             pupils.
Ms Yeats: Well the Asians are taken care of with E2L. They get a lot
(L)   of support and of course their culture is strong. They have
             a number of languages which they use and which are
             accepted in the school.

However, since the early emergence within the school of E2L, there had been little development in this area. The response to the Asian languages is an example of the wider process of curricular selection and evaluation of what counts as 'worthwhile' knowledge. In this case not all languages were considered to be of equal worth. European languages were seen as 'worthwhile' and so they were incuded on the timetable and were accepted by the examination boards as a subject of high status. Also, European languages were assigned high status in the hierarchy of school subjects, by being associated with 'high-ability' students, for whom at Kilby school one European language was recommended. Special arrangements were made for those students who were considered to be linguistically able to attend German lessons in a local school. In contrast to this, a negative attitude was adopted towards Asian languages. So, for example, when a group of Asian parents requested that mother-tongue teaching be included on the curriculum for students of Asian origin, the school management refused their request on the grounds that essential subjects would have to be dropped and that provision for learning these languages was already made within the area in out-of-school hours. Partly as a result of this exclusion, students who spoke two or three languages but had difficulties with English, particularly in the written mode, were labelled remedial and treated as slow learners. That these difficulties were not seen as a problem by the Liberal teachers which might be overcome by the introduction of mother-tongue teaching is an indication of their ideological selection of the use of Creole in the classroom as of particular significance in relation to Afro-Caribbean students' assumed 'problems'. Both Asian and Afro-Caribbean students would have benefited from the opportunity to use their languages within the classroom; that only the latter group were encouraged to, suggests that ultimately this selection is not based on educational or linguistic grounds but that of social control.

MM: Why has there been more concern with the language of Caribbeans than that of the Asians?

Ms Yeats: I wouldn't agree, a lot of work has been done for them. It's
(L)   institutionally established and so may be hidden but nevertheless it is there, and they are achieving a lot more than the West Indian boys. If we are to overcome, if they are to overcome their language problem, they must be encouraged to view their language more positively. Owen and Harold, for example [low stream students], are cooperating much more as a result of being encouraged to talk in their own dialect and this will increase their motivation to work.

The Liberal teachers' response to the Afro-Caribbeans' language emerged from the ideological construction, which many of them shared with the authoritarian teachers, of Afro-Caribbeans as 'problem' students. Both authoritarians and Liberals located the students' linguistic problems within the students themselves. Like many of the perceived 'problems' that were assigned to black youth, particularly those of Afro-Caribbean origin, the unexamined institutional material and social response of the school had been central in creating them and reinforcing those of the wider society. The authoritarian and Liberal teachers differed in their response to their common definition of the problem. The authoritarian teachers believed in a non-interventionist strategy based on standard English for all students. In practice their negative evaluation of black youth's language served primarily to discourage them from writing effectively and developing their ideas. The Liberal teachers theoretically argued for the acceptance within the curriculum of the black students' languages. However, as was argued above, in practice this has resulted in the implementation of a pluralist approach for 'low-ability' students and this association has contradictorily tended to reinforce the negative evaluation of Creole.

The hidden curriculum

Of equal importance in understanding the response of the authoritarian and the Liberal teachers to the ideological role of Kilby school in maintaining the dominant culture, is an examination of the transmission of values, attitudes, pre-dispositions and social skills. This is at times carried out overtly, for example, when teachers impress upon the students values of individual achievement and right attitudes to work. However, much of this form of learning is carried out through what has become known as the 'hidden curriculum', that is, the implicit transmission of these values and social skills.[12] Although the authoritarian and the Liberal teachers differed in their response to the students who rejected these values and social skills, both groups assume that the dominant values of the school were intrinsically worthwhile. Hence both groups, as the following incidences show, were responsible for the attempt, albeit unintended, which pervaded the whole school, to incorporate black youth into white cultural identities.

The morning assemblies have remained essentially Christian. The head-teacher and the deputy head, who were both practising Christians, believed that it was important to maintain the Christian religious heritage. So, for example, at the beginning of each academic year, New Testaments were distributed to all the first years. During assemblies, there were token gestures towards the Sikh, Hindu and Muslim religions, but these often amounted to little more than explanations of why groups of students were absent celebrating particular religious occasions, such as the Diwali and Eid festivals. Informally, many of the largely secular teaching staff were either ignorant of the students' religions, or critical of their religious observances, such as their frequent visits to mosques and temples, the Sikhs' wearing of turbans, and the Muslims' fasting during Ramadam. It was assumed that the students of Afro-Caribbean origin shared the traditional Christian values of the school. The beliefs of the Rastafarian religion, which a number of students identified with, were never formally acknowledged. Each morning at assembly this process of cultural incorporation was enacted as white Christian values were celebrated by the school management. The following talk is representative of the school authorities' insensitivity to the school's black population:

Mr Keegan: A lot of you have taken up wearing badges. I would
(I)   rather you did not, unless they are of significance. If you
                      are in the scouts or boys brigade then that is very
                      commendable. I was a scout myself. Also the scouts'
                      badge might get lost amongst the other badges, they just
                      look untidy. And there is a chance that some boy will
                      bump into you wearing the badges and it might catch
                      you.

Mr Keegan, the headteacher, considered this to be a value-free warning. For him, it was essentially concerned with appearance and safety. However, what was of significance for him was not necessarily the same for the boys. Six out of the 230 boys present were members of the scouts. Three of them were white. The students' badges indicated their identification with black popular culture, representing their appreciation of such figures as Bob Marley, Marcus Garvey and Aswad.

The teachers' understanding of the students' response to academic work highlighted the way in which both authoritarian and Liberal teachers assumed the neutrality of the dominant values of the school. Many of the teachers were critical of the students' lack of competitive spirit, especially among the Afro-Caribbeans. The following conversation concerned the annual internal examinations that were taking place:

Mr Walker: I can't believe it, every year it's the same. The noise in
(OD)   there is intolerable.
Mr Tetley: A lot of them have finished after half an hour.
(NR)
Mr Walker: They don't even try, half of them. I just don't understand
                      them, they just don't seem to have it in them to work
                      through a paper.
Mr Lynch: Well, you know my view on it Pete, I believe that we don't
(L)   teach them the necessary study skills.
Mr Walker: No it's more than that. It's their attitude, especially the
                      West Indians, they refuse to take exams seriously. Look
                      at the lot at the back, they had no intention of working.
                      They just want to disrupt it that's all.
Mr Lynch: But it's not simply a matter of . . . [interrupted] . . .
Mr Walker: No they want . . .
Mr Lynch: No, it's not just, it's a question of their motivation. I think
                      that we could do much more to explain that once they
                      leave here, they won't be surrounded by their friends.
                      They'll be on their own and they'll have to succeed on

their own and that's why working to their potential while they are here is so important.

The authoritarian and the Liberal teachers differed in their explanations of these students' attitudes to work and so suggested different solutions to the problem. However, both groups took for granted that the school's dominant values of individualism and competition were intrinsically worthwhile. They believed that if the students adopted a positive work orientation approach to the school, which was based on these values, then their resulting school success would guarantee work success. Both groups of teachers perceived the students' resistance to schooling in negative terms and failed to take into account that different class and cultural groups have access to different experiences and values. These differences can be seen, for example, between the teachers' value of competitive individualism and the anti-school students' forms of collective resistance, which are examined in the following two chapters.

Summary

The attempt to maintain and reproduce monoculturalism at Kilby school through the ethnocentric teaching materials and the hidden curriculum was achieved as a result of this shared educational paradigm. On the one hand, the Old Disciplinarians and the New Realists overtly rejected any reform of the curriculum in response to the majority black population. On the other hand, the Liberal teachers' commitment to a multicultural position was in practice reduced to a strategy of accommodation of the non-cooperative students. This resulted from the limitations and contradictions of their theoretical position which implicitly shared the same ground as the authoritarians in defining the 'problem' of schooling black youth in terms of the students themselves rather than the racist, gender and social class determinants of the school and wider society.

It is important to stress that the social relations of the school cannot simply be explained either in idealist terms of teacher consciousness or in functionalist terms of social control. The different remedies of the authoritarian and Liberal teachers in response to the assumed 'problem' of schooling black students were materially linked to the career structure of these two groups. In modern bureaucracies appointments and promotions are increasingly based on merit (Weber, 1948). For both groups, evidence of their professional competency was measured and evaluated by school management and their colleagues in terms of their capacity on a day-to-day basis to develop coping strategies in their management of the students (see Denscombe, 1980).[13] Two broad strategies of career mobility could be identified at Kilby school, that of the Old Disciplinarians and New Realists, based on the maintenance of institutional order by means of overt authoritarian practices. Hence, the disaffected students who openly challenged their authority presented real disciplinary problems which called for strong preventative measures. The response of the liberals was more ambivalent. Their institutional power and their future career progress was dependent on their 'success' in working with these 'problem' students. It was in their material interest to achieve consensus within the school by means of negotiation and to persuade deviant students that resistance to schooling was not in their interest. Furthermore, in the contracting teaching profession with little job mobility the expanding area of multicultural education provides fertile ground for aspiring Liberal teachers, who have demonstrated their ability to deal with 'problem' black students.

Teacher racism

One of the central concerns of this research is the question of how white teachers at Kilby school encountered the black male students of Asian and Afro-Caribbean origin. Recent Official Reports[14] on black youth's presence in schools, have mentioned the role of racism. This has tended to be superfically discussed in terms of 'another' factor contributing to their school 'failure'. However, there has not been a systematic analysis of racism and there has been little mention of teachers. At Kilby school, racism was prevalent throughout the white staff, including the school management, the teachers and the administrative and domestic workers. I shall examine this widespread racism with particular reference to the teachers' response to the black community and the system of racist stereotyping that operated within the school. While the Old Disciplinarians and New Realists tended to work explicitly within this framework, the majority of Liberals tended to work implicitly within it.

Teachers' response to black community

Many of the staff had been at the school for many years but they did not identify with the black community. Their hostility towards them was displayed in a number of ways. The following discussion took place between white school governors, senior teachers and white parents, after a meeting at which an Indian parent had asked for Punjabi to be placed on the curriculum. There was immediate identification by the teachers with the white parents, representing 7 per cent of the student population:

Mr Crisp: These meetings are a waste of time. Instead of having
(Teacher)   Indian languages in the school, they should be concentrat-
              ing on their kids being taught English. They should do
              something useful with what we taught them . . . [inter-
              rupted] . . .
Mrs Rose: It's like the old saying, when in Rome do as the Romans
(School   do. If we went to their country, we'd have to follow their
Governor) customs, and what about the white children here? What

	are they supposed to do while the Indian boys are learning their languages?
Mr Crisp:	They're the ones I feel sorry for. Like, just look at Walsall, they're opening up Indian schools. If I lived there I would demand Welsh schools for my children. All that extra money on the rates and if . . .
Mr Ford: (Parent)	They don't know what they want. They moan, say they're worried about the Nationality Act because they want to stay here. Then why don't they try and be more English? I'm glad to . . .
Mrs Rose:	It's just a few community leaders who cause all the trouble, especially the Sikhs. Most of the parents of the children here can't speak English so they couldn't even ask the questions.

The white staff's racist response was also displayed by the frequency with which they generalized from the particular behaviour of black youths to the social group as a whole. So, for example, when a white boy who attended the school was beaten up by two Asian boys for informing on them, the secretaries discussed the incident in racial terms:

Mrs Rogers:	It's awful not to be able to send your child to a school without getting bullied and beaten up. They're always onto the white boys here. I would take my child away I would.
Mrs Peters:	I wouldn't send mine to . . .
Mrs Rogers:	Well neither would I.
Mrs Peters:	My husband says that the Indians are all the same at work and that, and they gang up an' stick together.

The secretaries, like most staff at the Kilby school, were unaware of the large number of racist attacks on the black students. When they were informed of this, they reduced this racist verbal and physical assault to schoolboy rivalry.

Mrs Peters:	Youngsters are always mucking about, fighting an' all.
Mrs Rogers:	They're as bad as each other. Look at the gangs of boys walking home from here at night an' all.
Mrs Peters:	Yeah, going through the park causing trouble. Some of them people . . .
Mrs Rogers:	They should go straight home like mine an' keep out of trouble.
Mrs Peters:	They shouldn't go looking for it.
Mrs Rogers:	It's those mad skinheads. I don't like them. But I suppose they think they're getting their own back.

Most teachers had little contact with the black community, so tended to caricature the students' parents. Teachers' negative interpretations of the parents' behaviour might be read as a defensive mechanism to discourage their participation in the school. So, for example, when an Asian parent had asked for a progress report of his son after half a term at the school, Mr Green (OD), the boy's tutor, refused the parent's request. He explained his decision in the staffroom:

> I refused it because there's no point. How are we supposed to know if his son's a genius. Anyway, his parents can't probably read English. They'll want it in Punjabi next.

Another example of the teachers' unsympathetic response to parents was displayed after a fifth-year's parents' evening. The following comments were recorded:

Mrs Turner: (OD)
: They all want their bloody kids to be bloody brain surgeons.

Mrs Rogers: (NR)
: It's hopeless them bringing older brothers, no older than themselves. It's just a waste of our time. It's supposed to be a parents' evening.

Mr Beckett: (OD)
: Did you see William's mother coming in when it was all over, Just like her son, always late. Turn up when it pleases them. You can always see where they get it from.

The above three incidents may be interpreted in a positive way, in terms of the support that the black community is willing to give to the schools. First, that many immigrants, both black and white, tend to hold education in high regard as a means of escaping the unskilled sector of the labour market. Secondly, that the students' parents, if they are unable to speak English, are prepared to make sure that their children are represented at school. In the third case, Mrs Williams was a nurse at a local hospital who managed to get off early from a late shift.

The Liberal teachers, who were more sympathetic to the parents, nevertheless failed to make any organized contact with them. They assumed that they were reactionary on most educational issues.

Mr Hickey: (L)
: What can we do? Among white kids, the old working-class authoritarian behaviour is disappearing. Most of the parents are more liberal but not our parents. If you want the Asian and West Indian support, you're lost. They'll only back up the authoritarian lot here, as you know they often appeal to.

This caricature of the parents was frequently challenged during the research period, when I met them in their homes and on picket lines and anti-racist demonstrations. It would suggest that the response of the parents at Kilby school was one determined by lack of contact by the liberal teachers and the absence of organization rather than the parents' culture. It is against this background of the racist response of the white staff that I shall now examine the system of racist stereotyping in operation at Kilby school.

System of racist stereotyping[15]

There was a tendency for Asian male students to be seen by the teachers as technically of 'high ability' and socially as conformist. Afro-Caribbean male students tended to be seen as having 'low ability' and potential discipline problems.[16] This racial division was partly the result of the historical ideological legacy that the present staff had inherited. This was transmitted to the younger members of staff in a number of ways. First, senior staff advised younger teachers on the specific problems of having to deal with black youth. Mr Lyons (NR), who was on teaching practice at the school, described his introductory talk with the school management:

> I was told that I had to look out for the West Indians and what to do. If they went mad, we just had to leave them alone to cool down. There was nothing we could do, and things like that if they swore at us in their own language we must report it. They had a lot of trouble from them in the past.

Secondly, these powerful social images of the black male students were passed on in the staffroom to younger teachers. This often took the form of older teachers offering moral support to new teachers who might be having difficulties with particular classes. Stories were often told with racist overtones, of how 'old characters' on the staff had dealt with student confrontations, particularly with 'big West Indians'. The young teachers' specific problems were rationalized in terms of the racial composition of the school rather than the young teachers' inexperience, his or her personal inadequacies or the material constraints of an overcrowded, under-resourced school. This racial division of the student population was of central significance in the structuring of the social reality by the staff at Kilby school. However, its maintenance could not simply be reduced to historical structural determination. The school did not exist in a social vacuum and the racist stereotypes of the wider society were what teachers brought to the teaching situation. Mr Barlow (NR) recalled his initial reactions to his redeployment to the school:

> I didn't want to come here. I tried to find other places, anywhere. I'd heard all about the area, not the school itself really but about the problems of coloured kids, about the reputation of the West Indians.

You would read about them mugging old ladies round the place in the papers, but, and then the thought of having to teach them.

These racist images of the wider society were also an important element in the racial structuring of the social reality at the school.

Of equal importance to the maintenance of this racial division was that the present staff's perception of the 'ethnicity' of the black students tended to reinforce rather than contradict the historical social images and the racist stereotypes of the wider society. I interviewed Mr Lyons when he was on teaching practice and, as is shown above, he spoke of how negative racist typifications were passed onto him by teachers at the school. He was subsequently appointed to the school on a 12-month contract. I interviewed him again before he left the school and he spoke of how his perceptions of the students had developed:

> The West Indians are tough. I tried not to let anyone influence me in how I treated them but they look at you with wild eyes if you tell them to sit down. They are looking, expecting trouble. They are more pre-judiced than white people. The Asians are better, you tell them to do something an' they are meek an' they go an' do it.

This finding supports Rex and Tomlinson's (1979) and Wright's (1985) studies of teacher attitudes to black students, that the racist typifications with which they work tended to be reinforced rather than negated by student responses.

The following comments indicate the widespread acceptance of these teacher caricatures, which seemed to evaluate Asian students in technical terms and Afro-Caribbean students in social/behavioural terms. The Old Disciplinarians and the New Realists worked explicitly within this system of racist stereotyping. So, for example, Mrs Turner (OD) explained the im-proved examination results in terms of the changing ethnic composition of the student population:

> This is the first year I've had a class in which most of them could cope with the work as the exam results have shown. Without being too crude, if we're honest it's because we're getting Asians now and not West Indians. Though there's still a lot of thickies.

Similarly, Mr Beckett (OD) described explicitly his perception of the black students in these terms. He did, however, make a further sub-division between Jamaican boys and those of other islands. He assumed that most of the Afro-Caribbean students at Kilby school were of Jamaican origin and he claimed that he could identify them from their behaviour:

> There is a difference between West Indians and Asians, yes definitely. It's a question of attitude, temperament, sticking at the work. The West

Indians have a chip on their shoulder. That, that's why they act towards us in the way they do, aggressive. I do make a distinction between Jamaicans and the others, from other islands. The other islands are hard-working, achievement-orientated, but we have few of them here, David and one or two more.

Many of the Liberal teachers worked implicitly within the framework of the racist stereotyping. Mr Young was critical of the teachers' dominant social image of the Afro-Caribbean students. He was regarded by the other members of staff as a successful classroom teacher who had few disciplinary problems and coped effectively with trouble-makers. The following discussion took place after I had attended a number of his lessons. He assumed that I was helping a small group of students with language difficulties and so was not aware that I was observing his interaction with the students.

MM:　　　Do you think that you treat all the kids the same?

Mr Young: I like to think, no I mean I do try and consciously try to
(L)　　　treat them all the same but you, I suppose, unconsciously I label kids and react in certain ways. Kids who cause a lot of hassle say, or personality clashes, but generally I try to treat them all the same.

MM:　　　What about your treatment of Asians and Caribbeans?

Mr Young: Well, no, as you know I'm against the crude division that they make in this place. I try to treat the Indians and the West Indian kids, and the white kids, the same. I try to see them individually. There's good and bad in all and some days it's one kid and the next another. There are a few that are problems but it can't, it's not a question of them all being West Indian or anything like that.

Mr Young was surprised when I showed him how he had responded to a number of incidents involving students who had 'interrupted' the lessons. Although there were, out of a class of 34, only 5 Afro-Caribbeans, they had been identified nearly twice as many times, compared to the 27 Asian students and 2 whites, as causing an interruption. Most significantly, as Mr Young discusses below, was his perception of black youth of Asian and Afro-Caribbean origin, which was related to the criteria he used to define what constituted a 'classroom interruption'.[17]

I see, I would, I did come away, well I would've come away thinking that I was not working with the stereotypes, at least not those ones. It's amazing really, Jasbinder turning around for a ruler is legitimate, is seen as O.K. Richard [Afro-Caribbean] doing the same thing is regarded as interrupting and his behaviour is good generally. I don't think of him as one of the problems. I bet he's noticed that I treat him differently.

The stereotypes that Mr Young was aware that he worked with were part of what Lacey (1976, p. 60) calls the teachers' 'crude conceptual picture of the class', in which he classifies the students into such groups as ' "the bright boys", "the conformists", "the troublemakers", etc.' These crude typifications are developed as coping strategies in the management of classroom interaction (see Hargreaves, 1978 and Pollard 1982). What Mr Young was unaware of was how for the Kilby school teachers, this conceptual framework provided the basis on which there emerged the racist stereotypes that they employed within the school. At this level, the racist stereotypes functioned as a strategy of teacher survival. This example serves to illustrate the complexity of racist practices. This is of particular importance to those who tend to see these practices as exclusively the product of an extreme right-wing political position.

There were a number of occasions, which I recorded, when the Liberal teachers' implicit racist stereotyping was challenged by personal contact with groups of Afro-Caribbean students. For example, Mr Fearns (L) described his surprise at the positive interaction of such a group:

> You know that lot of third years, I was really surprised I've just got them in my tutor group. I always thought of them as sullen. They're a very sociable group once you get to know them.

Mr Banks pointed to the more positive aspects of the teachers' caricature of the Afro-Caribbean students. He made clear that the system of racist typification operating within the school did not simply consist of the caricature of the 'rebellious' Afro-Caribbean student and the 'conformist' Asian student. This would be too crude a construct and be challenged by the teachers' interaction with the students. For each group there was constructed an oppositional structure without which the racist stereotyping could not form a system of knowledge for the teachers who used it. So, for example, Mr Banks (L) described the behaviour of Afro-Caribbeans as truculent on certain occasions and as exuberant on others:

> If you are honest you must say that they are tougher to teach. I find them so anyway. But they are more, they have more character, more interest than the Indian or the white boys here. They are often truculent but they can also be full of exuberance. A lot of their teachers in the junior schools say that when they were with them they were mostly full of life but it's not the case here. But if you're talking to them they have a better sense of humour. But it has got a lot more easier with more Indians. I think that if you examine yourself you are prejudiced, and you must change it and it's tied up with [he pointed to his Christian cross that he wore].

Mr Banks, who was a committed Christian, identified with those

Caribbean students who shared his Christian zeal. He had organized a Christian club that 15 younger students attended.

The teachers' dominant social image of the Afro-Caribbean male students was that of 'trouble-maker'. However, they had developed strategies and tactics to deal with this social perception that they had created. What they found more threatening was the academically successful Afro-Caribbeans. It would seem that their caricature of the Afro-Caribbean students had developed exclusively in behavioural terms excluding a technical evaluation. Hence, the oppositional structure of this group consisted of an evaluative system of their temperament which varied from truculence to exuberance but did not include such technical categories as the measurement of academic achievement. They were assumed implicitly as a group to be of 'low ability'. Mr Lynch (L) discussed the teachers' response to academically successful Afro-Caribbeans:

> The teachers here can't cope with black lads who can stand up for themselves without being cheeky. Look at the Charles boys. Teachers hated them. Why? Because they were successful and probably going to be more successful than them economically. If a black lad talks back to a teacher as an equal, they have a special vocabulary for him, he's arrogant, truculent and so on. They go out of their way to humiliate him and if the lad walks away to avoid confrontation they get them for cheek. If yer a racist, the one thing you don't want is a successful black. Such lads have always found it tough here. I try and get them into colleges.

In contrast to this caricature, the Asian male students tended to be perceived in technical rather than behavioural terms, though the latter was not excluded. The oppositional structure of the teachers' caricature of the Asian students consisted of the positive perception of them as high achievers and the negative view of them as sly. In the day-to-day interaction between staff and students the Asian students were perceived as causing few disciplinary problems. However, many teachers explained their 'conformist' attitude in negative stereotype terms:[18]

Mr Walker: (OD)	I've never no, I don't think I've ever met an Indian who was interested, I mean really interested in learning, in education. All they're bothered about is science subjects and becoming doctors. They don't consider discussion as work. Can we write something.
Mr Tetley: (NR)	You talk to them and you can't tell if they're listening or not. They're such liars an' . . . [interrupted] . . .
Mr Walker:	I know, look at . . .

Mr Parks: (OD)	At least with the coloureds, you know where you are, with the Asians you just can't tell.
Mr Walker:	They may get into less trouble, I know that, but let's face it they're more sly and they've got no guts. The West Indian will go wild but at least he'll stand his ground. He's no coward. The Indians would stab you in the back.
Mr Parks:	And then say it wasn't them.

Much of the conventional research on 'race relations' calls for in-service training for teachers. The evidence at Kilby school suggests that it has little effect in changing racist attitudes.[19] Mr Gordon was a young teacher who was completing a part-time B.Ed. degree in multicultural education. Like many teachers he continued to hold contradictory ideas on questions of 'race'. In staffroom conversations, he often employed multicultural phrases and suggested a liberal position on these issues. However, his superficial stance was challenged by his support for openly racist verbal attacks by other members of staff. The following discussion took place in the staffroom with Mr Gordon relating details of how he had caught an Asian student cheating in an examination.

Mr Gordon: (L)	I threw out Ranjit Kumar for cheating in my exam today.
Mr Rogers: (NR)	You've got to watch them [Asian students], every year it's the same, we get a few of them caught. They're too sly to. They're so ambitious ye see, parents trying.
Mr Gordon:	I know, when I go along the Kilby road I see them pushing in the queues. Always trying to get things for nothing. It's their standards. I told Kumar if that's your standard that's fine out there but we're not, we don't accept it in this school.

Finally, we can see how the system of racist stereotyping operated in relation to the teachers' response to the students' sub-cultural groups. Teachers at Kilby school were aware of the significance of the student peer group interaction. A minority of Liberal teachers maintained that these peer groups were of central importance to the formation of the students' social development. However, most teachers saw these groups primarily in terms of a social base which strengthened the students' resistance to their authority. The following discussion which took place between Mr Lynch and Mr Winters, a probationary teacher, was representative of these differing views:

Mr Winters: (NR)	It's terrible the way the kids get into gangs. They come here as individual kids but after about two years they begin to form really strong groups and then the gang affects them more than us. It's a pity that we can't

	prevent them happening and then we could be more effective.
Mr Lynch: (L)	No, these lads haven't got much. These groups are very important to them.
Mr Winters:	Yes, but it's the trouble they cause that ... [interrupted] ...
Mr Lynch:	They form their identities through these groups. Believe me, they will need these mutual self-help peer groups to exist outside of here.

At Kilby school, teachers become experts at predicting the formation of particular sub-cultural groups. Usually during the students' third year, leaders of these groups were the first to emerge. Once they were publicly identified, their friends, when disciplined, were referred to as belonging to a particular gang. At this point, the authorities attempted to split up these groups. Below, the teachers are discussing what tactics to employ to counteract the growth of a sub-cultural group among the third-year boys:

Mr Walsh: (OD)	He's a real yobbo.
Mr Parks: (OD)	We're gonna have a similar clique by the end of this year as the present fifth year if we're not careful.
Mr Walsh:	He's got his yobs around him already. I told him to go down stairs. He just stared back. You know that arrogant look. Then Williams, Brown and Flash came and ... [Afro-Caribbean students] ...
Mr Griffiths: (OD)	Pickett?
Mr Walsh:	Yeah he was there. I couldn't believe it, third year. I told Brown there's no way he's coming into my group next year, but of course he just gave that stupid look.
Mr Parks:	Are they all in one group, the same class?
Mr Griffiths:	No not, that's the trouble. It's usually from 3:3 but some of them are in 3:1.
Mr Walsh:	I'm going to make sure he's put down to 3:2.
Mrs Turner: (OD)	His work's OK, in fact he's ...
Mr Walsh:	I don't care, it's his attitude to the staff. Well you know, he'll only talk to you if he has to, as if he's doing you a big favour and of course the other boys pick it up.
Mr Griffiths:	He's the most truculent kid I've met. Typical Jamaican, sucking his teeth and getting the others to go mad.
Mr Walsh:	I think the head should take them and tell them, warn them they don't hang around together while they're here, anyway, or they find another school. I mean just imagine them in the fifth year.

Mr Griffiths: We'll have to get him and a few others and they'll need a concerted trampling on. They'll need the full treatment.

The emerging third year Afro-Caribbean sub-cultural group were seen to be modelling themselves on the Rasta Heads. The school authorities realized the central significance of Rastafarianism. Its ideological strength within the context of the school was that it had not permitted white authoritarian or liberal accommodation and so, consequently, it had united the staff against it. The authoritarian teachers saw it as the most visible threat to the order of the school. The Liberal teachers were divided among themselves as to the significance of this ideology of resistance. The majority Liberal view and the institutionally more effective one, was represented by Mr Lynch, who argued that Rastafarianism acted against the interests of the Afro-Caribbean students, preventing racial integration and social mobility. Mr Fields, who believed that the school should be community-based, represented the minority view. At the time of the research there were only three teachers who defended the Rasta Heads' activities as a legitimate strategy of survival. Mr Fields, who remained within the culturalist perspective, explained how he had come to appreciate the positive effects of Rastafarianism in building up Afro-Caribbean youth's 'low self-image'. Harold, an Afro-Caribbean student who had a good disciplinary record, began in the fifth year to associate with the Rasta Heads. Mr Fields:

> I don't particularly like the Rasta movement. I know some who are OK, but generally they are devisive. But I've begun to see that from our kids' point of view it gives them high status, a role and it helps them to develop a positive image of themselves that a lot of West Indians lack. Look at Harold in my group, he used to be an Uncle Tom. It isn't enough to tap a kid on the head everyday and tell him we are pleased with him. Now he's a much fuller personality, beginning to work out an identity. Teachers go mad when we lose kids like him. They haven't chosen our way they reckon, fuck it, of course they haven't. It wouldn't make sense. They have to prepare themselves for living around here. I don't see it as a question of agreeing or disagreeing with the Rasta stuff. It's a question of understanding why it has emerged. But I don't personally think that this is the best course. We must work together more to build up our community.

Mr Fields' response was partly determined by the school authorities' reaction to Rastafarianism. As pointed out above, the headteacher and the deputy head were successful in creating a 'moral panic' among the staff concerning the Rasta Heads' behaviour.

The teachers' response to the emergence of a new sub-cultural group demonstrated a number of significant points in relation to the system of racist stereotyping operating within the school. First, that for most teachers, this group was seen exclusively in negative terms as a source of disruption to the school's authority. This perception of, and response to, the male students' resistance to the racist power relations of the school and the broader society demonstrates how for both authoritarian and Liberal teachers professionalism[20] operates as an ideological strategy for depoliticizing educational and moral questions and converting them into value-free administrative and technical 'problems' (Gramsci, 1971). By refusing to acknowledge the legitimacy of the students' behaviour and locating the 'problem' within the black youths' culture, the Old Disciplinarians and New Realists reinforced the view of the need for their authoritarian solution to the problem of maintaining order. At the same time they reproduced their professional role as power holders within the school. Similarly, many of the Liberals reproduced the dominant institutional social relations by adopting racist stereotypes, which served to prevent real knowledge of black youth and their location within the school and wider society. The Liberals' definition of the situation also served to expand the need for their professional diagnosis in such areas as the school testing and classification apparatus, remedial work and counselling in response to the students' assumed psychological and social deficiencies.[21]

Secondly, we can see the teachers' perception of the 'visibility' of the Afro-Caribbean students and in particular their strong reaction against Rastafari as an ideology of resistance. Thirdly, the third-year Asian students' resistance would appear to be 'hidden'. This is made clear if we examine the composition of this sub-cultural group. The Asian and Afro-Caribbean male students' resistance to schooling, as the main case studies show, tended to take place in separate groups; however, the third-year group that the teachers were discussing above consisted of six Afro-Caribbean students, four Asians and one white. Nevertheless, it was the Afro-Caribbean students who were selectively perceived as the main 'trouble-makers'. Fourthly, these social images can be seen to determine the teachers' mode of intervention, which operated on a racial basis. Here we can see how the system of demotion and transferals discriminated against Afro-Caribbean students. In the next section these selective mechanisms are shown to be of central causal significance to the over-representation of Afro-Caribbean youth in the lower streams of schools and in Special Schools.

Summary

A definite system of racist stereotyping which consisted of an oppositional structure for each youth group, was in operation at Kilby school. The Old Disciplinarians and the New Realists worked explicitly within this framework, while many of the Liberals worked implicitly within it. The dominant social image of the male students that emerged was that of the 'high-achieving conformist' Asian, and that of the 'low-ability truculent' Afro-Caribbean. However, this is not to argue that the teachers defined students exclusively in terms of this stereotyping. Nevertheles, these racist caricatures, which were often hidden, were of central significance in understanding how white state professionals encounter black youth. Furthermore, these racist social images were of primary significance to the stratification system in operation at Kilby school, which is now examined.

The process of testing and classification

The process of testing and classification in operation at Kilby school was the central mechanism which structured the students' school career. The main stages in a student's school career were first his placement on entry to the school; secondly, the 'choosing' of subject options at the end of the third year; thirdly, the preparation for and the taking of examinations in the fifth year and, finally, career advice, aptitude testing and applying for either a job or further education. During the research period, with few students getting jobs, 'youth opportunity' training schemes became of particular importance. The Old Disciplinarians and the New Realists defended this process, arguing from a functionalist perspective that it matched the students' talents, skills and abilities to the jobs for which they are best suited. The Liberal teachers and two of the Independents were opposed to the selective system. However, as it will be shown, their criticism was aimed at the present organization of this selective system but they did not challenge its theoretical base. There was a shared acceptance of such concepts as intelligence, ability and aptitude. Behind these ideologically constructed concepts, lie class and cultural power relations. That these power relations lay hidden is partly due to the Liberals' adoption of a cultural form of analysis which assumed the class homogeneity of the black community. This racial reductionism served to reinforce the teachers' perception of the division between the 'academically high-achieving' Asian and the 'low-ability, problem' Afro-Caribbean students and so structured the teachers' material and social response to these two groups. It is through this response as part of the wider institutional structures that racism was mediated.

System of stratification

A systematic policy of stratification operated within the school through a strict streaming procedure. Levels of intelligence were measured by an initial screening test on entry to the school. The boys were then placed in a four-stream stratification for all subjects except physical education, religious education and crafts for which there was mixed-ability teaching. This initial selection was of primary importance, as there was little movement between the streams.

Mr Raynor (L), who was responsible for the administration of the tests, was highly critical of their limitations.

They are not valid. They are diagnostic tests being used as an instrument of selection. They are given out in the first few days of the children arriving, which for administrative purposes make sense but the practice is educationally totally unsound. Children are just in from their junior schools to a new establishment, totally unsettled and there is culture bias. You might as well stream by throwing all the names in the air and picking them out at random.

For the Liberals, it was not simply a matter of questioning the validity of the testing procedure. Their main criticism was the selective nature of the stratification system. Each year, they argued for the introduction of mixed-ability teaching groups for the first 3 years. They were particularly concerned at the effect of the streaming process on 'low-ability' students. Mr Hickey (L):

The selective mechanisms are a hangover from the old grammar–secondary mod division. There has been a lot of research to suggest the harmful effects of this type of placement, especially the self-fulfilling effects of being labelled a failure, of being treated differently in the lower streams. It's not just the question of the child's perception but the effects it has on teachers, going into 3:3 for example, to those who are seen of low ability.

However, what the Liberals did not challenge was the theoretical basis on which the policy of stratification was based which defined intelligence as an absolute category. The Liberal and two Independent teachers who did not support streaming, nevertheless reified intelligence as a rare commodity. For example, Mr Wilts (I) employed this concept to explain the large failure rate in school examinations:

You cannot talk of failure in an unqualified way as you suggest. There are a number of variables involved. Remember that out of a hundred and twenty each year, you get about twenty who are capable of passing O-level. In fact, with the Grammar they take about four per cent of the cream, perhaps more. Even the CSE was only meant for the next forty per cent. An average is a grade three or four CSE but we put nearly everyone in for it, so they fail. But you must measure our success rate against the range of ability in a school like this.

Hence, the argument between the authoritarian, and the Liberal and the Independent teachers concerning the stratification system in operation within Kilby school took place within a shared theoretical educational paradigm which assumed that such psychological concepts as intelligence, ability and aptitude are value-free and reflect social reality (see Woods and Pollard, 1988).[22]

Mr Young: There will always be kids of low ability and those that are
(L)   brighter. But what a school must ensure is that all are
               treated equally, and that all have an equal chance of
               developing their own abilities, whatever they are, and
               they will naturally be different.

The Liberal teachers worked from within a social democratic educational
ideology which sees schooling as a meritocratic mechanism for achieving
equality of opportunity. This concept of equality of opportunity was developed in the late 1960s in relation to the question of the academic failure of
white working class youth. In response to the presence of black youth in the
school, the Liberals argued that in order to achieve equality of opportunity
there had to be an institutional acceptance of a plurality of cultures.

Mr Hickey: The last forty years of educational development has been
(L)   concerned with attaining equality of opportunity. I be-
               lieve that this is one of the aims I work with, and for the
               black kids it means accepting their culture, but in the
               main curriculum not just as an extra subject area.

The Liberals assumed that the plurality of cultures within the school would
co-exist equally. What is missing from their analysis is an awareness of the
power relations that exist between the dominant and minority cultures both
within the school and the wider society. So, for example, the Liberals were
unable to see that their view of knowledge served to maintain a monoculturalist class-based curriculum. They tended to see knowledge as a fragmented
collection of value-free commodities, and the school as a means of the
maximization of this cultural accumulation (see Whitty, 1985).[23] They did
not see the systematic ideological selection, transmission and evaluation of
school knowledge which reflected the dominant culture and so excludes the
cultures of the black community.[24]

Mr Lynch: In the past, we have selected a few of our top lads and
(L)   given 'em the best of our culture. A comprehensive, a
               multicultural comprehensive curriculum enables all the
               pupils, whatever their ability, white and black, to be
               given the chance of the best which has been passed on
               from the past in each of the subject areas.

Furthermore, they did not see the ideological role of the form in which
knowledge is organized. So, for example, the Liberal teachers were unaware
that the individualized learning programme that they had introduced into the
curriculum which was based on the students signing 'contracts', promising
personal behaviour modification, was reflecting particular social and economic interests.

The Liberals' plural culturalist perspective was located within a culturalist form of analysis which assumed that individual students' behaviour could primarily be explained in terms of their ethnicity. The teachers' dominant social images were of a 'strong' Asian and a 'weak' Afro-Caribbean culture. It is on the basis of these social images that the teachers tended to explain the differential educational attainment of Asian and Afro-Caribbean students at Kilby school, in terms of the perceived differences between the two groups. These categories, that teachers shared with the State and conventional 'race-relations' research, form the ideological basis of their 'common-sense' racism.

> Ms Yeats: The West Indian lads have special problems, specific prob-
> (L)   lems due to their background. A lot, I have to deal with, a
>   lot of them that have only one parent. Their mothers don't
>   know what to do with them. It's really tough on them. It's
>   no fault of theirs. Families that migrate split up but for
>   them it's more. Historically, they had to suffer the effects
>   of slavery, breaking up families and so marriage and
>   family life is missing. The Indians are almost the opposite.
>   They have a very strong culture. There are pressures on
>   them living in two cultures but their strong family back-
>   ground helps them through. So ye see, you can't simply
>   talk about Indians and West Indians as though they start
>   off equally in the education system. The West Indian lads
>   need much more support. The Asians have confidence in
>   themselves. All the literature will tell you that if the West
>   Indians are to do as well as the Asians they must have this
>   extra support by us accepting their culture within the
>   school, by giving it high status, by responding positively to
>   their special problems.

The Liberals, by accepting a cultural form of analysis, had assumed a class homogeneity of the black community. While they would tend to adopt a social class analysis to examine the academic achievement of white students, black students' results were simplistically reduced to a question of 'racial' origin. This racial reductionism served to maintain the system of stereotyping in operation within the school, reinforcing the teachers' perception of the division between the 'high-achieving' Asian male students and the 'low-ability' Afro-Caribbean males. An analysis of the parental occupation of the four streams in the students' first 3 years and the option groups in the fourth and fifth years at Kilby school at the time of the research revealed that students of a non-manual work background, most of whom were Asian, were over-represented in the top stream. This suggests that social class would appear to be a significant variable in explaining the differential educational attainment between the Asian and Afro-Caribbean male students.[25] However, this is not to suggest that this differential educational attainment can simply be reduced to the analysis of the objective variable of social class. Nevertheless, the teachers at Kilby school acted as though it was ethnicity that primarily determined the educational success of black youth. This was demonstrated in the relationship between the teacher racist stereotypes and their perception of and response to the middle-class students.

Becker (1952) developed the concept of the 'ideal pupil', to refer to that set of teacher expectations which constitute a taken-for-granted notion of appropriate behaviour (see Figueroa, 1974). Keddie (1971, p. 55) argues that of primary importance to the creation of the 'ideal pupil' are social class judgements of pupils' social, moral and intellectual behaviour. At Kilby school there was no significant Afro-Caribbean middle-class, with less than 10 of the 157 Afro-Caribbean students from a middle-class background. Among the Asian students, in each year, there was a small group of middle-class students. Teachers tended to identify with these students and saw them as constituting the 'ideal pupil'. This is not to suggest that middle-class Asian students simply reduplicated or reflected the dominant ideologies of the teachers. Nor is it to argue that the mutual identification of the teachers and the middle-class students was consciously created. There was an internal logic to the ideologies and practices of each group. However, their logics did intersect at important points. So, for example, the shared values of individualism, competition and careerism served to reinforce the teachers' differential response to the students with their positive response towards middle-class Asian students. It would seem that teachers also tended to extend the conformity of these students to the Asian group as a whole. This then served to make 'invisible' the resistance of working-class Asian students. The teachers' positive response to middle-class students, including those of Afro-Caribbean origin, can be contrasted with their negative evaluation of the working-class students' sub-cultural groups, that was examined earlier. However, although social class would appear to be a significant variable in explaining the students' behaviour and the teachers' response to their behaviour, the teachers nevertheless, continue to explain the students' response to schooling primarily in terms of ethnicity. For the teachers there is assumed to be an unproblematic class homogeneity among the black community.

The Liberal teachers were of central significance in two ways in the evaluation and classification of students in racial terms. First, their use of psychological terminology unwittingly functioned to legitimate the racist stereotypes operating within the school. The over-representation of Afro-Caribbean students in the lower streams and non-examination groups was rationalized in terms of their adoption of the 'common-sense' educational categories of ability, aptitude and attitude. Secondly, although the Liberals opposed the stratification system, they failed to see that their acceptance of its theoretical underpinning, that is, the conception of the limited supply of intelligence, served to reproduce, maintain and ideologically legitimate a strict classification of 'academic' and 'non-academic' students. It was through this existing framework that racism was mediated. In the context of Kilby school, this division became synonymous with the division between the Asian and Afro-Caribbean students. So, for example, the under-representation of the Afro-Caribbean students in the top streams and O-level examination groups led to a simplistic social perception of Afro-Caribbeans, as a social group, as predominantly non-academic, and their ethnicity as the causal factor. Furthermore, the Liberal teachers, due to their acceptance of these ideologically constructed 'common-sense' concepts, were unable to see that the above division was not the result of cultural differences, but as Lettieri (1976, p. 151) argues, this institutional division reflects the labour process of capitalist societies:

> Capitalism has allowed us to get used to living under a system in which intellectual and manual work tend to be incompatible with each other (p. 151).

Significantly, Lettieri adds, in relation to the teachers' ideological position:

> This mutual exclusion is, moreover, a characteristic feature of petty bourgeois ideology, which is horrified by the idea of manual work (p. 151).

The organization of the curriculum, which was based on this division and which served to reinforce the racist stereotypes of the 'academic' Asian and the 'non-academic' Afro-Caribbean is now examined.

Curriculum organization

The stages of the students' career at Kilby school were structured in order that the primary teacher concern was the needs of the 'academic' top stream. They had a number of material and social advantages. Although there was a shortage of classrooms, they had permanent teaching locations for each subject, while the middle stream students had to move to different classrooms for the same subject. Also, the top stream were given access to specialist classrooms, e.g. the science laboratory and the computer rooms, they tended to have the most experienced teachers, the first choice of subjects, preferential treatment on the timetable and more equipment and books. Of equal importance was the attitude of the staff to the students. The teachers regarded them with high esteem and had high expectations of them.

As a result of the organization of the curriculum in favour of the academic top stream, it was particularly the third stream that suffered. It was consi-dered of little importance on the timetable, receiving split teaching periods and inexperienced teachers, and it was vastly under-resourced. This system of structuring the curriculum led to a strict stratification policy. Mr Raynor (L), explained how students who were placed in the lowest stream on entry to the school, had little chance of upward mobility.

> It's a terrible dilemma when the children work very hard and technically they are ready to move out of the bottom stream because the third set is non-supportive of our boys. When I came here first I worked to get as many of them as possible out, but seeing what happens to them, we now keep them. They are sometimes disappointed but you can't promote them to the worse place in the school. It's only the top and bottom we cater for, but those at the bottom are stuck there. We have no choice.

At the end of the third year, the top stream were offered first choice of subject options and encouraged to take science subjects, thus relegating the two middle streams to non-academic subjects and a general course in science.[26] The next stage of this highly selective process was the placement of students into examination groups. The top stream were given access to the high-status GCE examinations, while the middle streams were placed in CSE groups. The remaining students were encouraged by subject teachers not to enter public examinations but to concentrate on practically orientated subjects. When they did choose examination classes, they were often discriminated against by being grouped together with an inexperienced teacher who had low expectations of them.

This organization of the curriculum and the resulting differential response of the teachers to the 'academic' and the 'non-academic' students disproportionately affected the Afro-Caribbeans who were under-represented in the top stream. This placement was not simply the result of the school's tests. In the early years, and particularly in the first year, the Afro-Caribbean students were well-represented in the top streams. However, as they moved up the school, they became over-represented in the lower streams. In the first year of the present fifth year's schooling at Kilby there had been 14 Afro-Caribbean students in the top stream. By the fifth year, there were seven and, of these, only three students were entered for O-level examinations. Similar patterns were to be found in each year. Of particular significance to these results was the process of promotion and demotion between the streams which was accepted by both authoritarian and the majority of Liberal teachers and which was ostensibly based on the criteria of ability and achievement. This process, which in practice was based on an arbitrary decision-making procedure, was informed by the teacher racist stereotyping and so discriminated against Afro-Caribbean students.[27] It is now examined.

Process of promotion and demotion

Several incidents recorded during the research period highlight the practices of this process and makes clear the teachers' differential response to the Asian and Afro-Caribbean students. On one occasion it was found that 35 students were in set one for English, so 3 of them had to be demoted. It was the responsibility of Mr Wells to choose the three students. He asked Mr Knight, a temporary English teacher, to select them on the basis of their last English test. Mr Davies complained that the boys that were chosen would have to drop French, but the three of them had received certificates in recognition of their high achievement in the subject. He argued that the decision should not be based on one test in English, but that all the teachers who taught the students involved should make a collective decision. Mr Wells refused to accept Mr Davies's suggestion and asked Mr Higget, the deputy head, to decide. Mr Higget suggested that the principal of, last in first out, should be applied, so those who joined the school during the year were put into a lower stream. Also, he argued that since one of them, Lloyd Cains, of Afro-Caribbean parentage, had come from a Special School, he would benefit from this placement. It is difficult to work out how Lloyd was to benefit from this demotion, but the deputy head's assumptions were not based on the advice of the educational psychologist's report from his former school. It stressed the need to create an educational environment in which Lloyd's self-image was allowed to develop positively. Lloyd was very upset by the decision. Two years later he was suspended for continual non-attendance. Mr Lynch maintained that the school authorities' arbitrary administrative decision-making had indirectly created a school deviant.

On another occasion, an Afro-Caribbean student, Denzil Wallace, was demoted from the top set in mathematics. The decision was challenged by his form teacher, Mr Snape:

Mr Snape: (L)	Mike, why has Denzil been put in 2:2?
Mr Walsh: (OD)	The results are over there. He scored below the pass mark.
Mr Snape:	But how has he done in the year?
Mr Walsh:	Terrible, his work rate is awful.
Mr Snape:	But how come it was never reported to me?
Mr Walsh:	Listen, I've got 32 in that class and I just can't be expected to follow up every pupil. I warned him a number of times this would happen.
Mr Snape:	But why send him down to . . .? [interrupted].
Mr Walsh:	Because I always stick by the tests.
Mr Snape:	But Mike, Denzil scored the highest marks in his year on the entrance test. Everyone . . .
Mr Walsh:	There are freak results every year. Every year, you get one that you can throw away. You're always against the tests, don't tell me you now think that they are infallible. Denzil's brother was just the same.
Mr Snape:	The junior school said that he was the best pupil that they

had in his year. Christ, I can't believe it when black kids do bad on tests, you blame them and when they do well you question the tests.

One further example of the arbitrariness of the decision-making process highlights the racial element that is often hidden behind what are assumed to be value-free administrative and educational solutions to institutional problems. Paul Edwards, an Afro-Caribbean student, was placed in the third set when he arrived at Kilby school. During his first term, some of his subject teachers were concerned about his behaviour. This was described in terms of his vagueness and his coming late and not being prepared for lessons. At the end of the first term Paul was demoted to the fourth stream. The following discussion took place during Paul's second term at the school. Mr Barlow and Mrs Turner had asked for a place to be found for Paul in a Special School. Mr Raynor challenged the recommendation:

Mr Barlow: We're only thinking what is best for him. He doesn't fit in
(NR) to the school.
Mr Raynor: What do you mean he doesn't fit in? What does he or
(L) what doesn't he do that so annoys you?
Mrs Turner: It's not as simple, as easy as that. It's that strange gazed
(OD) look. You find it with coloured children. He turns up late with no excuse.
Mr Barlow: Yes, that's it, and he's not upset by it, that's the thing that gets me. He keeps getting lost and he's not upset. A lot of these kids have terrible backgrounds and they react in strange ways, to us anyway, they react in strange ways.

Mr Lynch asked Mrs Parsons, an educational psychologist, to carry out a series of tests on Paul. She concluded that there was no psychological reason why Paul should be transferred to a Special School. Mr Lynch asked Mr Barlow and Mrs Turner to specify the educational reasons why he should be transferred. They felt unable to give concrete reasons. Mr Lynch accepted the findings of the educational psychologist and decided that Paul should remain at Kilby school.

Just as demotion was arbitrarily based on the perceived attitude rather than as was officially assumed the 'ability' of students, so similarly this same criterion was used in relation to promotion. Mr Parks (OD) justified this approach:

There are boys of relative higher ability in the lower sets, especially among the West Indians. I've told you before Johnson and Brown were marvellous at Maths, especially problem-solving. But it's their, it's the West Indians' attitude and that must decide it in the end. You can't promote a boy who is known to be a trouble-maker, who's a dodger. It will look like a reward for bad behaviour. We've always got to be looking behind our shoulder and asking ourselves what effect will this move have on the other boys?

This process was an essential element in the differential response of both authoritarian and Liberal teachers to the Asian and Afro-Caribbean students. It is important to draw together the main conclusions of the effects of the implementation of the decision-making process in relation to the system of promotion and demotion of students, their placement in examination groups, and their transfer to Special Schools. First, it can be seen that it was not only the sector of the Afro-Caribbean students who overtly challenged the authority of the school, who were racially caricatured as culturally deficient, but the whole group. Secondly, it was the conjunction of the system of negative racist stereotyping and the process of decision making which is arbitrarily based on behavioural criteria that served to discriminate particularly against Afro-Caribbean students. Thirdly, that what are complex social and educational issues were reduced to administrative problems. One of the central functions of the school administrative role, which includes the teachers' evaluation of students, is to deal with what is dysfunctional in the system. Due to the teachers' powerful social image of the social pathology of the Afro-Caribbean students they were 'seen' as the main cause of the dysfunction. Hence, the school authorities spent much of their time in dealing with 'problems' that they had indirectly created. This in turn served to maintain the dominant social image of the Afro-Caribbean students as 'behavioural problems'.

Summary

This chapter set out to examine an absence in conventional 'race-relations' research and official reports, that of the response of the teachers to the schooling of black youth. The different teacher ideologies and practices in operation at Kilby school were identified, with particular reference to curriculum organization and the system of racist stereotyping. These differences are important, but we may conclude from the above that the main institutional response at the school has been an attempt, albeit unintentional, to incorporate the majority black male student population. The Old Disciplinarians and the New Realists were unambiguously committed to this approach. The Liberal teachers, whose position was part of a wider social democratic approach to solve the assumed cultural deprivation of white working-class youth by means of equalizing opportunities, saw the monocultural position of the rest of the staff as the main cause of their failure to implement throughout the school a multicultural curriculum. However, we can see that the arguments of the differing teacher ideologies take place within a particular shared conception of what constitutes multicultural education. All teacher groups adopted the state's conception, which perceives black youth rather than racism as the primary problem. It is this perception of black youth on which are based the state's multicultural policies. The authoritarian and the Liberal teachers differed in their prescriptive remedies for these 'problems', particularly that of the 'under-achievement' of Afro-Caribbean students. The Liberals believed in an interventionist approach based on the state's multicultural policies, while the authoritarians argued for the maintenance of the traditional curriculum for all students. However, both groups worked from within the same educational paradigm, which assumes that education is essentially a politically and racially neutral mechanism which socializes students for adult roles and occupations. During the research period, I recorded many personal interventions by Liberal teachers, particularly by those who were moving towards an anti-racist position, in defence of Afro-Caribbean students, such as Paul and Denzil above. The main weakness of their approach was that they failed to develop a co-ordinated policy to deal with the differential treatment of these young people. Furthermore, they did not have the institutional support for such an approach, which would have served to make their response more effective.

Teachers are not as crude Marxists suggest, disinterested agents of an abstract capital or the state, functionally reproducing social control. Similarly, the proposed solution of culturalist analysis to the 'problem' of schooling black youth, that the implementation of a multicultural curriculum will develop positive teachers' attitudes to black students, is inadequate. It is within the teachers' material interests as power holders to maintain the dominant social relations of the school, including its racist structures. As a result of the limitations and contradictions of the Liberals' ideology and practices, they were unable to perceive how the ideologies of class, 'race' and gender interact at Kilby school. Hence, they were unable to resolve the problems that arise.

It is against this background of the operation of a process of depoliticization and deracialization that works from within a culturalist form of analysis and which results in the differential response of the Kilby teachers to the Asian and Afro-Caribbean male students that I shall locate the black students' forms of resistance, which is examined in the following two chapters.

Chapter 3

The Rasta Heads: Visible Form of Resistance

Introduction

It was shown in the last chapter that within Kilby school the teachers' racism, working within a culturalist perspective, operated on the principle of defining Afro-Caribbean and Asian male students as different. These cultural differences were seen by the teachers as the primary cause of their behaviour. An important element in the creation of these oppositional forms of student practices has been the way in which 'race-relations' research has perceived and reported the school experience of these two groups. Researchers have tended to focus on the 'under-achievement' of Afro-Caribbean male youth with the dominant explanation of this 'under-achievement' in terms of various theories of cultural deprivation. In contrast, the 'problems' of Asian youth have been reduced to questions of linguistic difficulties and the conflict of being 'caught between two cultures'.[1]

By working within this culturalist perspective that assumes that intrinsic ethnic differences between Afro-Caribbean and Asian cultures are essentially causal of their academic achievement, researchers have created a number of significant effects. First, they have produced powerful social images of the social problems that Afro-Caribbeans cause schools in contrast to Asian youths' technical difficulties. Secondly, this in turn has challenged the black community's argument that racism is the main cause of their children's school failure.[2] Thirdly, the emphasis on the 'passivity' of Asian students has served to underplay the resistance to schooling of sections of this group and so helped to make it 'invisible'. Finally, the culturalist perspective has assumed a class homogeneity of the black community.

In order to challenge the teachers' common-sense perception of 'rebellious' Afro-Caribbeans and 'passive' Asians, a more fruitful framework to adopt is that of the visible and invisible forms of resistance to schooling of these two groups. This framework enables us to see a disjuncture between the teacher–

student relations. Further, it shows that one of the main effects of the teacher stereotypes and the resulting mode of intervention was that they tended to highlight the perceived 'rebelliousness' of Afro-Caribbean students and the perceived 'passivity' of Asian students. It is important to emphasize that no conspiracy theory was involved here. It was not a question of teachers consciously denigrating Afro-Caribbean culture and elevating Asian culture. Rather, these oppositional stereotypes had an existence in the material reality of the social relations of Kilby school. It would appear that this was not simply a problem of false consciousness as they performed a particular function. The practices of the teachers based on these stereotypes attempted to reproduce the situation they believed to exist.[3]

Of equal importance to an understanding of the student forms of resistance was the response of Afro-Caribbean and Asian boys to the teachers' racist stereotypes. In other words, it was not only what happened to students that was of importance but also how they perceived and managed their experience of racism.

Two of the main case studies, that of the Afro-Caribbean Rasta Heads and the Asian Warriors, suggest that their response operated at two levels. At one level, in both groups there were elements of a sub-culture that inverted the dominant ideology of the school. At another level, this ideology was accommodated and this had the effect of creating a self-fulfilling prophecy. So, for example, the Rasta Heads adopted the response that was expected of them, and overtly challenged the authority of the school. The Warriors similarly responded to teacher expectations and on occasions while breaking the rules they adopted a low profile. Although this was the dominant sub-cultural response, it is shown that on occasions they broke through this ideology, challenged the teacher stereotypes and emphasized the unity of black students of Afro-Caribbean and Asian origin and their common experience of institutional racism.

Finally, it is shown that the student ideologies and practices cannot be explained in terms of individual psychological inadequacies or generational conflict.[4] The problem is not one of cultural deficiencies or divisions but a question of class location and institutional racism. It is important to locate the growth of black boys' sub-cultures of resistance both in relation to the dominant relations of society and in relation to the black community's response to racism. Hence, the Liberal teachers' prescribed solution of a more relevant multicultural curriculum, which was examined in the last chapter, has been overtaken and will not resolve the crisis of schooling black students.

School and society

Among teachers at Kilby school, there was a tendency to see groups and relations within the school in isolation from the rest of society. But as has been argued (*Race Today*, 1974, p. 171) concerning the self-activity of the

Brixton youth in resolving their homelessness by occupying local council houses:

> The strength therefore of the black squatting movement is the fact that it is rooted in Brixton's black community and has as its base the social organization of the youth. They visit and frequent the same youth clubs, they congregate in large numbers at social functions, originally molded into a single social unit within the schools.

Similarly, the Rasta Heads' resistance to schooling must be located in its social setting. This is examined in terms of the social function of sub-cultures for working-class youth, the relation between the Rasta Heads and their parents, and the response of the black community to the effects of the changing national socio-economic conditions on Kilby's local economy.

The Rasta Heads group could not be reduced simply to a black variant of working-class youth sub-culture. However, it did share much with parallel white forms, similarly located within the class structure. Brake (1980, p. 36) explains why these groups emerge. He argues that:

> Sub-cultures arise as attempts to resolve collectively experienced problems arising from the contradictions in the social structure, and that they generate a form of collective identity from which an individual identity can be achieved. . . . This is nearly always a temporary solution, and in no sense a real material solution but one which is solved at the cultural level.

Of central significance to the emergence of the Rasta Heads had been their response to the contradictions of schooling. Milner (1975, p. 204) describes such contradictions experienced by black children attending British schools:

> At present the black child spends the greater part of his working hours in a place that does nothing to confirm him in any important aspects of his identity. Effectively, he is treated as an English child, albeit a 'coloured' one, and with certain disadvantages. His own cultural originality is almost entirely ignored, so that he only receives that sense of himself from his parents out of school hours.

Within Kilby school there was little positive confirmation of the black students' identity. However, Milner's weakness is his assumption that black young people live in two dichotomous social worlds, the school and the home. The male peer group was of central importance in the formation of identity. The Rasta Heads' opposition to schooling was most immediately expressed through their dissociation from the formal sphere of schooling into the informal sphere of their sub-culture. A positive association took place and central to this was a process of Africanization which pervaded the students' resistance. Of particular significance was the ideological influence of Rastafari in building a black cultural nationalism.[5]

MM:	Do you think all young blacks are affected by Rastafari?
Kevin:	Of course.
Leslie:	Yeah because I'll tell you one thing before Rasta some people would not know them culture.
Kevin:	Yeah Rastafari tell you about your culture because if you ask my father for one where you come from he don't want to know about Africa. Him say my home is Jamaica.
Christopher:	Is yer roots really, you find out who you are.
Leonard:	I don't check for Selassie but I really respect 'em right, you know when I was at school I never knew I came, that our foreparents came from Africa. Rastafari helped me to find out more things about myself, who I am an' what's important.

Small groups of students at Kilby school overtly identified themselves as Rastas but its ideological significance was much wider. As Miles (1978, p. 22) found in his research:

For a larger proportion of black youth in England, a distinct identity and life-style, a stylization can be found in patois, a style of dress and appearance, and a music which is a blend of Jamaican and Rastafarian symbols and English experience and events.

Of equal importance to the formation of the Rasta Heads and the development of their ideologies and practices, as Cohen (1972) has argued concerning white working-class youth sub-cultures, was their relationship to the 'parent' culture.[6] Ms Brown, a black teacher working in Kilby, dismissed the explanation common among white teachers that Afro-Caribbean youth's 'deviant behaviour' was the result of generation conflict among the black community:

All the teachers, most of them and they are encouraged by the race-relations stuff they really believe that we [the black community] are split in two. I sometimes wonder who they're talking about. It's not true, it's not true that our parents come thinking the streets were paved with gold, just nonsense. They had expectations of improving life like all migrants. How come they don't say the Irish were looking for these golden streets? Over the last twenty, thirty years, they have been more disillusioned. But why wouldn't black parents understand the frustrations of their kids? My dad fought racism ever since he came here. Kids are doing it their way now.

Mr Wallace, a black local community worker expanded this view of the unity of the black community:

> You see the white experts always simplify things. It's part of the old rulers' principle divide and rule. In fact it's not simply a matter of the parents not wanting their kids to become Rastas or throwing them out if they do. Sure a lot of them don't want their kids to become Rastas for religious reasons or realistically they are more vulnerable to police harassment, but at the same time the parents, my parents have educated their young, not by intention, and perhaps all the more successfully for being unintended into what life in a racist society really means. In loads of things, like the problems of working for white people, how they're treated by white officials, if they move into white areas, lack of promotion, doing shit work, they hear stories of people being beaten up by the police, no respect for older members of our society, the list is endless. The kids have learnt well and try other ways of surviving, of beating the system but I think in many ways the black community has more unity than among white people because the whole of the black community suffer from racism. How stupid and typical of whites to assume our parents just accepted it. Do people just accept being treated as inferior?

In support of this argument, Hall *et al.* (1978, p. 353) have stated that no simple dichotomy can be made between the 'first-generation' Afro-Caribbean migrants and their children.

> The commitment of the first generation migrants to steady if unrewarding labour and the second generation to the life on the street and hustling rather than labouring are the principal forms in which the generation gap is articulated. . . . However, as the pressures on the colony community, from police surveillance and control, from unemployment and official racism have steadily increased so the division within the colony between the young and the old, between those who have chosen the respectable route and those who have chosen to hustle and survive, has been eroded and there has been an increasing tendency to close ranks internally in the face of a common and hostile threat.

For Hall *et al.*, the unity of resistance to racism of both 'generations' is linked to the changing economic, social and political changes during the 1970s. An unintended consequence of this analysis may be the assumption that prior to those socio-economic changes the 'first generation' passively accepted racism.[7] Mr Baxter, Kevin's father, cited these changing conditions as of significance to Afro-Caribbean parents' support of their children's critical response to schooling but also emphasized that the Afro-Caribbean community had fought racism since their arrival in Britain:[8]

> We hoped that our kids wouldn't have to do the bad work we had to do.

But it hasn't worked out like that. I have lived here for over twenty years and things have got worse and worse for black people in this area. I used to think it was Delroy's fault at first but it's been the same for the others. Like Kevin was suspended from school and then the teachers, the headmaster tried to get him for non-attendance. They tell me he's clever but they were never really interested in him. They told him he has a chip on his shoulder. I was told the same thing when I first came here and asked for a job in my trade. We had to fight to get our right jobs. They sent me all round the country, now there's no jobs round here. Kevin knows, his two brothers and all his friends are on the dole. So you can't really blame him.

Mr Baxter, like many of the parents interviewed considered that the most significant aspect of the national socio-economic changes was the effect of unemployment on the local economy.

A number of reports and research findings have concluded that in addition to the problems facing working-class youth with the collapse of the youth labour market, black youth also experience institutionalized racism.[9] During the research period I visited a number of local employers. The following interview took place at a local factory that produced machetes. His argument was typical, albeit unusually explicit, of their response to recruitment during the recent economic recession.

> MM: How come the older workers are all black and the younger ones white?
>
> Mr Banks: A few years ago we could only get coloured blokes, but now, well between you and me we can pick and choose, so it's only natural that we pick our own kids. They'd do the same.

For Mr Banks, 'our own kids' referred to white youth. The fact that nearly all the black boys seeking work had been born in Britain did not qualify them to be classified as British. Colour was the predominant criterion for selection. For students at Kilby school and their parents, this was a common experience of the racist structures of the local economy. It was awareness of these material conditions and particularly knowledge of the effect of mass youth unemployment on the racial division of labour that informed the Rasta Heads' resistance to schooling.

> MM: Do you think qualifications are important?
>
> Leslie: Put it this way, I know friends who have 'O'-levels and some of them have left school for two or three years and aint got nowhere. The teachers don't know, really know, what it's like out here. How can they? They may build up yer hopes then ye go looking for jobs an' they just look at ye and ye know, go away nigger.

MM: How do you know?
Leslie: Ye know, ye see it in his face in the way he looks at ye. It's
        something ye can feel, ye've seen it with teachers and cops en it?
        Ye haven't a chance with white kids looking for the same jobs.
        They think, the owners, I'll have you your white, and a lot of
        white kids haven't work.

The logic of this sub-culture was not one of failure, inability to do
examinations nor one of cultural deficiency, but one of questioning the
validity of academic success and qualifications in relation to the demands of
the local labour market. The relationship between the Rasta Heads' ideologies and practices and their perception of and preparation for work was
further highlighted by the question of their rejection of contemporary forms
of employment (Willis, 1977, p. 154). Black employees' subordinate position
in the labour market was explicitly linked to British imperialism and teachers
were seen as presenting as an historical phenomenon what the Rasta Heads
perceived as the present-day relationship between blacks and whites. As
Leonard said:

I don't see why I should work for England because England aint done
nothing for me. You can't say we're supposed to do good and work for
England. And you did this for us and this. You came to my descendent
country, right, your own free will. We couldn't stop it because you're
supposed to have the guns an' all that. It's because of the white man,
slavery, Africa. Because of slavery and that's the mostest thing about it.
Teachers make ye think slavery was in the past, well in this country
there's a new slavery, of bad work, that's what they did to the slaves. I
wouldn't work for no white man.

With the high rate of unemployment among black youth, the question of
refusal to work tended to be hidden. However, the dynamics of the racial
division of labour was seen to be extended to the Youth Opportunity
Programme, then in operation (Sargeant, 1981). Hence, the rejection of a
subordinate position in the labour market was transferred to these youth
'training' schemes which the Rasta Heads refused to attend. Christopher:

There's a lot of kids round here even if they could get a job wouldn't
take just any job. I wouldn't do no bad job, factory work an' all that for
nutton and the same with the YOP things, we wouldn't go on them. The
work is too low an' how ye gonna survive in this country on £20? It
cannot buy nutton. How am I gonna survive?

The above research suggests that the emergence and development of the
black sub-cultures within Kilby school cannot be explained simply in terms of
parallel white youth sub-cultures nor in terms of 'second-generation' devi-

ancy. Rather, it is within the social relations of these black boys' groupings, linked to its wider class and cultural dynamics, that their resistance to schooling can be more fully understood.[10] It is important to stress that this is one particular response to racism; however, different sectors of black youth, as the Black Sisters point out in Chapter 1, adopt and develop the various strategies of survival worked out within the black community.

Formation of a sub-culture: response to racism

The Rasta Heads' visibility

The two main case studies of the resistance to schooling of the Afro-Caribbean and Asian male sub-cultures, are examined in terms of visible and invisible forms of resistance. The following account was an example of how members of these two groups by responding to teacher expectations reproduced their visible and invisible practices of resistance. Kilby school was located at the end of a long drive. The visible presence of the Afro-Caribbean students was highlighted each day as they grouped together at the school entrance. This was the only entrance for most of the teachers who drove to school. They complained frequently about the students' presence there. Each week at assembly complaints were related from local residents and passers-by of the nuisance caused by these groups of students. In contrast to the Afro-Caribbeans, Asian students gathered together at the back gate of the school involved in the same illicit activity of smoking.

The Afro-Caribbean students can be divided into three groups, the Soul Heads, the Funk Heads and the Rasta Heads. One of the main case studies was based on the latter group. It was this group of anti-school students that was most likely to include the 'under-achievers' of conventional 'race-relations' research. It was also this group that appeared to be successfully developing forms of collective resistance to the dominant racist culture of the school.

The Rasta Heads group consisted of eight pupils: Kevin, Leslie, Christopher, Andrew, Neville, Clive, Michael and Leonard. They were all born in England of Jamaican parents. Kevin's father was a carpenter and his mother was a nurse, and Clive's father was a painter and decorator. The other students' parents worked in non-skilled employment, while Andrew's and Leonard's fathers were unemployed. Six of them lived in Kilby. Neville's and Leonard's families had been rehoused outside of Kilby during the last 4 years. The students had attended two local junior schools. Kevin, Leslie and Leonard began their secondary school career in the top set but were demoted to set two, during the second and third year at the school. They were entered for CSE examinations during the fifth year. Andrew and Neville who were placed in set two on entry to the school, were demoted to non-examination groups at the end of the third year. During their 5 years at the school, six of the Rasta Heads had been suspended and, in the third year, two of their friends were transferred to Special schools. The Rasta Heads were the most visible sub-culture within the school. Most of the staff regarded them as the main source of disciplinary problems, both directly through their uncooperative behaviour and indirectly through the effect they had on the rest of the school. Among the anti-school students, they had very high status and, among them, the Rasta Heads' encounters with the staff were a constant topic of conversation and a source of imitation. However, for the conformists, the Rasta Heads were seen as the main cause of the low academic ethos of the school.

Lack of teacher–student contact

Young Afro-Caribbeans have grown up in a racially stratified society, in which there is little contact between the black and white populations. In interviews many of the boys claimed that, other than teachers and white students at the school, they did not know any white people. Gilroy, a Soul Head, made the point that he did not know any white people outside of school but that knowing them would not have included visiting their homes:

> MM: How many white people do you know?
> Gilroy: Apart from teachers?
> MM: Apart from teachers.
> Gilroy: Apart from boys at school?
> MM: Apart from boys at school.
> Gilroy: None. I'm don't know any. I only know white people at school even, even Kevin Johnson, he knows 'em but he aint ever been in their houses even.

Some of the boys claimed that they had white friends at junior school but their friends' parents discouraged them from visiting.

The Rasta Heads argued that this racial division extended to the teacher–student relations within the school and that teachers had little contact with them. Furthermore, they argued that teachers knew little about the lives of black people, as they did not visit their homes or spend time in their communities. The only time when they met black adults was the formal occasion of parents' evenings. This lack of contact and out-of-school experience helped to create and maintain the teachers' stereotypes of black youth. The Rasta Heads resented the teachers claiming to have knowledge of the black community. They interpreted the teachers' claims as a strategy of attempting to ally their authority with that of their parents against them.

> Leslie: I don't know [white teachers].
> Kevin: Him don't wanna know.

Leslie: They only know your problems till ye get outside the gate, that's only school problems.

Kevin: Not even then. They don't know nothing about our ways, like when they say, I know what your mother will do, I know, they don't know.

Leslie: How can they know? They just guessing. They only say it to frighten you, to set your own parents against you, that's wicked.

Kevin: Like they say, I know your father, I know your father. An' I know for a fact him talk like he knows my father more better than me and he's my father.

White working-class students also experience a similar lack of contact with teachers, as Mays (1962, p. 180) points out:

The teachers in the school find themselves at the nexus of two distinct cultures with a correspondingly difficult role to play. Being themselves mainly conditioned by the grammar school tradition and the middle-class system of values, they have to make a drastic mental readjustment to be able to deal sympathetically with the people whose attitudes and standards are so different.

More recently, Willis (1977) found that teachers still had to make this cultural readjustment with white working-class students. However, there are important differences between the teachers' response to the two sectors of working-class youth. First, many of the teachers at Kilby school had emerged from the working class and tended to identify more easily with white students. Secondly, Kilby school was of particular social significance for the black boys, as it tended to act as a filter institution into white society. For these students, the teachers were seen to represent white society. White teachers' lack of interest and contact with the black community was one of the students' most immediate experiences of living in a racially stratified society. It was in interaction with them that the Rasta Heads' form of resistance emerged.

Formation of the Rasta Heads

Research suggests that anti-school boys' peer groups usually emerge during the third year of secondary schooling.[11]. A similar pattern occurred at Kilby school. Initially, the students never thought of themselves as a gang. Most of them lived in the same neighbourhood and attended the same junior schools. However, as the schools made more demands on them they moved into a closer friendship. This grouping of black boys took on a specific significance within the location of the school.

MM: When was the gang formed?

Kevin: We never classed ourselves as a gang right. Like I know Christopher, Leonard and Clive from junior school and others live close. But we came together more at the end of second year at this place.

Christopher: Really, yeah, at the end of the second year, start of the third en it, an' teachers kept at us for being together.

Kevin: Yeah teachers kept trying to break us up, and we was friends.

Christopher: But we just came better, more together. You just say alright, it comes to a time, it just seems you just walk around with 'em. You walk with 'em you know. Everywhere you go your just together. You just move into togetherness.

In interviews with junior school teachers, they frequently told me that they could not understand what went wrong with some of the 'nice coloured boys' once they went to secondary school. Howard, a Soul Head, pointed out that as black youth grew older they became more aware of what teachers thought of them and then they were able to read their past experience more clearly:

At junior school, teachers pretend they like black kids, as soon as you leave junior school and you get into secondary school, and you reach third, fourth and fifth that's when you learn, you realize how you are being treated and the problems in the past. As you get older you understand what you are.

By the end of the third year at Kilby school, there would seem to have occurred what might be called a process of dissociation at the same time as the emergence of the Rasta Heads' sub-cultural group. Most of the boys interviewed who were of Afro-Caribbean origin spoke of the Caribbean and Africa as their home:

MM: What nationality are you?
Leonard: Well, I'm Jamaican.
Andrew: West Indian, Jamaican, African, originated from Africa.
MM: Were you born here?
Andrew: Yeah English-born but originated from Africa.
Neville: You mean that, I don't really care much about that because that's just where I was born. I could have been born in Israel, my roots still go back to Jamaica and then to Africa.

Other students, who at junior school had identified themselves as black English boys, at secondary school identified exclusively with their Afro-Caribbean origins. Brake (1980, p. 115) suggests that:

One myth which was quickly dispelled for black and brown youth in Britain was the view that racial integration would grow through the educational system.

Many of the boys ritualistically, as though publicly cleansing themselves, claimed that they had never thought of themselves as English.

MM: Was there ever a time you would have thought of yourself as English?
Leonard: No, no never.
Andrew: Never, how could we?
Neville: Never.
MM: Did you ever think of yourself as English?
Kevin: Well when I was at junior school.
MM: Yeah.
Kevin: It didn't seem to occur to me. I mean I just thought of myself as English, English–West Indian, English–black then.

The Rasta Heads explained their dissociation from the dominant culture as a response to their growing awareness of racism.

Kevin: Now it's changed.
MM: Why has it changed?
Kevin: Well because some'ow or other I've come to know white people hated us.
Leonard: That is true.
MM: Till?
Kevin: When I was at junior school.
MM: Till when?
Kevin: Well, till I was in about fourth year of my junior school.
Leonard: That is true, that was then when you was younger, you understand what I mean. When you get older you soon learn.
MM: Did you think of yourself as English when you were younger?
Leonard: I didn't class myself, I didn't class myself as English at all. I don't feel proud to be English. I don't feel proud to be it.
MM: How did you find out?
Kevin: Well things just started happening. Just started to hear people talk about the police picking them up for nothing, an' things like that and then seeing films, all sorts of things. Hearing about the Ku Klux Klan, the National Front, things like that.

Much of the research on racism has tended to concentrate on individual attitudes of whites rather than the underlying social forces working together against the black community.[12] For the Rasta Heads, racism could not be reduced to the personal discriminatory attitudes of individuals. They were aware of the pervasiveness of white cultural hegemony.

> Leonard: Well I was born here right but I don't wanna class myself as English, you understand, I prefer to class myself as Jamaican 'coz I don't really feel English, you know what I mean? Because you know when like some of your kind of people talk about, when they say something about when good stock comes in and they say, oh, it's British, when they talk about it's British, they ent talking about black people. They're talking about you lot. It's not for us, do you understand what I mean? Like when they say you buy pork chops, it is British of course, or when you produce the rocket, it is British. It's not for black people. It's for your kind of people.
>
> MM: So does English or British mean white?
>
> Leonard: To me it's not supposed to be but that's what it seems to me to my opinion.
>
> Andrew: Very white.

Andrew and Leslie explained the logic of their dissociation from the dominant hegemonic control of the school. They argued that the price of integration was that black people had to embrace the racist culture of white society and the majority could not do this.

> MM: Say black people were accepted as English, would you want to be classed as English?
>
> Andrew: No, you, you can never change just like that. Long time, it cannot be the same. I don't feel English because everything that goes in Britain it's not really for black people. It's against black people, so how can we join it, that, become part of that.
>
> Leslie: How can you call it your country when you've got racialists against you. When you've got people like the National Front against you. You can't even get a job in their country. So how can you call it yer country.
>
> MM: You wouldn't want to be English?
>
> Leslie: Not I wouldn't want to be, though for sure I wouldn't 'coz of what I said, but can't be, just because you're born 'ere that doesn't say you is English.

Hall *et al.* (1978, p. 347) argue that 'race' performs a double function. On the one hand, it is a central element in the way in which the black working-class experience their lives, on the other, it serves to raise consciousness of their subordination. So, it can be argued that 'race' is the principle modality in which the black youth's process of dissociation from the dominant culture operates. It was within this framework that the Rasta Heads' sub-cultural resistance could be located (see Weis, 1985, pp. 27–57).

Elements of a sub-culture

One important cultural form of a sub-culture is its style which indicates membership of a particular group.[13] A. K. Cohen (1965, p. 1) maintains that:

> An actor learns that behaviour signifying membership in a particular role includes the kinds of clothes he wears, his posture and gait, his likes and dislikes, what he talks about and the opinion he expresses.

The Rasta Heads' visibility within the school was partly due to their generation of style. This included dress, hairstyle, posture, language and the wearing of Rastafari colours. The teachers had reacted against this, as it was perceived as a threat to their social control. There was a systematic attempt to prevent student identification with Rastafarianism. The wearing of dread-locks, hats, rasta badges or colours were banned. No distinction was made by the school authorities between those who identified with it spiritually and those for whom it was a more loose cultural association. Severe sanctions were carried out against boys who challenged the authorities' position.

As a result of the effectiveness of the teachers in prohibiting external identification with Rastafari, the Rasta Heads emphasized that it was cultural practices and attitudes that defined membership of the group. Also, it is important to remember as Clarke *et al.* (1976, p. 22) argue, it is not only possessions and objects that make a style:

> What makes a style is the activity of stylization. The active organization of objects with activities and outlooks which produce an organized group identity, in the form and shape of a coherent and distinctive way of being-in-the-world.

A central component of their 'being in the world' was their projection of an image of 'toughness'.

The Afro-Caribbean experience of British schooling can be read in terms of the building of a culture of survival. From his work in Britain, Dodd (1978, p. 599) describes this culture in the following terms:

> The culture of these 'black marginals' is based, like any 'culture of poverty', upon survival; but its emphasis is on style, movement, and talk. This may be confusing to the visitor until he realises that, in this culture, this is precisely how you survive. Roles and careers follow

accordingly. The black street perspective, a profound contemporary influence on West Indian youth in England and the Caribbean look to its history in the highly symbolic biographies of Marcus Garvey, Haile Selassie and nameless rebel slaves. Rebellion in fact is a primary concept in building a viable street identity . . . it is a taken-for-granted assumption about their manhood and their place in society, or, as they see it, outside society.

Black youth systematically encounter among white people situations of degradation and violence; groups of fascists verbally and physically assault them; shop-keepers assume they are all thieves; teachers, social workers and probation officers treat them as 'social problems'; while the police are seen as a force of occupation in their neighbourhood.[14] Hence the Rasta Heads' projected machismo image, which may appear to contradict the Rastafari philosophy of peace, was in their terms a realistic defensive strategy. They knew their collective image of toughness had protected them from the recent increase in racist attacks that many Asian youth have suffered.

MM: Is it important to act tough?
Christopher: In this country, yeah. You gotta survive en it? You can't let the white man use you all the time.
MM: Do you think you sometimes act tough when you don't necessarily feel that way?
Christopher: Yeah, yeah that's true, yeah that is true. You see it's the image. You've got to act tough to survive here, to survive in this country. If you are being picked on, do you understand? I mean, you've got to act tough. Like say two white kids right call you a black bastard, what you gonna say? Are ye gonna walk on? Truth and rights I wouldn't. I'd give them the same. I'd give them, ye white dis, ye white bastard, back the same way. It's the same with teachers and specially the beesman [policeman]. He tries to make you feel low. You gotta stand up for yer rights, en it?

This toughness is not merely based on physical criteria.

MM: Does a black guy have to be tough?
Kevin: It depends. You gotta act kinda tough. I mean there's two kinds of toughness. You can talk right and you can be physical. If yer just physical I wouldn't mix with that somebody. I want someone who can talk and is physical right. I don't want to mix with a stupid head-case, he will cause you unnecessary trouble. Most of my friends they have sense. You got to talk to the man.

It was by means of these thought out strategies of resistance that the Rasta Heads were creating a crisis for the school by refusing to accommodate to the status quo. In this manner, they prevented the authorities from maintaining control through consensus. They continually challenged the relations and institutions of the school and forced its authoritarian nature into the open; the 'tough' teacher confronted the 'tough' student.[15] They rejected the institutional rhetoric of racial integration in favour of their own preparation for what they called 'reality', that is, life as they experienced it.

Rejection of schooling

The Rasta Heads regarded their view of the world as being superior and more relevant than that of the school authorities. As Willis (1977, p. 42) found during his research of white working-class boys:

> Most essentially this counter-culture is organized around the coloniza-
> tion of symbolic spaces within the school, space left unpatrolled by the
> school authorities. The nature of this colonization is the introduction of
> meanings and social ambience which subverts the school. . . . This
> involves the development of a system of practices and a set of evaluative
> criteria, opposed to those sanctioned by the staff and aimed at maxi-
> mum distancing from them.

The Rasta Heads systematically arrived late for lessons, disturbed other students by demanding their seats at the back of the classrooms, continually interrupted teachers, tried to cause arguments, talked incessantly throughout lessons and slept when asked to complete written work. They did little homework, never prepared for school tests and refused to attend annual examinations.

MM:	Where do you sit in the classroom?
Andrew:	In the middle to the back.
Clive:	At the back really.
MM:	How come?
Clive:	How come? because it come naturally.
Andrew:	You don't head for the front.
MM:	Why not?
Michael:	I don't know, it just comes natural, you know.
Clive:	We wanna talk an' all that.
Andrew:	And fall asleep, you can't sleep at the front.

Much of the Liberal research on the educational performance of black youth has pointed to the role of the school in alienating students.[16] There has been little work, however, on the question of the students' rejection of the functions of schooling. The Rasta Heads' main sub-cultural activity was called 'just talk', which has much in common with Corrigan's (1979) concept of 'doing nothing', that is, that for a majority of working-class youth their main activity is the 'passing of the time'. For the Rasta Heads 'just talk' or moving with a friend or extending your dinner break was more important than the rigid structure of the school curriculum.

MM:	Do you come late for class?
Kevin:	Well sometimes, yeah.
MM:	Why?
Neville:	Just, I'm still talking.
Kevin:	Seriously though, I don't come late just for the sake of coming late.
Neville:	A lot of teachers believe that, you know, that we come late for the sake of coming late.
Kevin:	That's wrong, I'll tell you the truth now, I don't come late for the sake of coming late in the afternoons.
Neville:	For sure, I'll tell you one thing now though, if I was talking to a girl or a friend right, I'd rather talk to them.
Kevin:	Than rush to school for sure.
Neville:	Serious, and like I'm eating my dinner, if you don't eat your dinner when you rush to school, how can you do the work on an empty stomach? That's what I say.
Kevin:	Yeah, and we're late because we wait for each other an' move with them, so you're late en it?

Their conversations at the back of the classroom might be vivid details of the 'blues' [party] they had attended the previous night. They might need to take the day off, or sleep when they come into school as a result of their leisure activities.

For the Rasta Heads, there was no intrinsic meaning in the discipline of school work. Andrew and Clive offered a rational analysis of their refusal to work in lessons in terms of the subject content lacking relevance to their lives.

MM:	Why don't you work?
Clive:	Because most of those lessons I just cannot stand.
Andrew:	There's two parts to a lesson it's got to interest you.
Clive:	It's got to be interesting right.
Andrew:	And you have to be interested in it. Most of the teachers bore you to death and I want to go to sleep.
Clive:	Sometimes, even in Mr Parks' lesson I just drop asleep [Mr Parks was seen as a strong disciplinarian].
Andrew:	Boring. So 'ow can you be interested in a lesson that bores you to death and 'ow can a teacher say, why don't you work? I tell you one thing, I only do things I'm interested in, serious. I don't play chess, I don't play

	games like that. I don't read books I'm not interested in. I do it for a reason.
MM:	Do you read any books?
Andrew:	No I hardly read any books.
Clive:	It depends on the book.
MM:	What was the last one you read?
Clive:	I'm reading the Bible.
MM:	Why do you work for someone like Mr Parks?
Kevin:	Mr Parks? Put it this way I don't to tell you the truth.
Christopher:	You only work, only work when it is necessary.
Kevin:	These few weeks Mr Parks, someat must be wrong with him because I practically don't do no work for him. I'll tell you that now.
Christopher:	You only do it when it's necessary, when it's fully necessary.
Kevin:	Yeah, I sit down an' write things man but I won't give it in because what's the use? Give it in I get cussed, get shamed because I feel I can do better. I can write good essays sometimes but Mr Parks was right when I gave him my essays. I only did them because I had to do them. That's why they was boring. I was writing just for writing, so, so that's why I'll probably get a bad mark anyway.

The visibility of the Rasta Heads' resistance was related to their overt rejection of schooling. However, this could not be explained in terms of ethnic personality traits, as teachers frequently did, when they reduced this open confrontation to a question of Afro-Caribbean temperament. At Kilby school, resistance to schooling, as is shown in the next chapter concerned with an examination of an Asian sub-cultural group, was not an exclusively Afro-Caribbean response nor was it the only response of Afro-Caribbean youth, but the teachers tended to see the Afro-Caribbean boys as intrinsically deviant. This teacher perception created a self-fulfilling prophecy.[17]

One aspect of the visibility of the Rasta Heads was their overt rejection of the work discipline of the curriculum. But also of significance were the more subtle strategies of resistance that they had developed in their refusal to participate in the 'hidden rules' of classroom interaction. They rejected what Jackson (1968) describes as the unofficial three Rs – rules, routines and regulations – that students must learn if they are to be successful at school.

In the passage below, the Rasta Heads explained that 'sucking teeth' and 'bad looks' were natural for black people. In the context of the classroom, however, they took on a different meaning. The teacher expected the student to appear sorry when he was disciplined, even if the boy was only acting out the student role of subservience. The Rasta Heads refused to apologize. Sometimes, they automatically reacted when they were disciplined, to 'warn off' the teacher. But they were very skilful at setting up the teacher and often they would exploit the teacher's lack of experience and acted out being angry. When the teacher backed off and turned away, they laughed triumphantly behind his or her back.

MM: Sometimes when a black kid is disciplined in class, they suck
           their teeth and . . . [interrupted] . . .
Michael: It's just natural.
MM: Do you know that teachers are very offended by it?
Leslie: So what? He'll have to live with it en it?
Michael: He's got to book up on it all the time. That comes from the
           parents because you could be in yer house right and some-
           body says something to you right, it's natural, it's a natural
           look.
MM: Well what kind of look is it?
Michael: It's just will you cut it out or somethin' like that.
Leslie: Bad looks, bad looks, just like a warning off.
MM: Would you do it to your parents?
Neville: If they really get you mad.
Michael: Yeah, a warning off en it? Would you go up to somebody
           laugh with them, then talk them up and then beat 'em up.
MM: So you're . . . [   ] . . .
Michael: It's just like a warning off. You get, you get a snake, like a
           rattle-snake rattles done it, to warn off somebody, same as
           somebody gives you a bad look to warn off, to say don't go
           no further.
MM: Do teachers understand?
Michael: Teachers understand? No way. Teachers is white.

Rejection of teacher strategies

The Rasta Heads were creating a sub-culture of resistance to schooling which was essentially concerned with collective protection and survival. Their attitude constantly brought them into conflict with the school authorities. This opposition was expressed in their language in terms of, 'standing up for yer rights', establishing 'truths and rights' and refusing to be 'shamed up' by teachers. As Leslie said:

Alright then put yourself in my place. You get so mad, the teacher slap you up in front of your friends, and you feel shame, you feel low down before them. What do you expect me to do? Walk off, walk off. Here I tell the man to fuck off or just tump him down, that's what I say.

Teachers were frequently complaining that Afro-Caribbean students re-fused to be disciplined. This area of conflict, so essential to maintenance of order within the school, highlighted the visibility of these students. The teachers assumed that the problem lay in the black youth themselves, and their behaviour served to reinforce the teacher stereotype of the 'troublesome' Afro-Caribbean. However, for the students, as Kevin pointed out, this stereotype was the source of the problem. They maintained that inside classrooms they were confronted by white adults who treated them as inferiors.

Kevin: It's lowness, you feel lower than the other man, done it?
MM: So what?
Kevin: What do you mean, so what? Already yer looked down upon as more inferior right. Not just us lot, all, all black men. The Indian kids are treated better than us, so it don't make no sense to make yourself look more inferior than you're already claimed to be.

This might not necessarily be a case of overt racism on the part of a teacher. He or she might be more concerned with the maintenance of order, but the effect of the ethnically based stereotypes, was that it was often interpreted through the modality of 'race'. So the 'pressure' was on the black youth to defend himself in front of his friends. Extra pressure was added by the fact that his reputation of being 'tough' or 'soft' stayed with him outside of the school.

Clive: When you get out of school, they'd run jokes. They say ye get box up by the teacher, couldn't box him back, an' all that. They'd bring it up, shame man, shame.

The headteacher, Mr Keegan, had reacted strongly against the influence of Rastafari. As a result of this he had become a primary target of the Rasta Heads' opposition. They expressed the hostility between themselves and the headteacher in personal terms.

Leonard: I'll tell Mr Keegan right, how can you run a school on fear alone? Most of them, like first years are frightened to go to Keegan.
Clive: Frightened to death.
Andrew: Really scared of him.
MM: Aren't you scared of him?
Leonard: No, in the first year when him passing my heart would jump up you know.
Clive: We build up a confidence between us.
Leonard: In my mind I say, if Mr Keegan layed a hand on me I swear to god I'd tump him down.
MM: But you wouldn't?

Leonard: I would, truth and rights. I'd tump him back, don't care. He's just a normal man.

The 'fear' that Leonard pointed to pervaded the whole school. The teaching staff as well as the students were expected to bow to the wishes of the headteacher. Many of the teachers attempted to establish an authoritarian relationship with the boys which reflected that in which they were held by the headteacher. This was part of the necessary price that they paid for their limited social mobility and might underlie their resentment of the students who refused to conform. Like Corrigans' (1979, p. 51) Smash Street Kids, who told him that school far from teaching them anything only bossed them around, the Rasta Heads frequently saw the teachers as agents of social control. As can be seen from the following discussion, their attitude to teachers appeared to be somewhat ambivalent. Their objection to 'tough' teachers did not mean that they would cooperate with those who were more liberal, whom they rejected as being 'soft'.

Christopher:	Some teachers let you away with stuff, some don't.
MM:	Do you respect any teachers?
Michael:	Respect? How can you respect 'em when they don't respect you?
Christopher:	I don't respect teachers. They just go on tough. I know a teacher may go on tough for a certain time but the time will come when he gonna fall, that what I say. All dem teachers that go on hard I say they gonna fall soon.
MM:	What's bad about teachers you don't like?
Christopher:	All teachers think they're tough.
Michael:	He's attitude to tell you the truth.
MM:	What's that like?
Michael:	The way he goes on you know, bossy because he thinks he's bigger, well he is an' he uses it as a threat.
Christopher:	I hate most of all a teacher who expects you to live up to his way of life like Parks. He's like a beesman [policeman], 'I don't know how you'll turn out lad, I've known you five years, how you gonna end up?' He's like a prison warden or someat, serious.
Andrew:	Just like that example, because so many have been taught by him right and come out good means everybody else who goes in had to the same.
Christopher:	Yeah.
MM:	Don't you think a teacher should push you?
Michael:	If everybody have their own target dem have their own target done it? Everybody don't want to reach the same heights as another.
MM:	What about the teachers who aren't tough?

Clive:	They're all the same.
Christopher:	They can be the worst, tryin' to get you to do their things just like the tough ones, only with other methods.
Michael:	You can't trust a teacher but it's, it might be easier to get them soft ones.

Fundamentally, the Rasta Heads saw school as a battle between themselves and the school authorities. They rejected the various strategies worked out by the teachers. On the one hand, they objected to the harsh tactics adopted by some of the teachers, but they would not cooperate with the more human face of the same enemy. The Rasta Heads had watched their opponents carefully and learned that weak members of their group were legitimate targets for the teachers, especially the headteacher.

Andrew:	That's what Keegan does, especially when they're in trouble. He uses them to get full information.
Leslie:	He uses the past. Like he'll bring up, I know your father, I know you an' all that. He uses the weak, like he use the small ones.
Andrew:	Yeah, if you're ever in trouble right, an' you go to Keegan's room right an' you're the one who looks a bit frightened, right then he just says I got one now.
Leslie:	Yeah because I tell you Mr Keegan.
Andrew:	Look in his eyes.
Leslie:	Mr Keegan he's evil. You can look in him eyes. You ever look in the eye of a chicken.
Andrew:	Him vicious, he's got an evil look about him.

As a consequence of the implementation of these teacher strategies, they had become experts at perceiving any signs of weakness in the authorities and responded as they had unintentionally been taught.

Clive:	They hate us for getting new teachers an' soft ones, half of us don't turn up an' when we turn up, we just sit down in our group an' talk about life. If they cause us any trouble we talk him down, in a way we can get back at them for using us so bad, that's fair en it?

One of the Rasta Heads' most creative and effective cultural practices was their use of Creole (see Gilroy, 1987).[18] In most lessons they continued their 'talks' in Creole, thereby using language as a mechanism of white exclusion. This was not simply a form of group argot. Their resistance to teacher strategies through language took various forms – for example, in the formal domain of the classroom, they frequently answered questions in monosyllables. They were aware of the defensive attitude of teachers, and so they often challenged their authority by adopting the tongue of a defiant culture. Their language belongs to an oral tradition, which conflicted with the essentially written mode of the school. As pointed out in the last chapter, in their early years of schooling, Afro-Caribbeans are often viewed positively as possessing oral skills. The Rasta Heads' junior school reports detailed their high language competency. The teachers at Kilby school had not developed these skills. The Rasta Heads, aware that the official language of the school was a major instrument of their own deculturalization, had developed these skills in order to resist the teacher strategies.

Another significant aspect of the Rasta Heads' rejection of teacher strategies was their collective resistance to the teachers' attempts to divide them through the mechanism of the stratified streaming system. The teachers could not understand why so many of the Afro-Caribbean students of 'high ability' rejected individual social mobility. Among the Rasta Heads were some of the 'brightest boys' in the school who had been demoted from the top stream during their school career. They refused to allow a black élite to be created from among them.

MM:	Why have you gone from the top stream down to a lower one?
Kevin:	I's just it, en it?
Neville:	Teachers always saying we expect dis from you, you are different, you work hard. I don't think we're different, we're all the same. I mean we should be all treated the same en it?
Kevin:	Like Leonard him got brains, like Leslie, him got brains an' all of 'em but teachers them try to divide, separate friends.

The logic of the Rasta Heads' position in rejecting the teachers' strategies which were based on competitive individualism, was made clear in the following incident. During the research period, a fifth year named Harold, in the lowest stream, suddenly became troublesome. The teachers explained this in terms of his recent close association with the Rasta Heads. However, as a Liberal teacher sympathetic to the sub-culture pointed out, the Rasta Heads could offer Harold a sense of equality that their educationally liberal approach had failed to provide. This provides a good illustration of the contradictory relationship between the Liberal teachers' policy and its implementation. On the one hand, their students were more motivated to work. On the other hand, the students' confidence was undermined as they were aware of their low status in the school and the low value of their school work (Stafford, 1981, p. 71). In contrast to the official stratification system operating within the school and its central significance in defining student identities, there was no discrimination on academic grounds among the Rasta Heads.

MM:	Where do you learn everyone is the same?
Christopher:	Through reasoning sessions.

Kevin:	Reasoning sessions all about Rasta. I's the way you is. They have a reasoning session right. First they may choose a place right? It could be anywhere.
MM:	Do you have them at school?
Christopher:	We had one last week in the sports hall. No, I don't think they would let us have it in the school due to some certain reasons like . . . [interrupted] . . .
MM:	Like what?
Christopher:	Because when you have a reasoning session everybody is as one, you smoke the holy herbs en it?
Kevin:	You don't have to have a reasoning session with ganja right, that's only part of it.
Christopher:	No, all you really need is a Bible and everybody just as one.
Kevin:	Yeah everybody just as one.

The Rasta Heads were aware of the limitations of individual social mobility. They knew the cultural cost involved. Unlike the professional teachers, they could not invisibly move into white suburbia and white-collar jobs. Within the context of school, the symbolic significance of their smoking ganja could be interpreted as their rejection of the official strategies of competitive individualism and their collective celebration of unity and equality – 'everybody as one'. The Rasta Heads took on the hierarchical structures of the school and the punishments handed out. They built modes of resistance to all of them. Teachers had to learn to negotiate with members of the group, in order to avoid open confrontation in the classroom. The Rasta Heads realized this was an important sphere of movement that they had won within the school. Their success was based upon their collective resistance (see Weis, 1985, pp. 110–27).

Summary: not a question of relevant courses

Williams (1961, p. 122) has emphasized the central importance of the relationship between the schooling process and the dominant culture of the society. He has argued that:

The way in which education is organized can be seen to express, consciously and unconsciously, the wider organization of a culture and a society . . . the content of education . . . expresses . . . certain basic elements in the culture.

In a similarly critical response to the dominant school culture, the Rasta Heads perceived and challenged the intellectual and social hegemony of white society. This was most immediately expressed in terms of criticism of the Eurocentric curriculum content.

Leonard:　It's true at school you don't learn nuttan, not really. You don't learn nuttan about your culture. You just learn about Spain and France and great England. There's nuttan wrong with these countries, you know what I mean? But me, I don't wanna learn about that. I wanna learn about my own culture but they wanna us to learn about France. I hate French. I don't understand one word I'm saying. Even Asian pupils have difficulty, how come? They, some of 'em speak three and four languages, how come? 'Coz the only thing that matters is learning French, and even the teachers can't speak it.

It was not simply a question of the transmission and reproduction of the dominant culture within the school. Of equal importance was the relationship of the school to the cultural capital of black youth. Hall *et al.* (1978, p. 340) maintain that:

In education, the reproduction of educational disadvantage for blacks is accomplished in part, through a variety of racially specific mechanisms. The cultural capital of this sector is constantly expropriated, often unwittingly through its practical devaluation. Sometimes this takes the form of patronising, stereotypical or racist attitudes of some teachers and classrooms; sometimes the fundamental misrecognitions of history and culture, as much in the overall culture of the school as specifically through syllabuses and textbooks. /

The reproduction of these racially specific mechanisms of exclusion in operation at Kilby school were examined in the last chapter. Here Andrew, Kevin and Neville discussed one of the effects of these mechanisms, the cultural continuity of the curriculum for white children. However, their insight into the racist curriculum took place within the limitations of a culturalist perspective. So, for example, they assumed that the fight against fascism during the Second World War was irrelevant to the black community.

Andrew:　Why can't we have Black studies like at Moor Green? [a neighbouring school]
Kevin:　Yeah, why should we deal with that history. I don't know about World War II or World War I.
Andrew:　I'll tell yer for sure right, might be most of the white people in this school can go home an' say mom what happened in the World War II.
Kevin:　I couldn't do that.
Andrew:　She might say this happened. I say to my mom what happened in the World War II? She'll say what World War II? Nobody knows.

Neville: They can't say there's yer grandfather's medals an' all that stuff.
Andrew: He just wouldn't know what you're talking about.
Kevin: Yeah, serious why should we deal with history and geography what don't concern us? The majority in that class it don't really concern.

They raised the question of the introduction of Black Studies. However, most state attempts at making the curriculum more relevant for white working-class children have failed.[19] They have, however, led to the institutionalization of second-rate qualifications, for example Certificates of Secondary Education and City and Guilds courses. This institutionalized mediocrity supports the unequal job structure of the labour market. Similarly, Dhondy (1974, p. 45) points to the limitations of Black Studies, which he calls a 'Battle for Minds':

> The impetus that gave rise to Black Studies which was an inspiration to know yourself and feel your own power, drifted into the formalities of geography and history. Inevitably, this co-operation of the impulse and the demand killed the interest which black youth took in the 'subject'.

Dodd (1978, p. 600) maintains that the second- and third-generation blacks, through Rastafarianism, reggae and rebellion, are developing a radically new self-concept:

> They are positive statements of change, which adhere to a view of black people as the descendents of a disinherited cultural tradition, possessing its own manner, pride and a growing sense of its own value. They are performed in the Afro-American style as properties attaching expressively to the body and affectively to the behaviour – although most whites are unfamiliar with this style and tend to react with hostility – like the police.

Some of the teachers at Kilby school also reacted with hostility. They had little respect for black youth, whom they considered to be largely cultureless. They accepted the model of black youth as presented in much of the 'race-relations' literature (CRC, 1976; Watson, 1977) as a 'generation caught between two cultures'. This led to the Liberal teachers' prescription that the function of school is to offer a path of integration to the 'second-generation immigrant'. The Rasta Heads were representatives of the 'under-achievers' of many of the studies of Afro-Caribbean students (Tomlinson, 1981). They demonstrated the theoretical poverty of this type of research which informed the Liberal teachers' position and which reduced the social basis of black resistance to a collection of individual 'behavioural problems' that could be put right by the adoption of a Liberal multicultural curriculum.

The form of resistance of the Rasta Heads cannot be reduced to a simplistic psychological theory, such as motivational deficiency. As Dhondy (1974, p. 47) argues, the adoption of a more relevant course – for example, Black Studies – would not coopt these students:

> It is futile for a black studies course to attempt to encapsulate their culture. It's only text is survival, and it is bound by a rejection of the discipline of work that society offers them, and can therefore be called a culture of resistance. It is a culture antithetical to the idea of schooling and, so finally unco-optable.

Their material and social base was the black community and its resistance to racist structures. As Brake (1980, p. 65) has argued concerning working-class youth sub-cultures located in the inner-city, they have their:

> origins in structural conditions and [are] mediated by class, race and gender and further modified by the local working-class community and the local political economy.

  Rather than examining the Rasta Heads' ideologies and practices in terms of pathological behaviour categories, they can be seen, more than any other fraction of the working-class, to be consciously creating their own culture. In so doing, they are rejecting the model of white society presented by teachers, and resist institutional incorporation into white cultural identities (Hall *et al.*, 1978, p. 341).

Chapter 4

The Warriors: Invisible Form of Resistance

Introduction

The last chapter was concerned with the visibility of a sub-cultural group, the Rasta Heads. This chapter examines the 'invisibility' of an Asian male sub-cultural group, the Warriors, and the relationship between these two forms of resistance to schooling. The Warriors developed a specific response to their experience of racism.[1] As pointed out above, at one level they constitute a sub-cultural group which challenges the authority of the school. At another level, the Warriors respond to the teacher expectation of their 'ethnic group' and adopt covert anti-school practices. Also, the teachers working within a culturalist perspective which assumes a class homogeneity of the black community is of central significance in maintaining the teacher stereotype of the 'passivity' of the Asian students. In particular, teachers tend to extend to all Asian students the conformity of the middle-class Asian boys. I hope to demonstrate that an analysis of social background will help to reveal more clearly the students' expectations and achievements at Kilby school. More specifically, I examine the presence of working-class Asian male students in a sub-cultural youth group and their resistance to their experience of racism.

Formation of the Warriors

The Warriors group consisted of nine students: Amerjit, Arshid, Ashwin, Iqbal, Khalid, Kulbinder, Parminder, Raj and Sokhjinder. All of them were born in England. Arshid and Khalid were of Pakistani origin, the parents of the other seven were from India. When the research began, all their fathers were working in non-manual jobs in foundries and factories and five of the boys' mothers were working in local factories. During the research period, four of the boys' fathers were made redundant. The Warriors lived in Kilby, except Sokhjinder who had recently moved with his family to Kingston, a predominantly white area nearby. They all attended local primary schools. Amerjit and Parminder began their secondary school career in the top stream but were demoted to the second stream at the end of the third year. Arshid, Ashwin and Iqbal began and remained in the second stream, and Raj, Sokhjinder, Khalid and Kulbinder in the third stream. All of these students were placed in CSE examination option groups during the fourth year, but Kulbinder was demoted to a non-examination class at the beginning of the fifth year. Parminder gained five grade 1 CSEs and went on to a local sixth form college to take A-level examinations. His increased political conscious-ness, which developed partly as a result of visits to areas such as Southall, informed his later close identification with, rather than participation in, the group's practices. He maintained that these practices were of political significance but that of more importance was a politically organized response to racism in all its institutional manifestations. Parminder formed a close relationship with Amerjit, the leader of the group.

There were a number of peer groups throughout the school. For the anti-school students, the Warriors were seen as the best organized and toughest group and so were respected and feared. The group projected an image of toughness both to the racists outside the school, and to the teachers and students within. They acted as a model for younger students. For the more conformist boys, the significance of the Warriors was that they caused them trouble either directly by threatening them, or by refusing to cooperate with the teachers and so disrupting their lessons. Due to the teachers' preoccupation with the Rasta Heads, the Warriors as a group were often overlooked, though individual members of the group were regarded as disciplinary problems.

Brake (1980, p. 128) maintains that the findings of research on Asian youth conclude that they are absent from youth culture: 'Asians are rarely found in youth culture . . . and indeed are often absent from formal youth organiza-tions.' Working from within a culturalist perspective, he argues that this absence is the result of the Asian youths' 'strong cultural background' which serves to maintain unity within the community.[2] The Warriors explained their absence in the past from youth sub-cultures in terms of the control exercised by their families.

> Iqbal: I think there hasn't been gangs, not so much. It's parents, Asian parents, an' uncles an' everything press their children into education. They maybe beat them, but I used to get really shouted at, but I keep telling 'em education's no good there. They think if ye get CSEs it's good.

Although Afro-Caribbean youth groups emerged earlier and are therefore more visible, Asian youth groups are now developing within schools.[3]

Raj: When the West Indians came down to England they had much more freedom than the Indians. It was basically freedom but the Indians didn't have any, as much social freedom but the West Indians had, so they rebelled first, before the Indians. But now the Indians are rebelling. So we become rude boys and things. We know there en't nothing for us here. But our parents still press us.

Asian boys at Kilby School have identified with various white sub-cultural forms.[4]

Sokhjinder: There are some heavy metal, just a few you know, that I've seen in Kilby. I've seen Teds, Elvis followers, rockers, seen a few punks. There used to be two in this school, Sarwan and Allan, and there's Mods. They wear the odd earring and do their own hair.

Of more significance is the identification by the Warriors with the rude boy sub-cultural form.[5] As is indicated by their choice of name, they wish to project a tough image[6] that challenges the stereotype of the 'passive Asian'. They have adopted from the rude boys an anti-authoritarian attitude, particularly in relation to the police and teachers, the most visible agents of social control which impinge on their lives.

MM: What's the main one for the Warriors?
Ashwin: Most of us are rude boys.
MM: Why rude boys?
Ashwin: I think the main way, the main way why we call ourselves rude boys is 'coz we hate authority and school and the police. We like the music and the people.
Iqbal: Rude boys are tough. They can look after themselves. They go round making trouble, so kids are scared of them.

As was pointed out in the last chapter, the emergence of anti-school peer groups usually occurs during the third year of secondary schooling. The formation of the Warriors group followed this pattern. They claimed that when they first came to Kilby school, they were all conformists. During the third year, attitudes and orientations towards the school began to crystallize. The Warriors group came together as they found boys with a similar response. Their shared view of the school was that of a system of hostile authority and meaningless work demands.

MM: So you were good when you first came here?
Arshid: Only when I came here. I mean most of them in the first year you'll notice, they don't cause trouble and the same in the

second year. But in the third, fourth and fifth year, you get trouble off them.

MM: Well what happens in the third, fourth and fifth year?

Arshid: You just start to grow up, to grow up an' ye know if the teachers push ye round you stand up to them. You start talking back to him.

Ashwin: In the first and second years you don't know teachers that well. But in the third year we began to be better mates and stick together.

The informal group was the means by which the authority of the school was challenged and boredom alleviated. As Willis (1977, p. 23) argues:

Even though there are no public rules, physical structures, recognised hierarchies or institutional sanctions in the counter-culture, it cannot run on air. It must have a material base, its own infrastructure. This is, of course, the social group. The informal group is the basic unit of this culture, the fundamental and elemental source of all its resistance.

MM: Why go in a gang?

Khalid: It just happened en it?

Kulbinder: For company. You come to school and you look forward to seeing your mates.

Khalid: School is really a meeting place. You come at first to read and learn something, but then you come to see yer friends and talk about what you did the night before and arrange to go places and things. Maybe plan to disrupt a lesson or somethin', and look after yourselves.

The Warriors claimed that their group had no formal rules, but certain behaviour was expected. Perhaps of most importance was the obligation never to inform on group members:

Amerjit: When the riots were on, we thought we'd do our little bit to the collection. And Raj got picked up right an' there was about twenty kids involved. He didn't grass on one. Yer all mates, ye stick together. It's like some really strong organisation like the IRA. They don't grass on each other. They really are, that's what I like to see some strong group like that. Like the coppers were really getting on to Raj, but there was no way he was going to budge. To some people, authority is something good, something you can turn to, but not to us. It doesn't represent that to us. Someone I can turn to is my mates. They just represent something over ye, against ye,

> trying to split ye up 'coz they know when black people stick
> together we're strong. Mates always look after each other.

The formation of the Warriors group demonstrates that Asian students can constitute a sub-cultural group which challenges the dominant school culture.

Class and response to racism

Resistance to racism

This research was carried out at a time of increasing violence against black people. A Home Office Report (1981, p. 11) found that:

> The incidence of victimisation was much higher for the ethnic population, particularly the Asians, than for white people. Indeed, the rate for Asians was fifty times that for white people and the rate for blacks was over thirty-six times that for white people.

Similarly, a report by the Commission for Racial Equality (1982, p. 6) detailed the rise in racist attacks:

> In the past year, at least sixteen attacks on black . . . Council house tenants have been reported to the Community Relations Council, including one vendetta last month where fire bombs and stink bombs were posted through an Asian family's front door.

Asians have tended to be seen by racists as an easy target. As a result of these attacks there has emerged a number of youth organizations, most notably the Southall Youth Movement, the Bradford Twelve and the East London Bangladeshi Youth Association, to defend their communities. For example, as *Race Today* (1979, p. 52) reported:

> The election campaign of '79 will be remembered for the extra-parliamentary intervention of the black communities of Britain who have . . . taken to the streets to oppose the presence of the NF in their areas. The demonstrations called by the joint IWAs and SYM [Indian Workers Association and Southall Youth Movement] occupied the streets leading to the town. They were driven there by police equipped with riot shields.

The increase in racist attacks, many of which go unreported to the police, have led many Asians in Kilby to realize that they must organize to defend their community. The following discussion with Mr Swali, the father of Raj, took place on a demonstration to support the Bradford Twelve.

> We have to stick together and support each other. It's this place now, we could be next. There are a lot more attacks now in Kilby. I've seen it get more and more. The police don't care, you phone them and they come two hours too late or not at all. We must defend, protect ourselves.

A similar attitude to organized self-defence is adopted by the Warriors. A central element of their development as a group was their resistance to racism both within and outside the school. The Warriors' most immediate experience of racism was the verbal and physical abuse that they received from white gangs. During the research period, I documented the increasing number of attacks on the boys and their families (see C.R.E., 1988).

> MM: When did you become aware of racism?
> Kulbinder: I don't really know, it seems like always.
> Parminder: You come to experience it everyday. White people look at you in a special way, on buses, in shops, in town and all white places, they look at you. They're kind of suspicious all the time.

Although the harassment of the Asian community in Kilby is not confined to skinheads, they are seen as the most extreme and visible expression of white racism.

> Amerjit: I just noticed it for a long time. When yer, I think, when yer in junior school, you kind of don't know anything about racialism. You wouldn't understand what's meant. Ye hear names, but it's when ye get older whites seem to pick on ye, call ye really bad names and smash ye up, especially when there's a gang of whites together, skins and that, an' yer on yer own. They kind of act tough, call ye Paki bastard and smash ye up.

As a result of racists' presence at football matches, most Asian boys never attended local matches, although many of them are keen football supporters. They also knew that this was the location for the distribution of National Front and, more recently, British Movement propaganda.[7]

> Kulbinder: A lot of my friends have been attacked on their own an' a lot here. It's getting worse with the National Front and British Movement.

It is this evidence of racist abuse which may explain their absence from school football teams and their involvement in sports like hockey.

The Warriors are aware of the media coverage of 'race' issues. Despite the fact that racist attacks are frequently made on the black community, the media present selected 'black crime', and so create the image of the 'black mugger' waging war against white victims.[8]

Amerjit: The news an' papers an' all right, only talk about when say, when a black person mugs someone. What about the fucking National Front an' the skinheads and a lot of other white people hating us for, for nothing?

Kulbinder: Yeah, an' beating us up, even on the drive, in the park, everywhere. But they only go round in gangs. Twenty white kids got one Indian. I bet the judge would send him away.

On discussing the similarities and differences between black and white people, colour discrimination was felt by the youth to be the main difference.

Amerjit: Colour matters the most, especially if yer talking about being accepted. Like you can go to town or like on our trips out to new places an' no-one knows yer Irish, but they know I'm Indian en it, and you haven't even been born here.

However, none of the Warrior group would have liked to be born white.

MM: Do you wish you were born white?

Amerjit: No, the problem don't go away 'coz I'm born white. No, I'm glad to be Indian. It has its problems, but nearly all whites are bastards, so it's a stupid question en it?

Raj: How can you wanna be what you hate, no, never.

The Warriors demonstrate that 'colour' has its positive as well as negative elements for the black community. As is pointed out in *Race Today* (1975, p. 56):

This is not to say that there is no distinction between black and white immigrant labour. There is one important distinction, the second generation of white immigrants is not branded by skin colour. Those who are branded are able to maintain a continuity of struggle from new arrivals to new natives.

One of the effects of racist practices is that an 'unofficial geographical immobility' is forced on the black community. The boys in Kilby rarely visited other areas of the city. They felt isolated if they went alone and conspicuous if they went in a group.[9]

MM: Do you like living in Kilby?
Khalid: I would prefer to live in Kilby than a white area because you won't be so much on yer own. When ye go to a white place on yer own, they look at ye as if yer an alien.

Sokhjinder's family moved out of Kilby into a white area. His family regretted the move and were trying to return. They were constantly harassed and have had their windows broken on three occasions.

MM: You don't live in Kilby, do you?
Sokhjinder: No, we are in the Kingston area.
MM: Which would you prefer?
Sokhjinder: I prefer Kilby because people around it, you know, they're more friendly. Down there, they're complete strangers, nearly all white. I haven't mixed in. I wouldn't know how. I don't know how to get along with white people. I think most probably all of them hate us, so they keep attacking us, even the milkman, the boy who helps the milkman ran up the garden an' shouted 'Paki Bastard go home'. My mother and sisters are really scared.

Kilby is often described by white people as a depressed area, but this is not the experience of black residents. Despite the housing limitations and lack of social amenities imposed upon the inhabitants, they have positive images of their neighourhood. The boys express this in terms of their preference for living together in the security of Kilby. The residents have successfully recreated their own culture on the streets of Kilby, including shops to service their own community, workers associations, and churches, mosques and temples, which act as religious and social centres. The main road, with its Asian supermarkets, restaurants and cinemas, is a powerful symbol of their presence and permanence.

Arshid: This en't a bad area. I mean ye feel safe here. Ye feel at home. I know some friends who used to live in Kilby. They've moved out to Kingston. They really hated it 'coz they left everything here. I mean Asian people have made this place where ye feel good.
MM: What do you like about living in Kilby?
Ashwin: Put it this way, I feel safer in Kilby at two o'clock in the morning than any white area.

Class and racism

This image of Kilby as a defensive zone and more significantly the adoption of the strategy of community self-defence is not shared by all Asians. Britain means different things to different sectors of the black community. *Race Today* (1976, p. 123) describes it as follows:

> Neither is the Asian community of one mind. A middle-class has developed within. . . . For this group, Britain is experienced as quite a different place from those who have nothing to sell but their labour power. . . . Until recently, all appeared to be running smoothly. The concentration of attacks from outside had the effect of tearing the veil from the surface, bringing to the fore what the different sections stand for. The middle-class Asians do not want to fight. They prefer appealing to government ministers and the police to calm things down. Pressing on them are the mass of Asian families who have been facing the attacks on the ground. The latter stand for the mobilization of the strength and the power of the community in mass meetings, mass demonstrations and vigilante groups.

As was shown above, I examined the assumed class homogeneity of the black students at Kilby school. Most of the Asian boys' parents worked in foundries and factories before many of them were recently made redundant. A small group of boys of a non-manual work background attended the school. The latter group were over-represented in the top streams of the school and were not involved in the anti-school sub-culture. Two incidents that occurred during the research period highlighted this relationship between class and anti-school sub-cultural groups. First, the 1981 summer disturbances, in a neighbouring area, which the Warriors described as an opportunity to get even with the police and take advantage of goods. The middle-class students condemned the disturbances. They argued that the police were only doing their job and protecting property, including the supermarkets and factories owned by their families.

Permjit: It was just trouble-makers. They were just out to steal as much as they could.

Sukhdip: The police were around trying to stop trouble.

Vijay: You have to have law and order. We lost a lot of trade immediately after. It had nothing to do with, I mean the riots were not really protests against the police and racialism and all that. They were just, just trouble-makers destroying property in their own area.

The second incident concerned an industrial dispute in December 1982, in which 200 textile workers, mainly Asian women, with the support of the Sikh temples, the Indian Workers Association (GB), the local trades council, the local Labour Party and the Socialist Workers Party, demanded the reinstatement of three workers who were sacked for joining the Transport and

General Workers Union, the recognition of their right to strike and the implementation of the Wages Council Act of 1979.[10] The management issued termination notices to the strikers, redundancy notices to those working and threatened to close the factories. The dispute ended with the employees gaining their demands, except the reinstatement of the three sacked workers. As a result of a number of successful industrial actions in the region by Asian workers, the Asian traders responded by forming the Asian Trade Association. This development was described in a *Shakti* article (1983, p. 13) as follows:

> Some years ago it would have been quite easy to blame white racism for grievances of Asian workers. . . . Now things have changed. With the rise of a relatively under-developed black bourgeoisie, new tensions have emerged, particularly among Asian workers whose relationship with the management has turned on class lines.

Two students were interviewed concerning their understanding of the strike – Ashwin, one of the Warriors, whose mother worked at the factory involved in the dispute, and Mohan, whose family owns the company:

Ashwin: My mother prefers to work for Indians. She feels better with the other Indian women, but they just use this really. They show they don't care about them, just, just making lots of money, big cars and all that. I would never work for an Indian man. They don't pay you, like we joke a penny a day. We need the money but you have to strike and stick together if yer gonna get better wages.

Mohan's explanation of the dispute reflected the views of the local Punjabi press, that jealousy was the problem:

Mohan: It's not about wages like is said. Its trouble-makers who are jealous. There's lots of them in our society. How can it be about wages? If you go to other factories round here they pay less and have less room to work in for the machine. It's like I said to you before, at school you learn too much about workers' rights and nothing, they don't tell you about how difficult it is to have a business. We work a seven day week. White people can't understand. A family business looks after it's own people in our society. With us, they don't feel, they won't get any racial abuse. We don't need unions to tell us. You see it's simple, if wages go up our profits are small, and so you end up closing the factory and anyway look at them on strike, they have lost all that money, so it can't really be about more money.

The response of these two students to the strike reflects the development within the Asian community of a black business class and the organization of workers. This business class has emerged by exploiting the labour of Asian women. Women have increasingly come into the labour market during the 1970s, and it has been the members of the Asian Traders Association who have employed them in the Kilby area. The women's demand for union recognition and the response of the management demonstrates the class and gender divisions between these groups. The class division of the Asian community was reflected in the attitudes and practices of the students at Kilby School. This was demonstrated in the different explanations of racism given by middle-class and working-class Asian students, which reflected those of their parents. The former group described racist attacks as individual aberrations of white youth. It was basically a moral problem.

Mohan: It's only a small percentage that are racialists. We get white people in our shop, and my brother at the grammar school says that most of them are okay, so it must only be a few.

Permjit: It's the same with every group, some are good and some are bad.

Vijay: There is differences, like we don't get on with all black kids and some white kids might not like us. It's mainly the skinheads who cause the trouble, but Indian kids go looking for trouble too, getting drunk and picking fights.

The Warriors offered a political explanation of racism that included an awareness of the role of white imperialism in the past and the present.

MM: What percentage of white people are racists?

Amerjit: Nearly all of them.

Arshid: Yeah, they just hide it.

Ashwin: Anyway, I don't like them either.

MM: Like who?

Ashwin: The whites, I have always hated the Union Jack or whatever you call it and the Royal Family an' all them posh bastards looking down on us.

MM: Why?

Ashwin: Just hated, for what they did over in India. They tried to take control over the Indians.

Amerjit: They shouldn't have done that. Why did they? An' why did they go round torturing the negroes for in America like that?

MM: Who?

Amerjit: The bloody whites. They've robbed everythin' everywhere. An' they're still doing it today in Africa, Salvador, everywhere they go they rob.

Raj: They rob the countries before they free them an' then they starve. They won't let them come here or America now unless they've got lots of money.

Parminder, who worked for the Communist Party, helped to develop the Warriors' political consciousness. He made an explicitly political distinction between hard line organized racists, like those who are National Front voters, and those who are involved in racial abuse. He argued that the working-class was racially divided and that black people were treated as scapegoats for the frustrations generated within the organization of work:

MM: What percentage of white people are racists?
Parminder: If you were thinking of supporting the National Front, for them no per cent. But using things like 'there goes a Paki' or 'there goes a nigger', I think a very high percentage. The main point of being a racist is because you feel frustrated with your life. You feel everyone's abusing you at work, so you may as well abuse others as well. So you go round doing the same thing to black people and there's no unity.

Class and teacher racist stereotypes

Parminder's political awareness was not representative of the Warriors. They may have offered political explanations of racism, but their resistance to schooling was not informed by an organized political ideology. Parminder had an ambivalent relationship to the Warriors, whom he attempted to organize politically. They tended to ridicule his beliefs and especially his use of political language, but at the same time he was shown respect as an effective and articulate anti-racist speaker. The dominant ideological response of the Warriors remained within a culturalist perspective. However, Parminder was an important influence on the group's shifting on certain issues beyond the limitations of their position. Of particular significance, was their critical perception of the teacher racially-based stereotypes operating within the school. Once again, we can see in the students' explanations of these stereotypes, the class division of the wider Asian community.

The Warriors suggested that the teacher racist stereotypes were not based upon any real differences in the behaviour of Asians and Afro-Caribbeans. Rather, it was the teachers' classification and labelling processes, to which both groups reacted, which determined teachers' perceptions of students.

MM: Do you think that West Indians cause more trouble than Asians?
Ashwin: No, don't be stupid, that's what teachers think. The Indians cause just as much trouble.

Raj: The West Indians are more obvious some'ow. They're seen more easily.

Iqbal: It's not, it's not that they cause more trouble. Its teachers, they pick on them more.

Raj: They treat them differently. I think they think the West Indians are dumber than us.

They challenged the teacher stereotype of the 'ignorant Afro-Caribbean' by pointing out that it was 'high-ability' Afro-Caribbean students who were involved in the anti-school groups:

MM: Do you think they are more dumber?

Raj: No I don't.

Iqbal: No, because they can do as well as Indian kids, better than a lot of them. The ones who have been in most trouble were the brainy ones, like Kevin and Michael, in the first year they were the brainy ones, really brainy.

These racially-based stereotypes acted as powerful social images and were of central significance to the teachers' perception of their interaction with students. They served to highlight the perceived 'rebelliousness' of Afro-Caribbean students and the perceived 'passivity' of Asians. The Warriors claimed that the Afro-Caribbeans did not cause more trouble for the school authorities, but that they were officially 'seen to'. When an Afro-Caribbean student became a disciplinary problem, it was seen by the teachers as a frequent characteristic of being 'Afro-Caribbean'. Any disruptions caused by Asian students were seen as individual acts of deviancy and did not challenge the teachers' idea of being 'Asian'.

Ashwin: White people, teachers look on Asians as kinda quieter an' think they accept their ideas more, agree with them. They think they won't make trouble. It's things like that.

Iqbal: It's like this, if an Indian does something wrong, like one of us cause trouble they think it's just him. There's something wrong only with him an' all that. But if a West Indian does it, acts bad, they drag him off to the head. They'll really shame him up an' think another bloody West Indian making trouble.

Ashwin: That's what happened with us. But then I think they get scared of the West Indian kids more in the fifth year, Kevin an' all them. An' they think that they make others worse. An' Asian kids are more on, their own. If ye think all West Indian kids are bad ye gonna be scared of them when they get big.

Khalid maintained that these racist stereotypes also operated with authorities outside of school, especially with the police.[11]

> Khalid: It's like outside. The police pick on West Indians more. Ye see
> to them the Asians, they're not so suspicious to them. If they
> see Kevin an' his lot and if they see us they act differently,
> more tougher with them.

For the Warriors, the effect of these racist stereotypes, shared by the teachers
and the police, was to criminalize the behaviour of Afro-Caribbean youth.
    Ashwin's explanation of Afro-Caribbean youth's resistance to schooling
questioned another aspect of the racist stereotype adopted by teachers, that
of the individualism of Afro-Caribbean youth. Teachers frequently explained
Afro-Caribbean students' refusal to cooperate with authority in terms of their
inability to work together among themselves. Liberal teachers working with
the same stereotype often assumed that this was the effect of slavery.
Ashwin's argument challenged this dominant view. He claimed that due to
the influence of Rastafari, Afro-Caribbean youth were more aware of racism,
and that in the past they were more organized than Asian youth in developing
collective techniques to oppose it:

> Ashwin: In a West Indian community they have Rastas who tell them
> things more. It's like if you were an extreme Sikh. The Rastas
> tell you this society isn't good and you should reject it. They
> stick together more an' are more aware of what's going on
> instead of us.

Parminder supported this view, arguing that Afro-Caribbean youth had been
at the front of the rebellion in school against racism, but that now Asians were
as much involved in rejecting school:[12]

> Parminder: I think older Indians weren't so much together, didn't act
> together enough. Some were like my dad in the union. But
> the Rastas are really strong, that's why white people are
> scared of them or try to buy them off like here in Kilby.
> But Asians have learned, now they are more together all
> over the country and here. Like the third year gang, they
> are going to be really bad. The teachers hate them already.

The Warriors' critical analysis of the racist stereotypes in operation within
the school contrasts with the middle-class Asians' acceptance of the dominant
teacher ideology. Iqbal discussed the divisions that existed between the Asian
youth.

> Iqbal: Some Asians believe that they will be accepted in a general view

by whites because they think they're different, better than West Indians. An' that white people would prefer to aim at West Indian cultures an' they wouldn't like the West Indians as much because they [Asians] look more white, act more white.

The division between the Asian youth that Iqbal pointed to was a real division, but it could not be explained simply in terms of arbitrary differences between the youth. The sector of Asian youth that Iqbal referred to, tended to be represented by the middle-class at Kilby school. In interviews with the latter group, they argued that Afro-Caribbean students were mainly disruptive and anti-authority. The middle-class Asians identified with whites rather than Afro-Caribbeans and they believed that occupation and property ownership were more important than colour in determining their future relationship with white society. (Hanif Kureshi, in his film, *My Beautiful Laundrette*, vividly portrays these class divisions.)

Permjit: My father wouldn't have coloured people working for him. He prefers whites. The West Indians are always causing trouble.

Sukhdip: The West Indians are the main trouble at this school an' it's the same where they live, playing music all night, hanging out of their windows all day. They never work, most of them, thieving and begging.

MM: Do you think colour makes a difference?

Mohan: Like I said before, only a few, a small percentage are prejudiced. What job you are doing makes a big difference. Of course, no-one looks down on a doctor or an accountant.

Vijay: My brother at university does not have trouble. People may look down on you because you live in Kilby, not just because of your colour. Indian businessmen drive round in Mercedes, people look up to them.

This is not to suggest that the conflict within the black community between Asians and Afro-Caribbeans can be reduced to class location. One of the central limitations of the culturalist perspective, within which the youth sub-cultures worked, was the emphasis upon cultural differences. However, there tended to be among the working-class groups, like the Rasta Heads and the Warriors, a shared perception and response to racism that was not found among the middle-class Asian students. It is against this background of the class heterogeneous nature of the black community that I locate the resistance to schooling of an Asian male working-class youth sub-cultural group.

Resistance to schooling

Racism and dissociation from school

A central element of the development of the Warriors as a group was their resistance to racism, both within and outside the school. Asian youth at Kilby School have little contact with the white community. When they visit other areas, it is mainly places of black settlement or business activities, such as markets. Within Kilby they mix with other Asians and Afro-Caribbeans, but there are no white members of their leisure groups.

> Parminder: I know a few white people through the Communist Party.
> MM: Would other Asian kids know white people?
> Parminder: No, not normally. If they did know them they wouldn't keep in contact. But around here they're, it ain't very common.
> Raj: I don't know none except for teachers and Peter an' a few others here.
> Ashwin: Ye see when we go out, when we leave Kilby and go to London an' other places, it's to other Indian places like my sister lives in Wolverhampton.

The following discussions with the Warriors demonstrated their anti-racist position and their dissociation from white society. They critically celebrated their own cultural origins. As Brake (1980, p. 128) argues:

> Asian youth . . . can draw upon its own historical, cultural and religious traditions and importantly its own languages.

However, Brake fails to point to the limitations of their position. As is shown in the Warriors' discussion of nationality, their dissociation from white society remained within a culturalist perspective, as they tended to accept the conventional definition of culture as the primary determinant of behaviour.

> MM: What nationality are you?
> Raj: Asian en it? I'm Indian. I was born in England but I don't think of myself as English. I've got to stick to my culture ye see. You know my background.
> MM: What about you?
> Ashwin: I'm Indian, I was born over here but I think I'm Indian.
> MM: Well do many of the kids here think of themselves as English?
> Ashwin: No, none of us. No, none of them. They think they're Indian, an Asian person.
> MM: What about when you have kids?

Iqbal: They'll be Asian of course.
MM: Even if they are born here?
Ashwin: That doesn't, that, that makes them a British citizen that's .
           all. That's what we want, but it won't change ye.
Iqbal: It won't change who ye are. We'll still live in our society and
           whites in theirs.

It was against this background of living in a racially exclusive society that
there emerged an awareness of racism. For the Warriors, this developed at the
same time as their dissociation from school.

The Warriors expressed opposition to compulsory schooling. They saw the
formal side of school as irrelevant to their future lives. They suggested
training on the job as an alternative to the present arrangement.

MM: Have you worked much while you were here?
Amerjit: I've dossed all the way through.
MM: Why?
Amerjit: Just did. I didn't wanna work. I don't think school will do
           anything for me. I don't believe in schools. Let yer parents
           teach ye or learn at work or somethin', that would make
           more sense. I don't think many kids believe in the learning
           bit in school.

Raj and Amerjit's explanations of their dissociation from formal schooling
were representative of the Warriors' attitude to school. Raj was one of the
best hockey players in Kilby. He became disillusioned with the demands it
was making on him. Eventually he decided between the gang and school sport
and he chose the former. He thought it was better to make the decision than to
allow the school authorities to carry out their constant threats to ban him. He
saw, as many other anti-school students claimed, that his sporting skills were
being exploited by teachers to increase the school's prestige.

Raj: I hate school. They always say we done this for ye an' all that.
       What have they done? We made ye into, we gave ye our time. The
       school gets all the glory en it? The prizes and everything. In the,
       about in the fourth year, I started playing for myself and then I
       dropped it. I could just see they were just using me.

Many of the boys were highly skilled sportsmen. However, as they moved
into sub-cultural groups, they either withdrew from school teams or, more
often, the authorities banned them, using sport as an institutional mechanism
of exclusion. The staff argued that if the boys refused to cooperate in all areas
of school life, they should not be allowed to participate in selected areas of
high value to them.

Arshid's experience of school was shared by many of the students at Kilby.

Having learnt the basic literacy and numeracy skills, the school had little to offer him. Initially he was motivated to teach himself to read and write, but having achieved this task, he then found the formal side of school made few demands on him.

> Arshid: So when I first came here, I mean I had a reading age of, I read like a seven year old. I couldn't do anything, 'coz in our old school, the junior school, they thought there were a few of us who they thought had no chance in life. So, they used to give us jobs around the school. And I spent about six months building up tents. So I worked here, worked at home an' I learnt without them. I mean what else have I learned here in five years? Fucking nothing have I?

Strategies of resistance

The Warriors developed a number of strategies of resistance in response to the demands of the school. First, they were a constant threat to the teachers' control. Even when they did not carry out a planned interruption, their very presence in the classroom meant that the teacher had to negotiate his or her way through the lesson.

> Khalid: We do it all the time. We do it without thinking most of the time. We don't even realise we're doing it. But we're winding them up and they have to let the pressure off.

Due to the collective nature of the Warriors' strategies, the teachers' usual techniques of control – for example, the threatening of students, the use of sarcasm and the selection of weak students to make an example of – could not be employed with these boys. Amerjit explained the importance of the development of these collective strategies to disrupt lessons. One student would start an argument, the teacher reacted and he or she had a group of students against him or her.

> Amerjit: We do loads of things to interrupt them. Like we often get a teacher going just to get him annoyed. We arrange it between a few of us. Get in a, get in a group, and get a teacher, an' wind 'em up real bad an' cause a big argument.

He likened the student–teacher interaction to a fight which both sides must be seen to win. All teachers were opponents to attack, even Mr Parks and Mr Walsh, who were regarded as strong disciplinarians. The Warriors planned the disruption of lessons in which one of them had been disciplined in front of his friends.

Amerjit: We take them all on, even Parks and Walsh. We work our plans out, like when they shame one of us up in front of everyone.

They found most lessons boring. They had to sit through double periods of 60 minutes, often producing minimal work. Hence, the sub-cultural group acted as a resource base of diversionary activities. The more formal the lesson the greater the challenge to employ their diversionary skills. High status was accorded by the boys for the most creative response to the boring routine. They persistently interrupted lessons, by coming late, dragging chairs, laughing among themselves and arguing with teachers.

Raj: If one word sums school up, lessons an' all that, it's boring. It's just boring, same old things everyday.

Iqbal: It's more fun when yer supposed to be working. It's too easy in social studies.

MM: What kinds of things do you do?

Kulbinder: Oh, always being cheeky, late, coming late nearly every day. They say I'm very lippy.

The boys claimed that the teachers disliked teaching them and consequently often came late themselves and had little work prepared for lessons.

MM: Why do you come late so often?

Kulbinder: Why not? They do, they hate coming into us.

Iqbal: They sometimes tell us. Ye can tell anyway.

Kulbinder: So, I hate it as well. So I come late, it adds a bit of excitement.

Dhondy (1974, p. 46) argues that language is one of the most powerful weapons black students possess:

The culture of blacks . . . is capable of opposing this wedge of interests. To put it simply, if a large number of youth in a school speak only Punjabi or Gujerati, it becomes impossible to grade them into clever ones and thick ones. It becomes virtually impossible to treat them as anything but mass workers, produced to share a fate they resent and defy.

Language was of central importance to the Warriors' collective strategies of resistance to schooling.

Amerjit: We can easy make them mad.

Ashwin: When we are together in class we talk in Indian and they go mad.

Amerjit:	Yeah, they can't, they don't know what we're saying. And they think we are talking about them.
MM:	Are you?
Amerjit:	Not at first we didn't. But when we see them going mad, we all start laughing.

Bilinguists naturally adopt the most appropriate language for the situation. Asian students frequently spoke in Punjabi, Hindi, Gujerati or Urdu among themselves. However, the Warriors had learnt that teachers often over-react to this. Therefore, they used their languages as a means of excluding teachers. They also adopted the defiant language of the Rasta Heads, when they were confronted by the authoritarian attitudes of teachers.

Secondly, the Warriors' rejection of schooling was expressed through their attitude to school work. They primarily associated school work with writing. So their refusal to cooperate with the school authorities often took the form of avoiding writing tasks. The various strategies developed to achieve this were recalled with pride, for instance, coming late to lessons to miss the instructions, forgetting to bring a pen, breaking the pen the teacher gave you, claiming to have hurt your hand or just falling asleep. Members of the group attempted to go through the whole term without producing any written work.

MM:	Do you work in class?
Khalid:	No, I haven't done any writing for months.
Amerjit:	It depends on what kind of mood I'm in. If I don't want to, I don't. I just snooze off. Say we do dictation, we get lots of that, that's one thing I can't stand, so I snooze off. They could give us handouts. It's just to keep us quiet, so I do them a favour by nodding off.

Some of the boys claimed that, initially, they were keen to write well in English. However, teachers eventually destroyed this enthusiasm. Each year they were asked to do the same tasks; writing long essays, comprehension exercises and writing letters of job application. They continued to make the same mistakes each year and the teachers responded with the same negative comments. Often their work was not marked over long periods of time. So, eventually, they gave up trying to improve their writing skills.

Khalid:	We used to do it, but not now. In the second year, they didn't even mark the books, me an' Manjit's. We gave in our books and not even once did they mark it. We gave in our book every week. I even finished my book.

Copying was a common strategy for those who did produce work. The boys believed that the teachers' superficial marking was unlikely to discover this practice. Logically, they cannot see the point of homework when they had not worked during lessons.

MM: Is there much copying?
Arshid: Much? About one person does the work and about ten people copy it, changing it a bit. They never say anything about it.
MM: What about homework?
Amerjit: Too busy, waste of time.
Arshid: We don't do nothing at school, so we aren't gonna do it at night.

Within the school, great premium was placed by the school management upon silence in the classrooms. It was an institutionally accepted sign of a 'good' teacher. Iqbal indicated the ground that they had won for themselves in this area. Unofficially, most teachers expected little work from them and they were allowed to talk among themselves, as long as they didn't cause too much noise.

Arshid: I mean if ye want to say something, I just have to say it. I wanna say it then I get into trouble for saying it. I mean ye can't keep quiet for an hour, but they used to try an' stop us even whispering.
Iqbal: Some teachers, most of 'em now let us keep our coats on and eat in lessons an' talk at the back.

The Warriors' rejection of schooling was also expressed through a high rate of absenteeism among them. They frequently came to school to make arrangements with their friends for a game of pool in the local snooker hall or to visit a cafe in which to spend the afternoon. The response of the Warriors to their absence from school was an example of the way in which their resistance to schooling at one level was influenced by teacher expectations. The Rasta Heads in open confrontation with the teachers would often refuse to bring a letter from their parents explaining their absence. But the Warriors were more likely to bring a forged letter and so avoided further disciplinary action.

MM: Do many kids knock off time from school?
Khalid: Yeah, and the teachers don't know.
MM: What about registration?
Khalid: Just get forged letters. It's a whole business.
Sokhjinder: Ye can get yer brother or a friend. Lots of us do it.
Khalid: Teachers don't say much. Ye see you can get away with it, just say me older brother had to write it 'coz me parents

don't write English. The teachers seem not so suspicious
of Indian boys as Kevin an' that lot. They go mad at them
but they can't say their parents can't write. They don't
expect it from us.

So, the Rasta Heads were more frequently suspended for non-attendance.
The disproportionate numbers of suspended Afro-Caribbean students then
served to reinforce the teacher racist stereotypes of the 'rebellious' Afro-
Caribbean and 'passive' Asian student.

The solidarity among the Warriors enabled the high rate of absenteeism to
continue. Of equal importance was the support that they received from the
wider community.

Arshid: Ye know who is skiving it because ye know ye will share with
each other. Ye know an' ye never say anything about someone even if ye hate him. We don't grass him up. That is one
thing school is good at, no-one grasses on nobody.
MM: What would happen if they did?
Arshid: Ye just never would. Ye wouldn't think of it. Ye can't be
against yer own lot.
MM: But say somebody did?
Arshid: They'd probably, they'd be battered to death. Not by the
person who done it, by bigger friends outside of school. He'd
be beaten bad.

The Kilby teachers developed a number of strategies to deal with these
anti-school student practices. The Warriors' rejection of schooling was made
most clear in their response to these strategies.

Response to teacher authoritarianism

In *Learning to Labour*, Willis (1977) argues that most students accept the
relationship between themselves and the teacher as one of 'fair exchange'.
Teachers exchange knowledge and qualifications for respect and good
behaviour. However, the 'lads', the counter-school group, saw through this
basic teaching paradigm. Similarly, at Kilby school, the Warriors rejected this
assumed fair exchange and pointed to the essentially authoritarian nature of
the teacher–student interaction. Their challenge of this ideologically constructed concept led to a breakdown in the achieved consensus within the
school, which enabled the authorities to act as they did.

The Warriors maintained that when they first came to the school, they
cooperated with the teachers, but the teachers' response had caused them to
withdraw their cooperation. They now felt a lot of resentment towards them.
The teachers had minimum contact with them. Outside of lessons they tended
to ignore students except to discipline them. Raj interpreted the teachers'

behaviour as a general dislike of all students, irrespective of how they responded to their authority.

MM: What do you think of the teachers?

Ashwin: I hate most teachers. Some ain't bad like Mr Hickey or Mr Snape. You can have a laugh with them.

Arshid: They don't know nothing about us, about how we live.

Ashwin: Who wants to be like them? That en't success. It's a piece of piss their job is.

The Warriors were particularly critical of the authoritarian nature and arbitrariness of the teachers' behaviour that caused so much friction within the school. The boys refused to respond positively to the teachers' frequent changes of mood.

Ashwin: Its the way they treat ye that makes ye really bad. They keep getting on yer nerves for nothing. One minute they're laughing together, then they're going mad at some boy.

Raj: Like they pick on ye, do this, do that. They pick on little things, like I was having my dinner once. I'd never had this teacher before an' I did nothing wrong an' he kept getting at me, an' he got me the next day. This went on for a week. Then I suddenly realised, keep out of his way.

Ashwin: They always do that. They have to win in front of all the other kids.

Raj: They gotta boss ye around. They think if they snap their fingers we'll do what they say an' all this. Why should we?

The Warriors' perception of and response to the teachers' authoritarian behaviour was made explicit by Amerjit, the leader of the Warriors. He was quick-witted and verbally and socially very skilled. Teachers could not understand how a student of his ability refused to cooperate with them.

Khalid: Teachers always hate him.

MM: Why?

Amerjit: Don't know. They say it's my attitude.

Khalid: They're scared of him en it? 'Coz he stands up to them.

Amerjit: They think I'm, I don't want to work an' all this, an' I'm lazy. And my attitude towards them, because I don't treat them the way they'd like me to treat them.

MM: How are you supposed to treat them?

Amerjit: Yer supposed to treat them with respect. But I've got no respect for them.

MM: Why not?

Amerjit: Because I don't like them, the way they rule ye. They've got too much power and they've gotta use it everyday. They like to think they've got some authority. Ye see if yer doing something wrong, right, an' they don't say nothing, then there's no authority there. If ye see what I mean. That's why they really hate all us lot. We keep making them mad.

Amerjit's dislike of teachers was based upon the unequal distribution of power which he believed enabled them to dominate students. The Warriors developed subtle strategies of resistance that challenged this domination. In the following incident, Amerjit recalled how these strategies operated. He disliked Mr Elmes, but on this occasion he cooperated with him, in order to challenge the authority of Mr Winters, a new teacher, who had not learnt the 'hidden rules' of social control. He naively presumed it was primarily based on force. He had to learn the covert mechanisms of social control, which include techniques of moral persuasion, selection of weak students and the questioning of boys in private, away from the support of their peer group.

Amerjit: Like when in the fourth year, Winters.
Khalid: Yeah, he really shamed him up.
Amerjit: I was knocking the ball around in the yard an' he shouted a few times to come in. He started getting very heavy, an' I told him to piss off. Then Mr Elmes came an' told me to come in, and he was in charge, an' I walked straight in an' ye can imagine how Winters felt. Ye see he had no power.
Khalid: But he was only young an' he hadn't learnt yet that there's a limit ye can go to, an' ye can't go over the limit.
Amerjit: Because what he was after was power. That's what all teachers are after, power over someone. If they have power, they can tell ye what to do. They then feel good or something. And then he started pushing me an' I was gonna hit him back but he backed off an' it made him really mad. In the end he lost 'coz I kept cool an' he got really aggressive, an' he lost. As soon as he raised his voice and got extra he'd lost, en it?
Khalid: We all cheered him. Even the head thought he was a stupid bastard for getting involved with us.

The headteacher showed his disapproval of the way Mr Winters had handled the situation. Such incidents challenged the hegemony of the school and forced the staff to adopt a more coercive attitude to the boys and so revealed the real relations of domination operating within the school.

The Warriors' refusal to cooperate with the authoritarian teachers was extended to the Liberal teachers. Most of the latter group believed that the teacher–student relationship should be based on rational persuasion. Underlying their approach was the assumption that the boys' culture and position within the school was 'different but equal' to that of the teachers. However, that was precisely what was challenged by the Warriors. They dismissed the approach of these teachers as an attempt to coopt them. The Liberal teachers attempted to accommodate the Warriors' resistance to schooling. They believed that if issues of conflict were rationally discussed with the students, they would then see why their behaviour was not acceptable, and so alter it. They also saw this as the best strategy for containing further confrontation. An incident in the dinner queue one lunch period, which is discussed below, demonstrated the real contradictions between the students' social position in the school and that of the authorities. Mr Collins attempted to defend the rules of the school. He was surprised that the boys challenged the hierarchical structure of the school. For him it was there naturally, and one would not call it into question. For the students, situated at the back of the queue, it was a question of the most powerful being officially permitted to push in front of them. They were also critical of the privilege being extended to prefects, as a reward for their conformism.

Kulbinder: We just have big arguments.
Sokhjinder: They say listen to Amerjit, listen to Edward, do we fuck. They don't really listen anyway, like none of us were made prefects. Anyway, we pushed in the dinner queue and a fight started.
Ashwin: We was suspended. Our parents had to come up.
Sokhjinder: And after we came back we were supposed to discuss it in social studies. Well, Collins wouldn't listen to our side, not really.
Khalid: He'd made up his mind before he came in. What's the point in getting us to say our side.
Sokhjinder: We said, teachers, visitors an' prefects, all of them went to the front of the queue. It's kind of pushing in, so why can't we?
MM: What did he say?
Sokhjinder: He said it's privileges 'coz staff can't stand in queues, there's only thirty minutes for dinner. Well, what about us? We wait an' all these others push in an' there's nothing left for us.
Khalid: He knew he'd lost, so he changed a bit and said it maybe wasn't fair, but we better get used to it because that's the way the world is. It's rubbish, if yer got rules and things ye can change them. I ain't gonna let no white fuckers push me about.
Sokhjinder: He just supported them. He always does, in the end anyway.

Mr Collins was unable to persuade the boys, so he reduced his argument to a question of 'common sense', that the authority relations that operated in the school were the way things were in the 'real world'. From his own perspective, he assumed that if that was the way things were, then that was the way they must remain. However, he benefited from the present social arrangement. While the students, for whom the present arrangements were not of benefit, could not see why they could not be changed.

It was the function not the style of teachers that they saw as primarily determinant of school conflict. Sokhjinder attacked Mr Young's attempt to make them feel guilty about their behaviour. They instinctively felt that teachers could not be trusted.

MM: OK say a teacher tries to explain things and persuade you?

Amerjit: I'd go against him naturally.

Khalid: Some of them try it, but it's the same en it?

Sokhjinder: They're the worst, making ye feel bad for what ye did. The others just tell ye off. Mr Young gives ye all the shit about you've let us down an' we never thought you were the same as the rest, load of bollocks.

Amerjit: It's still authority. They're just using different methods to rule ye, do what they want. Like when they're interrogating someone they have a hard one and a soft one working together against ye. We hate them all.

In interviews with teachers from other economically depressed areas, such as Liverpool and Derry, they claimed that the students in inner-city schools viewed the teachers with as much hostility as the police. In the recent past, prior to the research period, this was not the case in Kilby. In the worsening economic climate, however, with its disproportionate effect on the black community, a similar view was emerging there. The collective practices and attitudes of the Warriors pointed to the growing contradictions of schooling for black students. *Race Today* (1975, p. 10) argues that this is the generation of black youth

whose very lives and lifestyle are in opposition to the production deal under whose yoke generations of the working-class have laboured.

As the crisis has become more visible, teachers have retreated into a more authoritarian stance. The boys gave details of the similarities between these authoritarian teachers and the police. They had direct experience of the repressive function of both state agencies of social control. Teachers have become experts at 'interrogating' students. In response the boys have developed techniques of counter-interrogation as each morning they were paraded into the headteacher's office for the ritual 'who did it'?

Parminder:	I hate authority. It's the same with coppers. I can't stand them. Teachers are like them, always trying to catch you out.
Iqbal:	They act just like them.
MM:	How?
Parminder:	Well, they tell ye what to do, so can coppers. In a way the coppers can arrest ye and the teachers do things the same like, coppers arrest ye and fine ye, teachers grab ye for something an' give ye lines or suspend ye.
Iqbal:	Both are suspicious of ye all the time. They look at ye as if you've done something wrong when they see ye. They try an' catch ye out. Ye can't trust them.
Parminder:	They interrogate ye the same.
Iqbal:	Yeah, getting the weak ones and trying to get ye to grass on yer mates.

The Warriors claimed that the individual teacher's power lay in his ability to back up his authority with the support of other teachers. They rationalized their group perspective in terms of the need to imitate this strategy in order to survive.

| Amerjit: | I always feel better, stronger when there's more than one. It's like we was stopped by coppers the other night when you left and he got extra but we stayed calm, an' when we walked round the corner another one was there. If we had cheeked the first one, he would of called the other one. Well teachers are like that in a way. They can always call or send ye to someone else, teacher in charge of yer learning, headmaster, deputy head, Higget here and all the rest. So ye must, ye need yer mates, ye must stick together to survive in this place an' out there. |

The Warriors believed that their collective techniques of resistance were effective in defending themselves against the school authorities. The conformists complained that the teachers were not tough enough with troublemakers. Teachers realized the strength of sub-cultural groups like the Warriors and adopted a strategy of negotiation with them. This often involved redefining what constituted unacceptable behaviour in the classroom in order to avoid confrontation.

| Arshid: | I mean ye talk back to teachers and yer mates back ye up an' it's going to spread. The other teachers, they're not going to put too much pressure on ye. |

Traditionally sub-cultural groups within the school system have been successful in winning ground for themselves. This success has been based upon the solidarity that these groups have built up among their members.

Summary

This chapter has attempted to establish the existence of resistance to schooling among a section of Asian boys at Kilby school and to explore the nature of this resistance in order to challenge the teacher stereotype of the 'high-achieving, conformist' Asian student. Such a group, the Warriors, were identified and it was shown that they adopted a sub-cultural response with many practices similar to the Rasta Heads in their resistance to authoritarianism and racism. However, the Warriors, as an anti-school group, tended to remain largely invisible to the teachers, with the latter's attention primarily focussed on the Afro-Caribbean students. The Warriors took advantage of this situation and on occasions carried out their anti-school practices covertly. The teachers' culturalist understanding of the students' social behaviour served to maintain the Warriors' invisibility, with the middle-class students' behaviour being assigned to the Asian boys as a whole. The disciplinary problems caused by members of the Warriors were explained by teachers in terms of personal deviancy and did not detract from the dominant social image of the 'conformist' Asian. However, the Warriors' response to teachers as part of their wider perspective of rejecting school cannot be reduced to a question of individual student deficiency. As the analysis of student social background demonstrated, class location informed the students' experience of and response to the dominant social relations of the school and the wider society and, through these relations, their experience of and response to racism.

Chapter 5

Postscript: Back to the Future

Where are they now?

I have kept in contact with many of the young men and women in the two studies. I made contact with all of the Black Sisters. I had more difficulty in tracing some of the Rasta Heads and the Warriors. Eventually, I contacted all but three of them. Khalid had returned to Pakistan with his parents. Parminder had moved to another area and no-one knew where Michael was. I had recorded their post-school/college 'careers' since completing the two studies at Kilby school and Connolly college and was aware of their contrasting lifestyles. In order to review the studies and to discuss their present situations and how they saw the future, I interviewed each of them individually and in groups, bringing the young men and women together.

The Rasta Heads and the Warriors had left Kilby school 3 years earlier. Since then, they were involved in a number of youth training schemes, part-time and temporary full-time jobs. At the time of interviewing, only two of them, Andrew and Iqbal, were working.

Leslie: I meet a lot of them from the school, down the club and I know only four that got jobs, proper jobs.

Christopher: I tried loads of places but there's nothing, not for us anyway.

Iqbal: I work for my cousin, in his shop. I keep looking around but there's nothing.

Andrew: I got a couple of jobs for a while since I left but they only want you for a couple of months. Now I got this one, doing electrical work. It's OK. Ye can get a lot of hours which pushes up yer wages an' I get to drive. I'm saving up for a car. Ye have to work hard all the time to prove that yer good for them. I hope that they keep me on.

Kulbinder:	Remember you used to have that record, *Ghost Town*, it's really like that here now, just dead.
Kevin:	I finished a training scheme thing then did a community thing. I was stuck in a training centre. We were nearly all black. We knew white kids who got sent to factories and then they get the jobs not us. I do my own private business to get by.
Leonard:	Any jobs there are go to the whites. When they did up all the houses by the park, you couldn't see any West Indians working on it, an' this is our area. You can see the way they look at ye when ye go for a job. I wouldn't go on any fucking training scheme. They don't really train ye, just shit work an' shit money.
Sokjinder:	I used to think I wouldn't take just any job like my dad had to but I get depressed. It's boring all day an' my parents keep on at me. They think I don't try but I've looked everywhere. There's nothin' at the job-centre. I'm going to move soon.

At the time of being interviewed to review the studies, the Black Sisters had left Connolly college 9 months. Since leaving, two of them, Chhaya and Minakshi, were working in the Civil Service, at a local Department of Health and Social Security. Five of them, Nihla, Smita, Hameeda, Wendy and Judith had gone on to higher education. Leonie was repeating her A-levels in order to get a place at university and Joanne was unemployed.

MM:	Was the Civil Service the first job that you applied for?
Chhaya:	We looked around a bit and applied for a few jobs. It seemed to offer more security.
MM:	How did you find it?
Minakshi:	We were lucky we got in the same section. We settled in quite quickly. To be honest, I think they wanted a few Asian faces around the place to deal with the Asians coming in. They are always talking down to them.
Chhaya:	They shout at them as if they are deaf or stupid, they have all the stereotypes of the Asians, living off the dole and working at the same time; that they're sly. The Asian men cope better but I feel sorry for the women.
Minakshi:	They hate us 'coz we keep sticking up for them. Telling them what they are entitled to, what they can claim.
Joanne:	I was thinking of applying for the Civil Service but I don't think that I could take it. I feel sorry for them on the dole but I would get depressed working there and I would be bored doing office work. I have applied to a few places but they say that I am over-qualified or that people with

degrees have got the job. I think that they just don't want me. I feel bad after all the study. You're kind of forced into doing some kind of community work which I wouldn't really mind but it's nice to have the choice to do what you want, especially after working for it.

MM: What's it like at university?

Judith: It's funny, all the teachers ask you, how is the course? How is the place? They don't ask you, what's it like for a black woman? Well that's the bit that's always there. I went up to administration for something and she said you've had yours. I told her I hadn't. She argued, I remember you this morning. The same old reaction. She probably saw a black face or a black hand across the counter and thought, there can't be many of her kind here.

Wendy: I share a flat with a white girl, real middle-class. It's full of them. She's a typical white liberal, telling me what it's like to be black. She's OK. I have to learn to live with her.

Smita: What amazes me is here are all these people with all these brains and they don't know anything about life, nothing about real life.

Judith: I have joined the Afro-Caribbean society and the black women's group. Ye need their support, especially from the women.

Hameeda: You feel very isolated. I get, I go home a lot, I miss it.

MM: Are you glad you went?

Wendy: As always, yes and no. It's good to prove that black people are just as good as them.

Hameeda: You mean better [joking].

Wendy: But it's not real. A lot of the students, they don't know anything like Smita said, they have no common sense. It's just a bit more leisure time for the rich kids before they take up their big jobs with their parents.

Nihla: It's nothing like ye think it's going to be. The lecturers are as bad as the students. They're more interested in parties and sleeping around then learning anything. The course work this year is really easy. The A-levels were harder.

Smita: Universities are strange places. We meet the white people there on equal terms. Our pasts are different, we went to different schools, live in different areas, and we will go our separate ways after but for a while we are thrown together. The racism is still there beneath the surface but it's less here than anywhere else, perhaps.

Judith: Yeah, it's like a massive international community, though there are still divisions, we are still black.

MM:	Do you think you will move away from the black community?
Wendy:	I never had a problem with being black. I was always proud to be black. I think that it's more difficult with the class question.
Smita:	I think the same. Like, I still identify more with Asians and all black people than I do with whites at university.
Judith:	I think that the problem is that others, other black people will, don't see us like that. Like Kevin [Rasta Head] yesterday. They thought we were snobs, looking down on them, using big words and all that.
Leonie:	I still think that they would feel closer to us than to whites.
Judith:	Probably, and of course it is more complicated because we are women. Black men are very sexist, like all men and they can't cope with their women doing better than them.
MM:	Do you think they [the Rasta Heads and the Warriors] were a bit jealous of your success?
Wendy:	Maybe, a bit.
Leonie:	I don't think so. I don't think that it's really that. It's the idea that we think that we are better. I don't think that they see us as better.
MM:	And do you?
Smita:	Of course not.
Joanne:	I think that middle-class women, black women would say yes but we don't. We know what the schools do to you and it's difficult when you're young to know how to respond. We did it our way. A lot of our friends did it their way like them.
Smita:	We know that we are the lucky ones that got through.
Joanne:	Yeah, and it's harder for them in some ways. Teachers seem to make more trouble for them.
Smita:	They've got worse stereotypes for them, and we know like we said that the students at university are not better than them, no brainier or whatever.

Review of the studies

Hameeda:	I read bits of it, about us and what they [the Rasta Heads and the Warriors] were saying.
Joanne:	It's really good. I've read through most of it. I think that you have really captured what it's like for black kids at school.
Raj:	It's easier for them [the young women] 'coz they, you all speak the same language en it? I read the bits about us.
Kevin:	I read all the bits about us. It's like having yer history

written down but I can't see why anyone else is interested in it. It's just the way we are.

Raj: I had forgotten some of the things you wrote about. I probably wouldn't tell ye now.

Leonard: I would. Reading it reminded me that I thought ye were a nutta, talking about blacks all the time but you were interested in us, helped us, so I thought we can trust him, an' I still do.

Leonie: I think that you prefer them in a way because you admire their anti-authority.

Arshid: I don't. Even now you an' them are closer than us, yer all successful, yer more together than us.

Raj: Yeah, them. Yer always telling us we are sexist an' all that. You influenced them more. They followed ye. We went our own way.

Judith: You admire their freedom. We're stuck in the system and so are you.

Kevin: Go on it's true en it, you would love it if we all chose your way like them?

MM: Yeah. I would've liked to see more of you get through 'coz I think that it gives ye more chances, more choices about the way ye live yer life and there's so many of you not getting through. But, there are other ways of making it.

Joanne: Why did you choose us?

MM: An accident really. Ended up in Kilby and living here, I began to see what it was like. And, then at Connolly you lot were always getting at me.

Kevin: We was like a gang of mates with someone who could help us. I used to forget that you were writing about us, an' you did sometimes!

Andrew: We had some great times dent we?

MM: Do you think that the way I see things gives a true picture of yer lives?

Raj: What do ye mean?

Judith: Well, you can't give an objective view of . . . [interrupted] . . .

Kevin: There she goes again, using big words.

Judith: I mean it's bound to be biased, your being for black people but it was because of that, that we talked to you as we really felt. You knew what you thought about us, you were more aware, but for most white people they hide it and pretend they see us as just the same as them but at the same time they treat us differently. As long as you make it clear in your study where you stand then it's OK. That's Weberian! [joking]. You reported our view of things.

Arshid: Like when that woman, that white woman came into school asking us all those questions about someat. She was objective but we just med things up. It was none of her business but we trusted you an' anyway we spent so much time together, you knew what we were like. An' ye let the teachers have their little say, usually it's only them that's talking.

Amerjit: My dad reckoned I took more notice of you than him. He used to say 'he's a funny teacher, why doesn't he teach ye somethin'.

Joanne: For a white man you didn't do too bad really. But like you say you had to change the way you saw things like we did and that's what you wrote.

Judith: In a way you see our lives as being worse than we do because you have an alternative to measure it against. But in another way it's worse for us because you can go on with your life. Tomorrow you can leave Kilby and go to your white areas. But we are always black living in a racist society. You can't really know, feel what it's like for a black woman. That's why I think that although what you have done is good, I think black women should carry out their own studies.

Hameeda: How come then that the Asian teachers at our old school never understood us better than him?

Student responses to school/college

MM: Do you think that their [the young women's] approach to school was better than yours?

Andrew: I think that they have more brains and worked harder.

Christopher: No, it's not that. I wish in a way I had more O-levels. It would . . . [interrupted] . . .

Amerjit: It wouldn't have made no difference. I know friends with qualifications and they can't get jobs. No-one in Kilby gets jobs, even the white kids!

Joanne: You can't say it was a better way for us. We all did it in different ways, trying to survive it, school.

Leonie: I don't think that there's anything great about what we did but we proved that black people have the brains and can be successful, in their terms [the teachers]. I'm glad we did it our way.

Arshid: I hated school, writing and all that stuff, so I wouldn't want more of that. I want a job and more O-levels wouldn't have helped would they?

Leonie:	They might have. How come so many of you mucked about? You got the brains?
Amerjit:	We had a really good time mucking about. Ye never really thought about getting exams. I wouldn't mind having them. But the teachers kept pickin' on ye, so you just had to do something to let them know that they couldn't just put ye down all the time. You had to challenge their power over ye.
Judith:	They picked on us as well but we weren't going to let them win.
Amerjit:	I don't know, it was different then. In a way your right we let them win, that is true. But in another way we won as well, they never beat us completely.
Leonard:	But they [the teachers] got at us everyday, especially us. They really hated us. You couldn't just let them keep ye down.
Judith:	Did you have to act tough?
Leonard:	Yeah, sure, there was pressure on us to come on tough. I don't think girls have to.
Hameeda:	But you gave into the pressure of yer mates as well.
Sokjinder:	Ye have to stick by yer mates. If ye have to choose between teachers an' yer mates, ye choose yer mates en it?
Kevin:	I don't think we really had a choice. We weren't that bad in the first and second year but they forced us to be bad.
Leonie:	They said you were stupid so you acted it out.
Kevin:	In a way, yeah. But it was so boring, all that work. We wanted to enjoy life an' we had a great time an' now we have something to look back at. You had a boring time, pleasing the teachers and letting them boss ye about, an' yer still doing it in a way.
Amerjit:	That stuff ye learn's not important. It's nothing to do with us, nothing to do with life. They try to make us feel we are nothing but when we're together, acting together, we were strong. It made ye feel ye were someone, someone important. The other kids respected us. We were right.

Inner-city rebellions

Christopher:	It was like with the riots. It's the excitement, all acting together.
Amerjit:	We heard it was on. Some of our mates called an' we

went up. For once we had control of everythin'. The coppers were scared of us. If ye stick together, at school or on the street, ye can win. All the people were passing stuff along, helping each other.

Kevin: We all went up to see what was going on. It looked like justice had come an' it was burnin' down.

Ashwin: It was great fun, really exciting.

MM: Why was it so exciting?

Christopher: Usually it's boring round here but then it was great, everyone out on the streets.

Leonard: It doesn't just explode. There are a lot of little incidents. Me and him are often stopped [by the police]. Like when you left us off from that cafe. They stopped us and asked us, what we had in our bag. They ent got no right to do that and to abuse ye while yer standing there.

Joanne: They are always looking for trouble, looking for excuses to put you down. It all mounts up. They beat my brother up and he's never been in any trouble.

Judith: In Bristol, Brixton, Tottenham and Handsworth black people have rebelled in this way. They try and make out that there is something inside of us that causes it. It's not true. All through history in this country and elsewhere when people are oppressed, they rebel. The problem is this rotten society not us. It turns whites against blacks and men against women and the police against the community they're supposed to be protecting. In this society there is a law for the whites and a law for the blacks. And let's remember, even their own statistics shows that black people, both Afro-Caribbeans and Asians, are the victims.

MM: A lot of white people think that it was mainly young Caribbeans that were involved.

Iqbal: They are talking through their arses. We were all together, Asians an' West Indians an' whites, young people and older ones.

Amerjit: The papers and the telly talk about all this. It's not true. It wasn't planned like they say. It wasn't about drugs an' it wasn't only the black kids fighting. It's all very simple to explain why it happened. Like she says, this society hates us an' keeps us down because we are not white like them. That's the truth an' we have to deal with it in our own way, in different ways. This is one way.

Hameeda: It's like that black community leader, your mate, said on TV. He doesn't riot 'coz he doesn't have to. Well it's the same for us. We [the young women] don't have to

	show our protest in that way but like he says that's one way. And it can't be about drugs 'coz there's more at university than round here.
Minakshi:	I've got a job and all of us [the young women] might get good jobs. We will be able to move about more than them [the Rasta Heads and the Warriors], experience more. So they will probably feel more frustrated than us.
MM:	Are your critical of the rebellion?
Hameeda:	No. It's not our way but when you keep treating people in a bad way, discriminating against them, one day they will fight back, like this.
Judith:	I would always defend those who are involved in it and women were involved in it as well. Not all of the things, like the policeman who died, I don't agree with that. The police are terrible to us but I don't think that we should behave like them.
MM:	What about in South Africa?
Judith:	That's different. There, blacks have no rights. They've tried all the other ways. There the whites are trying to wipe them out, pretend they don't exist in their own country.
Kevin:	It's like you used to say about Ireland. Ye try all the peaceful ways, marching an' everything an' if nothing changes an ye see yer family an' yer friends put down and beaten up all the time, there comes a time when you will see justice an' some will take up violence.
Leonard:	If ye look at our history, black people have always been forced into it.
Leonie:	I think that black people in this country have a lot to learn from the South African youth in resisting oppression. We all come from the same oppression.
Leonard:	If there wasn't so much violence against black people then blacks wouldn't have to fight back. It's the whites that start it. We are only defending ourselves.
Judith:	So really you have to choose which side you're on and really there is no choice. When the police shoot black people, they try and show that the family were criminals and so deserved it. They wouldn't do that to whites. But it's easy to do it to blacks because this society sees all black people as criminals.
Amerjit:	That's true. When did ye hear someone ask, do you support white violence. But they do most of it.

The future

MM:	What of the future?
Leonard:	There's no future in this country for our people. This is a wicked country for the black man.
Amerjit:	Ye can't think of the future. It's not gonna be any different to now.
Leonie:	It's got much worse for black people. There aren't many jobs around, so we aren't going to get many.
Clive:	It's OK for you. My parents come down on me 'coz I'm, I haven't got a job.
Leonie:	Not really. I'm talking about all black people. It's getting worse and worse.
Clive:	There ent no jobs so ye gotta get by with yer own business. They just keep giving ye the training schemes. I think a lot of people have learnt now that they're no good. I think in the future people will just refuse to have anything to do with them.
Ashwin:	Even if ye do get a job, they give ye the worst ones, and it's so boring an' they don't treat ye good. It's shit money, ye can't even live on.
Christopher:	Ye just have to learn to survive when yer out there. That's why our way at school helped us for now. We can look after ourselves. It's not so bad.
Kulbinder:	There's nothing for us 'cept our mates. We still most of us still see each other round the place.
MM:	What do you do?
Leslie:	We spend a lot of time down the snooker hall, down the cafe, just talking.
Kulbinder:	Yer lucky. I have to look after my nephews an' do things round the house.
Iqbal:	I spend some time at a friend's house. Go down the cafe. Look about for work from friends. I get little bits.
Neville:	There ent much to do, a couple of parties, go round to yer girl friend's house. Sit round talking, go down to the club. I still play football a lot.
Judith:	If you get back to the future. I think we have to make the future good. You don't have to give up and act their stereotypes. That's what they want. Then that gives them more power to treat us worse and we feel bad and start fighting among ourselves.
Amerjit:	That is true. After the riots the coppers have got much tougher. They lost out that night but like you say they will get their plastic bullets an' then they will come after us. They have to show their power just like the teachers

at school. If they lose one fight, then they have to win the next one. An' they will force us into a fight that we will lose, that's how they work. If we stick together like they do, we will be stronger.

Leonie: If the National Front grows like in France, the white people won't protect us. If the oil runs out, they'll say, we've had enough of you lot, go back to where you came from.

Kevin: We wouldn't accept that. We'd fight back, we were born here. I want my share of the goods however I get them.

Minakshi: I think that they will try to kick us out. We will be the scapegoats. That's why we have to stick together just to survive. Just like at school, in our different ways.

Joanne: Tiocfaidh ar la! [Gaelic – our day will come. Written on the walls in the Republican areas of Northern Ireland].

Chapter 6

Conclusion

A number of implications arise from the above examination of teacher ideologies and practices and student responses and resistances at Kilby school and Connolly college. This is a complex issue involving the two interconnected levels at which racism operates within the education system. At one level, racism is mediated through the existing institutional framework of the schooling process. Here, as the socio-cultural theorists (Bowles and Gintis, 1976; Bernstein, 1975) have argued, schools can be seen as latently recreating the social relations of the wider society, including such structural divisions as those of class, 'race' and gender. This is achieved through a number of pedagogical practices which serve selectively to reproduce the dominant culture by differentially skilling, both technically and socially, different social groups for their future place within the socio-economic division of labour. However, this reproduction, as the young people above make explicit, is not automatically or mechanically achieved as the more deterministic theorists suggest. As Carrington (1983) argues in his ethnographic study of Afro-Caribbean youth, the school system should be seen as a site of struggle. Commenting on the position of teachers, he maintains that:

> the conservative face of schooling . . . must be regarded as contingent rather than pre-given. To accept a politics of education and policy initiatives within education, whether to tackle race, class or gender based forms of educational disadvantage, is to accept the specificity of institutions such as the school and to recognise that teachers . . . whilst not totally free, are not 'automatons', 'passive objects', 'cultural dupes' or the mere bearers of the mode of production (p. 62).

At a second level, racially specific mechanisms, such as the system of racist stereotyping, are identified in operation. These mechanisms are linked to the former level, that of the existing institutional framework, but it is in response to these specific mechanisms that racially explicit policies can be formulated. In other words, there is scope for individual local authorities to adopt anti-racist and anti-sexist measures within schools that challenge institutionalized discrimination against male and female black youth.

The state, both at a national and local level, has a disastrously poor record in response to the presence of black students within the school system. Historically, having shifted from a 'colour-blind' approach to a multicultural perspective, the focus of attention became the assumed 'problems' of the black youth. These were divided into social and disciplinary categories. The former was essentially explained in terms of various forms of cultural deprivation theories. The latter was concerned with the 'problems' that the black youth caused the school. However, there has been a general silence on the question of the problems caused by the school due to its racial structuring. As Green (1982, p. 23) points out:

> There is a common tendency in much educational writing on race to allow that critical slippage from 'the problems encountered by' to the 'problem of'. Given the way in which the state frames the issues in terms of the 'problem' posed by blacks rather than the problem of racism, it's little wonder that people should read state policies not as remedies for racism but as ways of dealing with blacks.

The Kilby school and Connolly college students' responses, as part of the widespread evidence of black youths' resistance to schooling and the relatively higher levels of black youth unemployment, demonstrate the inadequacies of many multi cultural educational programmes to improve life-chances of black youth.

Sivanandan (1983, p. 9) suggests a way of overcoming the limitations and contradictions of conventional 'multicultural' practices by adopting an explicitly anti-racist approach:

> In the field of education ... it is important to turn ethnicity and culturalism into anti-racism. But this involves not just the examination of existing literature for racist bias (and their elimination) but for the provision of anti-racist texts ... and not just an examination of curricula and syllabuses but of the whole fabric of education: organization and administration, methods and materials, attitudes and practices of heads and teachers, the whole works.

From my research, it is evident that a priority for such a policy should be to address the issue of the absence of teachers from conventional 'race-relations' research and, in so doing, to examine the racism within the teaching profession and its underlying material base. The adoption of the strategies that Sivanandan outlines above should not be seen in isolation but as a necessary part of a broader anti-racist response. As Hatcher (1987, p. 199) argues:

The task now facing the movement for anti-racist education is to continue to construct a growing web of connections at school, local and national levels, between what happens in classrooms and the wider political struggles outside, in the form not only of campaigns to implement or defend specific reforms, but also of a comprehensive programme for anti-racist education in schools, around which unity can be built among the social forces capable of installing it.

Such a strategy may point to possible future alliances between black parents, students and progressive teachers who challenge the hegemonically determined view of a depoliticized and deracialized school system, thereby locating the 'problem' of schooling black students not within the black community but within the racially structured class society. This in turn would challenge the existing social and material differential response to black students of Afro-Caribbean and Asian origin, which was seen to be operating within Kilby school and Connolly college.

Equally important in examining racism in the teaching profession is the question of black teachers' experience of working in schools. While carrying out this study, I made contact with a number of black teachers. They all spoke of the under-representation of blacks, the mechanisms operating against their promotion and their isolation in mainstream schooling (see Gow, 1988). They were particularly critical of the pressure to become the multicultural teacher in their school. Local authorities and teacher unions and associations need to give higher priority to these concerns, if these teachers are to attain equality of career opportunity. Furthermore, anti-racist initiatives should be carried out with full consultation with black teachers, non-teaching black school staff and black community organizations, who have long experience of developing strategies of resistance to racism. Of particular importance here is the 'black voluntary school movement', which has developed in response to the failure of mainstream schools to meet black students' needs (see Chevannes and Reeves, 1987, pp. 147–69). State schools have much to learn from this community-based initiative, which may serve as a model of good practice.

Another implication of these studies which arises from looking at student–teacher relations, is the question of the significance of the students' implicit understanding of the school process. Through the framework of the existing power relations, multiculturalism is ideologically presented as a legitimate educational strategy and the anti-school students' perspective is perceived as an illegitimate response. This view is reinforced by much of the literature on youth sub-cultures which over-emphasizes the negative aspect of the students' resistance to schooling. A similar criticism may be made of the Kilby school study. This is partly the result of the nature of the school's institutional authoritarianism which prevents the development of formal mechanisms which would democratize teacher–student relations and provide student representation. There is no formal acknowledgement of the students' perspective, of how to manage the school, as a legitimate view. Hence, their practices ideologically appear as the irrational, illegitimate activities of a minority of irresponsible trouble-makers. This negative view is further reinforced by the lack of organized political structure that is found among youth sub-cultures. So, for example, the latter groups' ideology does not appear as rationally legitimate as that of student unions in higher education. Frith and Corrigan (1976, p. 11) discuss the dilemmas facing the National Union of School Students in organizing anti-school students:

> Can classroom struggle contribute to class struggle? This is precisely the problem of the [CP organized] National Union of School Students. . . . They have found it difficult to attract support from school 'failures'. Their members have a commitment to education which makes the NUSS a useful organization; the children who smash windows haven't. This doesn't make the latter correct, class conscious or revolutionary, but it does mean that the NUSS has to work out how to recruit them. Without the 'failures' the union isn't even creating union consciousness – these stroppy pupils leave school untouched by any organized form of politics and the NUSS is left in an elitist position.

Although they adopt a narrow social democratic view of political consciousness, Frith and Corrigan do point to a real limitation in student organization that was prevalent among the Rasta Heads and Warriors.

Nevertheless, contrary to the immediate appearance from the case studies of the students' exclusively negative response to schooling, an alternative reading is possible, that was empirically found among the Rasta Heads and the Warriors, that of their positive, progressive view of the reorganization of Kilby school. These elements of inventiveness and cooperation, which have been examined in the substantive work, included democratizing teacher–student relations, linking learning in the school with learning in the wider community and the decoupling of school and work. It is important to stress that these elements were not rigorously defined by the students. However, in the Rasta Heads' and Warriors' rejection of formal schooling, there is implied a radical critique of the existing structures and processes, and an alternative progressive form of education. This progressive outlook is highlighted in the Black Sisters' response. Their insightful distinction between education and schooling enabled them to acquire high-status qualifications while, at the same time, perceptively offering an explicit critique of present-day schooling. The radical creativity of the students' perspectives can be seen by contrasting their position with that of the Liberals' multicultural position which assumes the maintenance of the existing social relations within schools. Ultimately, the progressive basis of the students' position derives from their understanding of the black community's needs. In this they go beyond multiculturalism which, based on racist stereotypes, provides no real solution to the black community's actual cultural and material situation.

Policy-makers and practitioners, such as teachers and future teachers, have much to learn from students about their understanding of school. It is, for example, the students who experience directly the material constraints of the increasing contradiction between what has been a major function of schooling in industrial societies, that of the preparation of students for work, and the emergence during the early 1980s of mass youth unemployment, as a long-term structural phenomenon. As indicated in the previous chapters, such contradictions create different student responses. The Black Sisters' survival strategies are most effective; those of the Rasta Heads and the Warriors may appear to be less so. However, as shown in the postscript, the students did not see it this way. Although shifting my research away from examining the transition from school to work, which proved to be too ambitious a plan, I continued to collect data on the Kilby school boys' first 6 months post-school experience. These findings are outside the scope of this study, but one general trend is pertinent. For the anti-school boys, the fact that ony two of them and few of the rest of the students in their year got a job confirmed for them the realism of their response to schooling, as Kevin assessing their approach indicates:

> We're all the same now, no-one's got a job, a real job. School made no difference, it can't if yer black. You see we knew, that's the real difference between us and them [the conformists]. They believed in the teachers, they don't know, they don't live in reality. We were proved right, we were right to have a good time, en it?

The Kilby school students' failure to find work was reflected in the general employment situation for the area. The Kilby careers service informed me that of 1890 youths of school-leaving age in 1982, by November of that year only 4 per cent had found what they called 'normal employment'. One of the main 'limitations' of Willis' (1977 p. 145) 'lads' was that their cultural 'penetrations' into the school process were undermined by its mystifications, such as the boys' rejection of mental work, their sexism, racism and violence, which served to bound them back into the manual sector of the labour market to which they as members of the working-class were structurally destined. The Rasta Heads' and the Warriors' resistance to school shares some of these limitations. However, with the disappearance of many of these manual jobs to which they were destined, and more generally within the wider society in which they have little power, both as students within the school and as part of the black working-class within the wider community, such collective strategies of resistance make sense, albeit limited (see Solomos, 1986).

Understanding student–teacher relations is not an easy task. The issues that have been examined in this book are not only of significance for the black community but are part of a wider concern with the schooling of working-class youth as a whole. A study of the encounter of white middle-class professionals and black youth serves to highlight the dynamics of this process which are often hidden. More specifically the research hopes to make a contribution to the concern with the schooling of black students. This book has attempted to demonstrate that racism is of primary significance both in terms of the racial structuring of schools and in the students' resistance to racist and sexist structures and processes. Such a view is shared by Bryan *et al.* (1985). Writing of black women's lives in Britain, they point to the importance of education:

> . . . the very fact that black women are still fighting, despite the obstacles and sacrifices involved, to gain a valid education bears witness to the crucial importance education continues to play in our lives. Our struggles, after years of second-class schooling, confirm that we have not given up and no amount of racism and discrimination can deter us, now that we have come this far. This refusal to give in and accept the confines of our race, class and sex has been the single most important factor of our survival in Britain (p. 88).

Finally, this research has been carried out at a critical time for the inner-cities, with the recommendation of the introduction of plastic bullets for use in future disturbances. At a time of decreased spending on social science research, white policy-makers and welfare practitioners, such as teachers, have little understanding of the 'different reality' that the black community experience living in the economically under-resourced inner-cities in the mid-1980s. I hope that this book helps to inform their understanding by presenting a detailed examination of how schooling for black female and male youth is a central part of an alienating social response to them, that results in their experience of a 'different reality' from the white population both at school and in the wider society. It is in their response to this experience, involving creative strategies of survival, that they can be seen as 'young, gifted and black'.

Notes

Introduction

1 Throughout the book I have referred to people of Asian and Afro-Caribbean origin as black. The term highlights their common experience of white racism in Britain. Racism may take different forms for the two social groups and is gender-specific, as is demonstrated in this book (see Sivanandan, 1982).

2 Pseudonyms are used for the area, the school, the college, the teachers and the students to maintain confidentiality. Since carrying out this research, all of the students and many of the staff involved in the study have left Kilby school. This includes a complete change in the school management. The present headteacher and deputy head have incorporated an anti-racist perspective into the curriculum.

3 'Race' and 'race relations' are in quotation marks to highlight the fact that these concepts are socially and politically constructed rather than based on scientific findings. For a discussion of the problematic nature of the terms, see Husband (1982).

4 See Ballard and Driver (1977) for a further explanation of the 'ethnic approach'. See also Banks and Lynch (1986) for a more recent development of this approach.

5 Theoretically a division has been created between a 'strong' Asian culture and a 'weak' Afro-Caribbean culture. The development of Afro-Caribbean culture has been explained largely in terms of British imperialism; that is, it underwent a process of acculturation. In contrast, Asian culture did not suffer this fragmentation to any significant degree. But as Lawrence (1982, pp. 111–12) has argued, these social images are caricatures.

6 The most stimulating of recent work on the analysis of racially structured societies has come from Marxist (Hall, 1980; Sivanandan, 1978, 1983, 1985a), quasi-Marxist (Castles and Kosack, 1973) and left-Weberian (Rex, 1973; Rex and Tomlinson, 1979) theorists. See Dummett (1984) and IRR (1982a, 1982b) for a very clear exposition of English racism. See Hiro (1971) and Fryer (1984) for a history of black people in Britain. See Marable (1985) for a discussion of racism in America.

7 Meyenn (1979, p. 103) points to the level at which links may be found between what are often presented as competing perspectives. Like Meyenn, I found that the

theoretical difficulties of seeing linkages between the perspectives depended on the level of analysis and, like him, I drew on the different traditions.

8 Duffield (1984) develops Barker's work by examining the similarities between 'new racism' and what he calls the 'new realism' of the Liberal establishment with the shift from assimilation to integration.

9 Similar findings on the relations between white teachers and black youth can be found in Wright (1985).

10 In 1965 the Department of Education and Science explicitly defined the role of education as the 'successful assimilation of immigrant children'.

11 Hatcher (1987, p. 185) reminds us that the 'new multiculturalism' acknowledges the existence of institutional racism but by remaining within the 'ethnic relations' framework it excludes a structuralist explanation of racism in a class-divided society.

12 Methodological concerns tend to be overshadowed by theoretical issues in much research. However, they do have a certain autonomy; so, for example, methodology allowed and pointed to the importance of examining the teachers' ideologies and practices as well as those of the black boys. This enabled me to understand how racism operated at Kilby school. See Hammersley and Woods (1987, p. 283–317) for a debate on ethnography. Carr's (1983) question, 'What is History?' and the answer he suggests provides much insight for the parallel question, 'What is Sociology?'

13 My thanks to the OUP's anonymous reader for clarifying these criticisms.

14 My own work has much in common with these American studies of students' responses to contemporary schooling. In particular, like them, I have tried to describe the students' lived culture in relation to the wider society.

15 See Bates *et al.* (1984).

Chapter 1

1 As a result of their close contact with each other, their college teachers referred to them as the 'black girls'. It was as a variation of this title that I coined the name the Black Sisters, which the young women initially accepted in a light-hearted manner. As the study progressed, they developed a political reading of the name, emphasizing black female solidarity.

2 Anyon (1983, pp. 19–23), discussing gender development in America, describes it as an 'active response to . . . the contradictory social messages regarding what they should do and be'. In order to develop the dynamics of this concept, she adapts Eugene Genovese's (1972) account of how black slaves appropriated the ideology of paternalism in order to resolve the contradictions of their existence as human beings and slaves. Genovese argues that the majority of blacks neither totally accepted nor overtly fought the system of slavery but rather adopted strategies of 'accommodation *in* acts of resistance, and resistance *within* accommodation' [Genovese's emphasis].

3 The use of the concept of resistance within accommodation to describe the young women's response to schooling is not to suggest that theirs was a strategy of conformity in contrast to the Warriors' and the Rasta Heads' strategies of resistance. Historically, in all dominant institutions and societies, the survival strategies of the oppressed have been a mixture of rebellion and acceptance (see, for example, Roberts, 1984 and IRR, 1985). The main point here is that there are

a range of strategies available to young blacks. See Giroux (1983) for a discussion of resistance in education. Aggleton (1987, pp. 120–33) provides a most imaginative framework within which to examine theoretically different modes of resistance and contestation, the former being concerned with challenges against 'relations of power structuring relationships between groups', and the latter being challenges against 'principles of control operating in particular settings' (p. 24). Pollard (1985) provides a detailed account of primary school students' strategies of conformity, negotiation and rejection.

4 See Griffin's (1986, pp. 95–115) article entitled 'It's different for girls: the use of qualitative methods in a study of young women's lives', where she discusses the male norm in academic research. See also McRobbie (1980).

5 The limited number of British studies of young black women's schooling include Sharpe (1976), Fuller (1980) and Riley (1985).

6 Davies (1984, p. 172) and Griffin (1985, pp. 15–16) point out that the meanings of female conformity and deviance are more complex than the traditional studies of boys has suggested. At one end of the continuum, one finds McRobbie's (1978) description of the solidarity between girls and the importance of the concept of 'best friend', and at the other end is Llewellyn's (1980) account of the individual isolation of the non-examination girls.

7 See, for example, Wilson (1978), Davis (1981), Hooks (1982), Carby (1982a, 1982b), Bourne (1983) and Bryan *et al.* (1985).

8 Cicourel and Kitsuse (1963) found similar processes in operation in America, where students who were qualified to continue high-status courses, were counselled to 'drop out'. Within Britain these processes are likely to become more important as student profiling increases, creating further barriers for young blacks' progression in the education system.

9 See Note 14, Chapter 2, for examples of this research, whose primary focus has been male Afro-Caribbean youth. One of the most effective critiques of this type of research is provided by Stone (1981, p. 86), who writes: '. . . during the time social scientists have been busy proving that black people have negative self-images based on white stereotypes, blacks have been busy living in accordance with their own world-view'.

10 The notion of young blacks being 'caught between two cultures' is a central argument of the dominant ethnic approach in 'race relations' (see Note 5, Introduction). Lawrence (1982, p. 122) points to the influence of the Community Relations Commission in employing the 'cultural pluralist' approach with its focus on ethnic minorities' 'cultural conflict' and 'identity crisis'.

11 Sociological analyses of women and education, including such work as Sharpe (1976), Wolpe (1977), Deem (1978), Stanworth (1981), Walker and Barton (1983) and Arnot and Weiner (1987) have examined in great detail the way in which schools have created particular 'female routes', including such processes as sex-role stereotyping, and the resulting teacher expectations, curriculum differentiation on the basis of gender, the sexist discourse of much of the learning material and the preparation of students for the labour market and housework, based on the sexual division of labour. This research, employing different theoretical explanations, has provided important insights into the way in which school structures, processes and practices result in young women 'Learning to Lose' (Spender and Sarah, 1980). However, more recently, it has been suggested that there may be a tendency in some of the above work, by implicitly adopting a

passive conception of socialization to be overly deterministic. A more useful definition of socialization is provided by Lacey (1977) who sees it as 'the adoption or creation of appropriate strategies'.

12 Griffin (1985, p. 30) describes the different pressures from white teachers and career officers on Asian and Afro-Caribbean students. She writes: 'Asian students were frequently labelled as "over-aspirers" and their Afro-Caribbean peers as "under-achievers".'

13 Amos and Parmar (1981, pp. 139–40) provide a detailed examination of the racist stereotypes that inform teachers' perspectives.

14 This absence of gender is also found in official reports. As Mirza (1986, p. 39) points out, 'Gender is an issue in the race and education debate, yet one can read through the entire 806-page Swann Report and find a complete absence of any substantial and conclusive research with regard to the educational experience of black girls.'

15 Bourne (1983, p. 20) warns us of the danger of '. . . taking a practice out of its socio-economic context, by attributing it to a country or culture, rather than to an historical stage, feminists are well on the way to racial stereotyping. Instead of seeing that arranged marriages, circumcision, dowries and so on have been part of all our histories, they attribute the customs not to an epoch or to a social formation but to a racial group.' Placing the Black Sisters' and the Warriors families' social arrangements within their socio-economic context was not difficult for me as my extended family in Ireland adopt similar arrangements.

16 See Note 5, Chapter 2. Bryan *et al.* (1985) look at the meaning of Rastafarianism for black women.

17 For example, one of the main themes of Irish traditional and contemporary poetry and music is that of 'returning home'. See Conner (1985) for a detailed analysis of the experiences of recent Irish immigrants in London (see also Curtis, 1985 and Hickman, 1986).

18 Chigwada (1987, pp. 16–17) warns of the potential dangers of teachers marking their own students' GCSE work.

19 Teachers' authority is traditionally assumed to be based on the fact that they have subject knowledge which students do not possess. Here we see the inadequacy of this assumption.

20 For example, Willis' counter-school group, the Lads, were most scornful of the pro-school students, the Ear'oles.

21 The Black Sisters talked of various derogative names that they were called at school, such as 'choc-ice' and 'coconut', that is, black on the outside and white on the inside.

22 The young Asian women also pointed out that Asian students frequently repeat courses in the sixth form and so achieve qualifications at a later age than their white peers.

23 For a more positive reading of young male Afro-Caribbeans' involvement in sport and music, as a strategy of challenging the dominant white stereotypes of blacks in this area, see Carrington (1983). Bryan *et al.* (1985, p. 199) point out that black men and women historically have challenged cultural imperialism through the creation of black art and culture.

24 In making this point, I do not wish to underplay the qualitative curricular change presently taking place in inner-city schools. It is important to stress that there has been a significant curricular shift for the 14–18 age group in the last few years,

from 'the liberal-humanist education paradigm to a technicist training paradigm' (Moore, 1984, p. 66) with the introduction of such courses as the Certificate of Pre-Vocational Education and the Technical and Vocational Education Initiative. Furthermore, it appears that in the present 'enterprise culture' with the rise of the Manpower Services Commission and the 1988 Education Reform Act, the logic of this change will continue with schools being run on the model of small businesses.

25 Bryan *et al.* (1985, pp. 213–14) provide a critique of the image of the 'powerful' black matriarch'. As Chigwada (1987, pp. 14–18) points out, black girls are neither 'victims nor superwomen'.

Chapter 2

1 Within sociological theory, the concept of ideology is a highly problematic term. Apple (1979, pp. 20–21) identifies two main traditions; first, that of the Marxist 'interest theory' in which ideology is seen as a system of ideas which serve to legitimate vested interests of particular socio-economic groups. Secondly, the tradition of 'strain theory' developed by Durkheim and Parsons which perceives the main function of ideology as 'providing meaning in problematic situations', enabling groups to interact. This chapter will analyse the educational ideologies within a particular school, Kilby comprehensive, in terms of what Finn *et al.* (1977, p. 147), who have developed the former meaning, see as the ideological work of the school; 'their institutional structures, their disposition of knowledge, their pedagogic relationships, their informal cultures and organization' and the relationship of these ideologies to the more general ideologies at a national and local educational level. See Finn *et al.* (1977) and Apple and Taxel (1982) for a discussion of ideologies 'about' and 'in' education.

2 There has been a wide range of attempts to describe ideologies of education, including ideologies at a national level, of particular schools and individual classrooms (e.g. Williams, 1961 and Hammersley, 1977). Meighan and Brown (1980) offer a critical analysis of these studies.

3 See Barrat (1986, pp. 42–56) who makes a distinction between the psychological view of the stereotype with its focus on individuals' attitudes, such as prejudice, and the sociological view, that locates stereotypes within the wider context of society and the ideological function they serve in reproducing the dominant power relations. Referring to the work of Perkins (1979), Barrat argues that, 'Even though we may not "believe" the stereotype it remains as part of our consciousness and works as a shorthand technique for conveying a complex idea' (ibid., p. 45). Throughout the book I am using the concept of stereotype in the sociological sense. I argue that idealist analysis which reduces racial stereotyping to a question of teacher prejudice creating deviant black students is insufficient to explain the complex social interaction of teachers and black students. Rather, the process of racism involves concrete practices linked to the objective material conditions and expectations both within the institution and the wider society. At different points in the book, I shall expand on how specific racist stereotypes within the context of education were grounded in the material reality of the social relations of Kilby school and Connolly college.

4 Hegemony is a key concept in Gramsci's (1971) work. It refers to the way in which an alliance of social groups enables leaders to exercise power not by simple domination of ruling class ideas but by winning and shaping consent for its leadership. It produces a 'world view' which both legitimates and mystifies the

power of the dominant groups. It affects all areas of daily life, informing the common-sense beliefs of individuals. However, Gramsci emphasized the contradictory nature of common sense with dominated groups at the same time holding onto their own views of the world. An implication of Gramsci's concept employed in this book, is that teachers' everyday thinking and practices are hegemonically determined. Andy Hargreaves (1981, p. 305) points out that this untested thesis is not suggesting that teachers adopt a particular monolithic ideology but, rather, they hold a variety of views; however, '. . . the central issue is that while teachers hold a range of views about education . . . they do so in definite and unquestioning limits. Beyond these limits lie a set of educational and social practices which would be viewed by most people as potentially threatening to the existing order of capitalism . . .'

5 The establishment of the problem, in terms of under-achievement, in particular of Afro-Caribbean students, the dominant explanation, in terms of cultural disadvantages, and the proposed solution, in terms of the adoption of a multicultural curriculum, reflects the educability studies of the 1960s, which focussed on the socio-cultural deprivations of working-class students and suggested the implementation of compensatory education, in order to attain equality of opportunity. For a further discussion, see Keddie (1973) and Carby (1980).

6 See Hammersley (1977) for comparative material.

7 This concept of 'new realism' anticipated its wider adoption as a political strategy by sections of the Labour Party and trade union leadership in response to the ideological dominance of contemporary Toryism. It is presently a major theme in teachers' pragmatic response to the government's restructuring of education.

8 See Woods (1977) who describes 'teaching for survival'.

9 Further material on the function of humour in schooling can be found in Stebbins (1980).

10 Although socio-cultural reproduction theories, such as those of Bourdieu and Passeron (1977), Althusser (1971), Bernstein (1975) and Bowles and Gintis (1976) are not specifically concerned with the question of black youth, they do provide scope for an examination of black youths' social location in the schooling process and their preparation for the wider society. The above work informs my analysis of Kilby school and Connolly college. Weis (1985, p. 162) offers a critique of the over-deterministic approach of Bowles and Gintis. Similarly, I would argue that 'student cultures' do have a relative autonomy from wider institutional and economic forces that has not been examined by early work in this area. Dale (1982) provides a lucid account of the relationship between education and the capitalist state.

11 For examples of racism in school textbooks and children's literature, see National Union of Teachers (1979) and Dixon (1982).

12 Sharp and Green (1975) and Apple (1979) argue that the hidden curriculum must be historically and socially located within the power relations of existing society. See Weis' (1985, pp. 77–82) discussion of 'the dialectic of the hidden curriculum'.

13 See Denscombe (1980) for an explanation of 'keeping 'em quiet'.

14 The Rampton Report (1981) and the Swann Report (1985).

15 In recent years there has been much research in the general area of teacher typification. More specifically in relation to black students, Rist (1977, p. 279) examines the multi-faceted and multi-dimensional aspects of American teachers' expectations. He notes that: 'The variables of race and ethnicity have been documented . . . as powerful factors in generating the expectations teachers hold

of children.' Rex and Tomlinson (1979, p. 199) point out that in Brittan, little research has been carried out on the changing cultural base in majority black schools and more particularly little work is available on teachers' perceptions of students in these schools. They refer to two examples of the limited research in this area, that of Brittan (1976) and Giles (1977).

16 More recently, work has been carried out on white teachers' perceptions of black students. This work includes Eggleston *et al.* (1985) and Green (1985). See, particularly, Wright's (1985) ethnographic study of the school experience of Afro-Caribbean students in two comprehensives in the West Midlands. All of these researchers found that white teachers worked with negative stereotypes of Afro-Caribbean students, emphasizing their 'behavioural problems'.

17 See Hargreaves *et al.* (1975, p. 17) who applied labelling theory to schools.

18 As is shown in Chapter 4, the Asian young women reported that their secondary school teachers held similar negative caricatures.

19 This is not to suggest that attitudes cannot be changed. Rather it calls into question the limitations of multicultural courses.

20 The ideological nature of professionalism has been examined by a number of researchers including Finn *et al.* (1977) and Ginsburg *et al.* (1980).

21 Chessum (1980, p. 124) describes the large 'network of state agencies and professionals who took responsibility for selected aspects of the welfare and control of the pupils in and out of school. The schools were expected to cooperate with these bodies. . . . Psychologists, social workers, child psychiatrists, staff of special schools and educational welfare officers were examples.'

22 This uncritical reliance on psychology points to the gap between sociological theory and teacher practice. Waller (1967) remains one of the best accounts of sociology and teaching.

23 See, particularly, the work of Bernstein (1975), who is one of the most influential theorists in this area, on the role of education in cultural reproduction in a class society. He sees educational knowledge as a most important determinant of the structure of school experience. Williams (1961) provides insight into this area, with his concept of 'the selective tradition', that is, the ability of those in positions of power to define what constitutes legitimate knowledge and to represent their history and culture as constituting civilization, thus excluding other cultures or presenting them in a sub-standard form. Social phenomenologists, such as Keddie (1971), who has developed this idea in her work on the social construction of classroom knowledge and later work such as Young and Whitty (1977), have addressed themselves to the limitations of the earlier theory, particularly the problem of the relativistic view of knowledge. A limitation of the above work is that having concentrated on class ideologies, little attention is paid to the significance of ideologies of 'race'.

24 This points to a central weakness of multicultural education, that anti-racist education attempts to address (see Bryan *et al.* 1985, pp. 79–80). See also ALTARF (1984), Brah and Deem (1986) and Cohen and Bains (1986). Offe (1984) discusses in relation to structural inequalities.

25 The Rampton Report (1981) found that Asian children as a group were performing on a comparable level with white children, but that Afro-Caribbean children on average were under-achieving. Reeves and Chevannes (1981) are critical of the Report for failing to take into account such variables as class and gender.

26 See Ball (1981, p. 128) for a discussion of the constraints on what he calls the

'professed ideology of free choice of subjects and examination level open to pupils'.

27 Wright (1985) found a similar decline in the relative school position of students of Afro-Caribbean origin and provides evidence to support the explanation offered in this book that school processes, such as ' "gateways", streaming, banding, setting, suspensions and remedial units' operate disproportionately against the interests of these students.

Chapter 3

1 See Goldman and Taylor (1966), Taylor (1981) and Tomlinson (1981) for overviews of this research. See Amos and Parmar (1981) and Lawrence (1982) for criticisms of this research approach.

2 Throughout the research period, I attended meetings of black parents and teachers concerning racist practices in the local schools.

3 See Thomas (1928) who maintains that, 'if men see situations as real, they are real in their consequences'. This concept is of particular significance in the study of racism where there is frequently a large gap between the objective and subjective dimensions of social reality.

4 Allen (1982, p. 147) points out that the explanation of black youths' resistance to schooling in terms of generational differences has an earlier and more specific history in relation to the sociology of youth during the 1950s and 1960s.

5 As Hebdige (1979, p. 36) comments: 'Somewhere between Trenchtown and Ladbroke Grove, the cult of Rastafari had become a "style": an expressive combination of "locks", of khaki camouflage and "weed" which proclaimed unequivocally the alienation felt by many young black Britons. Alienation could scarcely be avoided: it was built into the lives of the young working-class West Indians in the form of bad housing, unemployment and police harassment.' See also Hebdige (1976, 1987) and Campbell (1980) for further discussion of the history of Rastafarianism and its significance for young working-class blacks in Britain.

6 This is of particular importance for black youth, which is often misread by 'race-relations' theorists, who do not address themselves to the question of the political structure of the black community. Behind this apolitical stance is hidden an appeal to national homogeneity, as Carby (1980) maintains. She (ibid., p. 2) attacks the assumed nationalist consensus of official reports and documents, arguing that, 'Inherent contradictions and conflicting interests . . . within and between racial, sexual and class groupings are contained by and subsumed under an apparent unity of interests.' See also Gilroy (1981, p. 212) for a critique of conventional approaches, which he argues, impose their own Eurocentric models of political activity onto blacks. For him, the 'community' is a vital analytical concept for an understanding of the black community's political structure and activity. He writes: 'Localised struggles over education, racist violence and police practices continually reveal how black people have made use of notions of community to provide the axis along which to organize themselves.' It is within this context that I examine the students' resistance to schooling.

7 The image of 'rebellious' black workers and children is to be found in the early 'race-relations' literature (e.g. Banton, 1959; Patterson, 1963; Davidson, 1966).

Hence, their response to racist practices cannot be reduced to the Nottingham/ Notting Hill rebellions of 1958. However, a reading of the current literature of this history suggests the absence of such a response. More recently, a number of theorists have addressed themselves to the question of the black community's resistance to racism since their arrival in Britain. So, for example, Joshua *et al.* (1983, p. 1), in examining the 1980 'Bristol riot', argue that this was not a recent phenomenon, but rather that 'collective racial violence', understood politically 'as an expression of political struggles and aspirations of the black communities settled in Britain', has been an integral part of the history of black settlement in Britain throughout the century. Sivanandan's (1982) historical analysis is the most comprehensive account of the black community's political structure and resistance to racism. He traces the move from resistance to open rebellion in the early 1980s and locates within this process the growth of the unity between the Afro-Caribbeans' and Asians' struggles. See James (1980).

8 Dhondy (1978, p. 81) has described the growth of black student and parent movements, who organized around various educational issues, such as banding, busing and Educational Sub-Normal schools. He points out that, '. . . there was a black movement in education in this country from the time that our children began to be schooled here. Its spokesmen were the parents of young blacks who were born here or brought here from the West Indies, from India, Pakistan and Bangladesh and Africa, as dependents.' See also Bryan *et al.* (1985, p. 78) for details of the central role of women in these movements, for example, in leading the campaign against 'sin bins', i.e. disruptive units.

9 See, for example, Stares *et al.* (1980) and Smith (1980).

10 See Hall *et al.* (1978), Sivanandan (1982), Gilroy (1982) and Gutzmore (1983), who have developed a class analysis of black youths' social location and their ideologies of resistance.

11 See, for example, Hargreaves (1967), Lacey (1970), Willis (1977) and Ball (1981) for a discussion of polarization/differentiation processes.

12 Including, for example, Rose *et al.* (1969) and Khan (1979).

13 Hebdige (1979, pp. 5–19) is the classic text here. He combines Barthes (1972) semiotic approach (semiotics is the study of the life of signs in society) and Gramsci's (1971) concept of hegemony in order to analyse the meanings of youth sub-cultures. Having explored the insights of these two theorists, Hebdige writes: 'Style in sub-culture is then pregnant with significance. . . . Our task becomes, like Barthes', to discern the hidden messages inscribed in code on the glossy surfaces of style, to trace them out as "maps of meaning" which obscurely re-present the very contradictions they are designed to resolve or conceal' (p. 18).

14 Similarly, one of the main concerns of conventional 'race-relations' research has been the assumed 'social problems' of Afro-Caribbean male youth, including patterns of deviant behaviour and negative attitudes to authority, particularly the police, negative identity problems, homelessness, as a result of conflict with parents, and their educational and employment problems. See John (1981).

15 The Rasta Heads 'toughness' also informed their conception of their masculinity. Like Willis' Lads, the Rasta Heads were overtly sexist and felt that they had the implicit support of most of the male staff for their views. In a racist society, gender relations between blacks takes on specific meanings. See Carby (1982b), who points to the limitations of white feminism for black women. A view shared by the Black Sisters. The best material on gender relations has been written by black

novelists, such as Baldwin, Walker and Angelou. Lorde (1985, p. 267) writes, 'As Black people, we cannot begin our dialogue by denying the oppressive nature of *male privilege*. And if Black males choose to assume that privilege, for whatever reason, raping, brutalizing, and killing women, then we cannot ignore Black male oppression. One oppression does not justify another. As a people, we should most certainly work together to end our common oppression, and toward a future which is viable for us all. In that context, it is shortsighted to believe that Black men alone are to blame for the above situations, in a society dominated by white male privilege. But the Black male consciousness must be raised so that he realizes that sexism and women-hating are critically dysfunctional to his liberation as a Black man. . . . Until this is done, he will view sexism and the destruction of Black women only as tangential to the cause of Black liberation rather than as central to that struggle . . .' [Lorde's emphasis]. See Weis (1985, pp. 21–6) who discusses gender and student culture.

16 See, for example, Jeffcoate (1979) and Willey (1982).

17 The best known work in this area is that of Rosenthal and Jacobson (1968). Sharp and Green (1975) are critical of the phenomenological approach to this concept that reduces it to a question of teacher consciousness. However, as Apple (1979, p. 140) argues, in pointing to the limitations of labelling theory and its resulting self-fulfilling prophecy, he is not suggesting that, '. . . one should throw out social phenomenology or labelling theory. Instead one combines it with a more critical social interpretation that looks at the creation of identities and meanings in specific institutions like schools as taking place within a context that often determines the parameters of what is negotiable or meaningful. This context . . . is the nexus of the economic and political institutions, a nexus which defines what schools should be about, that sets the limits on the parameters.'

18 Gilroy (1981, p. 210) maintains that an aspect of primary importance to the specificity of the black struggle is the centrality of cultural forms of resistance. Here 'race' is not reduced to a question of ethnicity or custom but rather racist and anti-racist ideology and black resistance are seen as an element of class conflict. He writes, '. . . the politics of black liberation is cultural in a special sense: Coons, Pakis, Nignogs, Sambos and Wogs are cultural constructions in ideological struggle. Cultures of resistance develop to contest them and the power they inform, as one aspect of the struggle against capitalist domination which blacks experience as racial oppression. This is a class struggle in and through race.'

19 Chessum (1980, p. 115) lists the limitations of the social democratic view of education as the central element in attaining equality of opportunity.

Chapter 4

1 Green (1982, p. 30) argues that there is a need to examine how racism operates in differential ways against Asians and Afro-Caribbeans. This may then lead to an understanding of how these groups respond to and manage their experience of racism. Also important, as Parmar (1982, pp. 245–6) points out is the influence of patriarchal relations, for example, on immigration legislation.

2 For example, Ballard and Ballard (1977, p. 44) maintain that Asian youths' generational conflict tends to be a temporary adolescent rebellion, with the youths resolving their problems in their later teens. This perception of limited inter-

generational conflict among the community, with its emphasis on the central unity of the extended family network, serves to heighten the sociological and psychological focus on the assumed generational divisions among Afro-Caribbeans. Furthermore, the differential education attainment of the Asians and the Afro-Caribbeans has been explained in terms of ethnic differences. So, for example, Cashmore and Troyna (1982, p. 16) present Asian youth as culturally secure, experiencing few social problems and, consequently, adopting a conformist approach to school, which results in their high academic achievement.

3 During the research period, a number of Asian youth gangs were formed in the local area.

4 This is an interesting additional aspect to Hebdige's (1979, p. 45) observation that, 'We can watch played out on the loaded surfaces of British working-class youth cultures, a phantom history of race-relations since the war.'

5 See Hebdige's (1979, pp. 36–7) description of the rude boy as an archetypal rebel. He writes: 'The rude boys formed a deviant sub-culture in Jamaica in the mid to late 60s. Flashy, urban, "rough and tough", they were glamourized in a string of reggae and rock steady hits.'

6 Like the Rasta Heads, this projected 'tough image' informed their perception of their own masculinity, which in turn reinforced overt sexist discourse, attitudes and practices to female peers and teachers. See Foucault (1979) for a discussion of the history of discourses about sexuality and the operation of power. The latter was particularly evident, for example, when the Warriors discussed future marriage arrangments. This is a complex area of social behaviour that I am presently examining. As Griffin (1986, p. 104) points out, '. . . research on men has seldom examined the influence of gender relations or masculinity (one recent exception is Wood, 1984)'. However, what should be challenged is the racist notion, held by many teachers at Kilby school and Connolly college, that Asian males are intrinsically more sexist than white men, particularly white middle-class men, due to cultural determinants.

7 For examples of white working-class racism, see Cochrane and Billig (1984).

8 See Hall *et al.* (1978) for a discussion of the construction of negative images of black people in the media. They describe how the term 'mugging' came to symbolize the crisis of law and order in the early 1970s, while at the same time associating street crime with young male Afro-Caribbeans. More recently, the media have misrepresented the findings of the inquiry into Manchester's Burnage High School, suggesting that anti-racist policies were responsible for the death of an Asian boy, Ahmed Iqbal Ullah. See Dummett (1988) and John (1988) for a discussion of this and for evidence of racist attacks on black people.

9 At the time of the research there were an increasing number of young Asians, female and male, including the Warriors, who were involved in leisure activities outside of Kilby in the city centre. This was a recent development.

10 Sivanandan (1982, p. 32) records the central importance of the women's struggles 'at the factory-gate, on the streets, in the home, at the schools and in the hospitals', to the black community's resistance to racism. See also Sivanandan (1983, p. 4).

11 For further information concerning the relations between the police and the Asian and Afro-Caribbean communities, see Moore (1975), Institute of Race Relations (1979) and Gutzmore (1983). A number of incidents during the research highlighted these relations within the Kilby area.

12 There was a developing awareness of common interests between the Warriors and the Rasta Heads, that was reflected in the wider society (see Gilroy, 1981, p. 217). Widgery (1986) writes of the potential for developing awareness of common interests between white working-class and black youth, citing Rock against Racism as an important example of how this unity can be achieved. More recently, in London, June 1988, the same spirit of unity was displayed at an anti-apartheid concert to celebrate Nelson Mandela's seventieth birthday.

References

Aggleton, P. (1987). *Rebels Without a Cause: Middle Class Youth and the Transition from School to Work*. London, Falmer Press.

Allen, S. (1982). 'Confusing categories and neglecting contradictions', in E. Cashmore and B. Troyna (eds.), *Black Youth in Crisis*, pp. 143–58. London, Allen and Unwin.

ALTARF (1984). *Challenging Racism*. London, All London Teachers Against Racism and Facism.

Althusser, L. (1971). *Lenin and Philosophy and Other Essays*. London, New Left Books.

Amos, V. and Parmar, P. (1981). 'Resistances and responses: the experiences of Black girls in Britain', in A. McRobbie and T. McCabe (eds.), *Feminism for Girls: An Adventure Story*, pp. 96–108. London, Routledge and Kegan Paul.

Anyon, J. (1983). 'Intersections of gender and class: Accommodation and resistance by working-class and affluent females to contradictory sex-role ideologies', in S. Walker and L. Barton (eds.) *Gender, Class and Education*, pp. 19–37. Lewes, Falmer Press.

Apple, M. W. (1979). *Ideology and Curriculum*. London, Routledge and Kegan Paul.

Apple, M. W. and Taxel, J. (1982). 'Ideology and the curriculum', in A. Hartnett (ed.), *The Social Sciences in Educational Studies: A Selective Guide to the Literature*, pp. 166–78. London, Heinemann.

Arnot, M. (1986). *Race, Gender and Education Policy-making*. E333, module 4. Milton Keynes, Open Univeristy Press.

Arnot, M. and Weiner, G. (eds.) (1987). *Gender and Politics*, Milton Keynes, Open University Press.

Ball, S. J. (1981). *Beachside Comprehensive*. Cambridge, Cambridge University Press.

Ball, S. J. (1987). *The Micro-politics of the School: Towards a Theory of School Organization*. London, Methuen.

Ballard, R. and Ballard, C. (1977). 'The Sikhs: the development of South Asian settlements in Britain', in J. L. Watson (ed.), *Between Two Cultures*, pp. 21–56. Oxford, Blackwell.

Ballard, R. and Driver, G. (1977). 'The ethnic approach'. *New Society*, 16 June, 543–5.

Banks, J. and Lynch, J. (eds.) (1986). *Multicultural Education in Western Societies*. London, Holt, Rinehart and Winston.

Banton, M. (1959). *White and Coloured: The Behaviour of the British People Towards Coloured Immigrants*. London, Jonathan Cape.

Barker, M. (1981). *The New Racism*. London, Junction Books.

Barrat, D. (1986). *Media Sociology*. London, Tavistock.

Barthes, R. (1972). *Mythologies*. London, Paladin.

Bates, I. Clarke, J. Cohen, P., Finn, D., Moore, R. and Willis, P. (eds.) (1984). *Schooling for the Dole?: The New Vocationalism*. London, Macmillan.

Becker, H. S. (1952). 'Social class variations in the teacher–pupil relationship'. *Journal of Educational Psychology*, 25, April. (Cited in M. Keddie (1971), 'Classroom Knowledge' in M. F. D. Young (ed.) *Knowledge and Control*, p. 125. London, Routledge and Keegan Paul.

Bernstein, B. (1975). *Class, Codes and Control, Vol. 3: Towards a Theory of Educational Transmissions*. London, Routledge and Kegan Paul.

Bourdieu, P. and Passeron, J.C. (1977). *Reproduction in Education, Society and Culture*. Beverly Hills, Sage.

Bourne, J. (1983). 'Towards an anti-racist feminism'. *Race and Class*, **XXV** (1), Summer. London, Institute of Race Relations.

Bourne, J. and Sivanandan, A. (1980). 'Cheerleaders and ombudsmen: the sociology of race relations in Britain'. *Race and Class*, **XXI** (4), 331–52.

Bowles, J. and Gintis, M. (1976). *Schooling in Capitalist America: Educational Reform and the Contradictions of Economic Life*. London, Routledge and Kegan Paul.

Brah, A. and Deem, R. (1986). 'Towards anti-racist and anti-sexist schooling', *Critical Social Policy*, 16, pp. 66–79.

Brah, A. and Minhas, R. (1985). 'Structural racism or cultural difference: schooling for Asian girls', in G. Weiner (ed.) *Just a Bunch of Girls*. Milton Keynes, Open University Press.

Brake, M. (1980). *The Sociology of Youth Culture and Youth Sub-cultures*. London, Routledge and Kegan Paul.

Brent LEA (1983). *Education for a Multicultural Democracy*. London, Brent LEA.

Brittan, E. M. (1976). 'Multi-racial education. 2. Teacher opinion on aspects of school life – pupils and teachers'. *Educational Research*, 18, 182–91.

Bryan, B., Dadzie, S. and Scafe, S. (1985). *The Heart of the Race: Black Women's Lives in Britain*. London, Virago.

Burgess, R. (1984). 'Headship: freedom or constraint?', in S. J. Ball (ed.), *Comprehensive Schooling: A Reader*, pp. 201–26. Lewes, Falmer Press.

Campbell, H. (1980). 'Rastafari: culture of resistance'. *Race and Class*, **XVII** (1), 1–23.

Carby, H. V. (1980). 'Multicultural fictions'. Occasional Stencilled Paper. Race Series: SP No. 58. Centre for Contemporary Cultural Studies, University of Birmingham.

Carby, H. V. (1982a). 'Schooling in Babylon', in Centre for Contemporary Cultural Studies (Race and Politics Group), *The Empire Strikes Back: Race and Racism in '70s Britain*, pp. 183–211. London, Hutchinson/CCCS, University of Birmingham.

Carby, H. V. (1982b). 'White women listen! Black feminism and the boundaries of sisterhood', in Centre for Contemporary Cultural Studies (Race and Politics Group), *The Empire Strikes Back: Race and Racism in '70s Britain*, pp. 212–35. London, Hutchinson/CCCS, University of Birmingham.

Carr, E. H. (1983). *What is History?* London, Penguin.

Carrington, B. (1983). 'Sport as a side-track: An analysis of West Indian involvement in extra-curricular sport', in L. Barton and S. Walker (eds.), *Race, Class and Education*, pp. 40–65. London, Croom Helm.

Cashmore, E. and Troyna, B. (eds.) (1982). *Black Youth in Crisis*. London, Allen and Unwin.

Castles, S. and Kosack, G. (1973). *Immigrant Workers and the Class Structure*. London, Oxford University Press and Institute of Race Relations.

Chessum, R. (1980). 'Teacher ideologies and pupil dissaffection', in L. Barton, R. Meighan and S. Walker (eds.), *Schooling, Ideology and the Curriculum*, pp. 113–29. Lewes, Falmer Press.

Chevannes, M. and Reeves, F. (1987). 'The black voluntary school movement: definition, context and prospects', in B. Troyna (ed.), *Racial Inequality in Education*, pp. 147–69, London, Tavistock.

Chigwada, R. (1987). 'Not victims – not superwomen'. *Spare Rib*, 183, 14–18.

Cicourel, A. V. and Kitsuse, J. (1963). *The Educational Decision-Makers*. Indianapolis, Bobbs-Merrill.

Clarke, J. and Willis, P. (1984). 'Introduction', in I. Bates, J. Clarke, P. Cohen, D. Finn, R. Moore and P. Willis *et al.* (eds.), *Schooling for the Dole?: The New Vocationalism*, pp. 1–16. London, Macmillan.

Clarke, J., Hall, S., Jefferson, T. and Roberts, B. (1976). 'Sub-cultures, cultures and class: A theoretical overview', in S. Hall and T. Jefferson (eds), *Resistance Through Rituals: Youth Sub-cultures in Post-war Britain*, pp. 9–74. London, Hutchinson/CCCS, University of Birmingham.

Coard, B. (1971). *How the West Indian Child is made Educationally Subnormal in the British School System*. London, New Beacon Books.

Cochrane, R. and Billig, M. (1984). 'I'm not National Front myself, but . . .'. *New Society*, 17 May, 256–9.

Cohen, A. K. (1965). 'The sociology of the deviant act'. *American Sociological Review*, 30, 1–14.

Cohen, P. (1972). 'Sub-cultural conflict and working-class community'. Working Papers in Cultural Studies 2, University of Birmingham.

Cohen, P. and Bains, H. (1986). *Multi-Racist Britain*. London, Hutchinson.

Commission for Racial Equality (1982). Racial Attacks. Cited in *Post and Star*, March 18, p. 6.

Commission for Racial Equality (1988). *Learning in Terror: a survey of racial harassment in schools and colleges*. London, C.R.E.

Community Relations Commission (1976). *Between Two Cultures: a Study of Relationships between Generations in the Asian Community in Britain*. London, C.R.C.

Conner, T. (1985). *Irish Youth in London Research Report*. London, Action Group for Irish Youth.

Corrigan, P. (1979). *Schooling the Smash Street Kids*. London, Macmillan.

Cross, M. and Smith, D. I. (eds.) (1987). *Black Youth Futures*. Leicester, National Youth Bureau.

Curtis, L. (1985). *Nothing but the Same Old Story: The Roots of Anti-Irish Racism*. London, Information on Ireland.

Dale, R. (1982). 'Education and the capitalist State: contributions and contradictions', in M. W. Apple (ed.), *Cultural and Economic Reproduction in Education: Essays on Class, Ideology and the State*, pp. 127–61. London, Routledge and Kegan Paul.

Davidson, R. B. (1966). *Black British*. Oxford, Oxford University Press.

Davies, L. (1984). *Pupil Power: Deviance and Gender in School*. Lewes, Falmer Press.

Davis, A. (1981). *Women, Race and Class*. London, Women's Press.

Deem, R. (1978). *Women and Schooling*. London, Routledge and Kegan Paul.

Denscombe, M. (1980). 'Keeping 'em quiet: The significance of noise for the practical activity of teaching', in P. Woods (ed.), *Teacher Strategies: Explorations in the Sociology of the School*, pp. 61–83. Hants, Saxon House.

Department of Education and Science (1965). *The Education of Immigrants*. Circular 7/65 London, HMSO.

Dhondy, F. (1974). 'The Black explosion in schools'. *Race Today*, 6 (2), February, 44–50.

Dhondy, F. (1978). 'Teaching young Blacks'. *Race Today*, 10 (4), May/June, 80–6.

Dixon, B. (1982). *Now Read on: Recommended Fiction for Young People*. London, Pluto Press.

Dodd, A. (1978). 'Police and thieves on the streets of London'. *New Society*, 16 March, 598–600.

Driver, G. (1980). *Beyond Underachievement*. London, Commission for Racial Equality.

Duffield, M. (1984). 'New racism . . . new realism: two sides of the same coin'. *Radical Philosophy*, 37, 29–34.

Dummett, A. (1984). *A Portrait of English Racism*. London, CARAF.

Dummett, A. (1988). 'Death in the playground', *The Tablet*, 28 May, pp. 610–11.

Dummett, A. and McCrudden, C. (1982). *Government Policy and Legislation*. Unit 7 of Open University Course E354. Milton Keynes, Open University Press.

Edwards, V. (1986). *Language in a Black Community*. Clevedon, Multilingual Matters.

Eggleston, S. J., Dunn, D. K. and Anjali, M. with the assistance of Wright, C. (1985). *The Educational and Vocational Experiences of 15–18 Year Old Young People of Ethnic Minority Groups*. A report to the Department of Education and Science. Warwick, University of Warwick.

Everhart, R. B. (1983). *Reading, Writing and Resistance: Adolescence and Labour in a Junior High School*. London, Routledge and Kegan Paul.

Figueroa, P. E. (1974). 'West Indian school-leavers in a London borough, 1966–67'. Unpublished Ph.D thesis, University of London, London School of Economics and political Science.

Finn, D., Grant, M. and Johnson, R. (1977). 'Social democracy, education and the crisis', in *Working Papers in Cultural Studies 10: On Ideology*. London, Hutchinson/CCCS, University of Birmingham.

Foucault, M. (1979). *The History of Sexuality*, Vol. 1. Harmondsworth, Penguin.

Frith, S. and Corrigan, P. (1976). 'The politics of education'. Paper presented to the Conference on Political Economy and Schooling, Bells Park College, Hertford.

Fryer (1984). *Staying Power: The History of Black People in Britain*. London, Pluto Press.

Fuller, M. (1980). 'Black girls in a London comprehensive school', in R. Deem (ed.). *Schooling for Women's Work*, pp. 52–65. London, Routledge and Kegan Paul.

Genovese, E. D. (1972). *Roll, Jordan, Roll: The World the Slaves Made*. New York, Pantheon.

Giles, R. (1977). *The West Indian Experience in British Schools: Multi-racial Education and Social Disadvantage in London*. London, Heinemann.

Gilroy, P. (1981). 'You can't fool the youths . . . race and class formation in the 1980s'. *Race and Class*, **23** (2/3), 207–22. London, Institute of Race Relations.

Gilroy, P. (1982). 'Police and thieves', in Centre for Contemporary Cultural Studies (Race and Politics Group), *The Empire Strikes Back: Race and Racism in '70s Britain*, pp. 143–82. London, Hutchinson/CCCS, University of Birmingham.

Gilroy, P. (1987). *There Ain't No Black in The Union Jack: The Cultural Politics of Race and Nation*. London, Hutchinson.

Ginsberg, M. B., Meyenn, R. J. and Miller, H. R. (1980). 'Teachers' conceptions of professionalism and trade unionism: an ideological analysis', in P. Woods (ed.), *Teacher Strategies: Explorations in the Sociology of the School*, pp. 178–212. London, Croom Helm.

Giroux, H. (1983). *Theory and Resistance in Education*. London, Heinemann.

Glaser, B. and Strauss, A. (1967). *The Discovery of Grounded Theory: Strategies for Qualitative Research*. London, Weidenfeld and Nicolson.

Goldman, R. J. and Taylor, F. (1966). 'Coloured immigrant children: a survey of research studies and literature on their educational problems and potential in Britain'. *Educational Research*, **8** (3), 163–83.

Gow, D. (1988). 'Blacks still hit by Racism in Schools', *The Guardian*, 16 March, p. 10.

Gramsci, A. (1971). *Selection from the Prison Notebooks*. London, Lawrence and Wishart.

Green, A. (1982). 'In defence of anti-racist teaching: a reply to critiques of multi-cultural education'. *Multiracial Education*, **10** (2), 19–35. London, NAME.

Green, P. (1985). 'Multi-Ethnic Teaching and the Pupils self-concepts in Annex B. The Committee of Enquiry Into the Education of Children from Ethnic Minority Groups', in *Education For All*. London, H.M.S.O.

Griffin, C. (1985). *Typical Girls?: Young Women from School to the Job Market*. London, Routledge and Kegan Paul.

Griffin, C. (1986). 'Its different for girls: the use of qualitative methods in the study of young women's lives', in H. Beloff (ed.), *Getting Into Life*, pp. 95–115. London, Methuen.

Gutzmore, C. (1983). 'Capital, Black youth and crime'. *Race and Class*, **25** (2), 13–30. London, Institute of Race Relations.

Hall, S. (1980). 'Race, articulation and societies structured in dominance'. *Sociological Theories: Race and Colonialism*. Paris, UNESCO.

Hall, S. (1987). 'Getting it right on race'. Talk given in Birmingham, 24 November, Politics in Motion, Marxism Today.

Hall, S. and Jacques, M. (eds.) (1983). *The Politics of Thatcherism*. London, Lawrence and Wishart/Marxism Today.

Hall, S. Critcher, C., Jefferson, T., Clarke, J. and Roberts, B. (1978). *Policing the Crisis: Mugging, the State and Law and Order*. London, Macmillan.

Hall, S., Ouseley, H., Vaz, K. *et al.* (1986). *A Different Reality: An Account of Black People's Experiences and their Grievances Before and After the Handsworth Rebellion of 1985: A Report of the Review Panel*. West Midlands County Council.

Hammersley, M. (1977). *Teacher Perspectives*. The Open University Course E202. Schooling and Society Block 11. The Process of Schooling. Units 9 and 10. Milton Keynes, The Open University.

Hammersley, M. and Woods, P. (1987). 'Methodological debate: ethnography'. *British Educational Research Journal*, **13** (3), 283–317.

Hargreaves, A. (1978). 'The significance of classroom coping strategies', in L. Barton and R. Meighan (eds.), *Sociological Interpretations of Schooling and Classrooms: A Reappraisal*, pp. 73–100. London, Nafferton Books.

Hargreaves, A. (1981). 'Contrastive rhetoric and extremist talk: teachers' hegemony and the educational context', in L. Barton and S. Walker (eds.), *Schools, Teachers and Teaching*, pp. 303–30. Lewes, Falmer Press.

Hargreaves, A. and Woods, P. (eds.). (1984). *Classrooms and Staffrooms: The Sociology of Teachers and Teaching*. Milton Keynes, Open University Press.

Hargreaves, D. H. (1967). *Social Relations in a Secondary School*. London, Routledge and Kegan Paul.

Hargreaves, D. H., Hestor, S. and Mellor, F. (1975). *Deviance in Classrooms*. London, Routledge and Kegan Paul.

Hatcher, R. (1987). ' "Race" and education: two perspectives for change', in B. Troyna (ed.), *Racial Inequality in Education*, pp. 184–200. London, Tavistock.

Hebdige, D. (1976). 'Reggae, Rastas and Rudies', in S. Hall and T. Jefferson (eds.), *Resistance Through Rituals: Youth Sub-cultures in Post-war Britain*, pp. 135–53. London, Hutchinson/CCCS, University of Birmingham.

Hebdige, D. (1979). *Subculture: The Meaning of Style*. London, Methuen.

Hebdige, D. (1987). *Cut 'N' Mix: Culture, Identity and Caribbean Music*. London, Comedia.

Hickman, M. J. (ed.) (1986). *The History of the Irish in Britain: A Bibliography*. London, Irish in Britain History Centre.

Hiro, D. (1971). *Black British, White British*. London, Monthly Review.

Home Office, (1981). *Racial Attacks*. London, HMSO.

Hooks, B. (1982). *Ain't I A Woman: Black Women and Feminism*. London, Pluto Press.

Husband, C. (ed.) (1982). *'Race' in Britain: Continuity and Change*. London, Hutchinson.

Inner London Education Authority (1979). *London English Papers: Helping Pupils to Write Better*. London, Learning Materials Centre.

Inner London Education Authority (1983a). *Race, Sex and Class, a Policy for Equality: Race*. London, ILEA.

Inner London Education Authority (1983b). *Race, Sex and Class, Anti-racist Statement and Guidelines*. London, ILEA.

Institute of Race Relations (1979) *Police Against Black People* London, IRR.

Institute of Race Relations (1982a). *Roots of Racism*. London, IRR.

Institute of Race Relations (1982b). *Patterns of Racism*. London, IRR.

Institute of Race Relations (1985). *How Racism Came to Britain*. London, IRR.

Jackson, P. W. (1968). *Life in Classrooms*. New York, Holt Rinehart and Winson.

James, C. L. R. (1980). *The Black Jacobins: Toussaint L'Ouverture and the San Domingo Revolution* (Revised edition). London, Allison and Busby.

Jeffcoate, R. (1979). *Positive Image: Towards a Multi-Cultural Curriculum*. London, Chamaeleon.

Jenkins, R. (1966). Speech to the National Committee for Commonwealth Immigrants, 23 May.

John, G. (1981). *In the Service of Black Youth*. London, National Association of Youth Clubs.

John, G. (1988). 'Glimmer of light in the racist gloom', *The Guardian*, 3 May, p. 25.

Joshua, H. and Wallace, T. with Booth, M. (1983). *To Ride the Storm: The 1980*

Bristol 'Riot' and the State. London, Heinemann.

Keddie, N. (1971). 'Classroom knowledge', in M. F. D. Young (ed.), *Knowledge and Control*, pp. 113–60. London, Collier/Macmillan.

Keddie, N. (ed.) (1973). *Tinker, Tailor . . . The Myth of Cultural Deprivation*. Harmondsworth, Penguin.

Khan, V. S. (ed.) (1979). *Minority Families in Britain: Support and Stress*. London, Tavistock.

Kirp, D. L. (1979). *Doing Good by Doing Little: Race and Schooling in Britain*. London, University of California Press.

Lacey, C. (1970). *Hightown Grammar*. Manchester, Manchester University Press.

Lacey, C. (1976). 'Problems of sociological fieldwork: A review of the methodology of Hightown Grammar', in M. Hammersley and P. Woods (eds.), *The Process of Schooling: A Sociological Reader*, pp. 55–65. London, Routledge and Kegan Paul.

Lacey, C. (1977). *The Socialization of Teachers*. London, Methuen.

Lambart, A. M. (1976). 'The Sisterhood', in M. Hammersley and P. Woods (eds.), *The Process of Schooling*, pp. 152–9. London, Routledge and Kegan Paul.

Lawrence, E. (1981). 'White sociology, Black struggle'. *Multi-racial Education*, 9 (3), 43–8. London, NAME.

Lawrence, E. (1982). 'In the abundance of water the fool is thirsty: sociology and Black "pathology" ', in Centre for Contemporary Cultural Studies (Race and Politics Group), *Resistance Through Rituals: Youth Sub-cultures in Post-war Britain*, pp. 95–142. London, Hutchinson/CCCS, University of Birmingham.

Lettieri, A. (1976). 'Factory and school', in A. Gorz (ed.), *The Division of Labour*, pp. 145–58. Sussex, Harvester Press.

Llewellyn, M. (1980). 'Studying girls at school: The implications of confusion', in R. Deem (ed.), *Schooling for Women's Work*, pp. 42–51. London, Routledge and Kegan Paul.

Lorde, A. (1985). 'My words will be there', in M. Evans (ed.), *Black Women Writers*, pp. 259–68. London, Pluto Press.

Marable, M. (1985). *Black American Politics*. London, Verso.

Mays, J. B. (1962). *Education and the Urban Child*. Liverpool, Liverpool University Press.

McCall, G. S. and Simmons, J. L. (eds.) (1969). *Issues in Participant Observation: A Text and Reader*. New York, Addison-Wesley.

McRobbie, A. (1978). 'Working class girls and the culture of femininity', in Women's Studies Group, CCCS (eds.), *Women Take Issue: Aspects of Women's Subordination*, pp. 113–28. London, Hutchinson.

McRobbie, A. (1980). 'Settling accounts with subcultures: a feminist critique'. *Screen Education*, 34, 37–49.

Mead, G. H. (1934). *Mind, Self and Society*. Chicago, University of Chicago Press.

Meighan, R. and Brown, C. (1980). 'Locations of learning and ideologies of education: some issues raised by the study of "Education Otherwise" ', in L. Barton, R. Meighan and S. Walker (eds.), *Schooling, Ideology and the Curriculum*, pp. 131–52. Lewes, Falmer Press.

Meyenn, R. J. (1979). 'Peer networks and school performance'. Unpublished Ph.D, University of Aston in Birmingham.

Miles, R. (1978). 'Between two cultures: The Case of Rastafarianism'. Working papers on ethnic relations, no. 10. SSRC Research Unit on Ethnic Relations, University of Aston in Birmingham.

Mills, C. Wright (1970). *The Sociological Imagination*. Harmondsworth, Penguin.

Milner, D. (1975). *Children and Race*. Harmondsworth, Penguin.

Mirza, H. S. (1986). 'Black girls and the Swann Report'. *Multi-cultural Education Review*, 5, Spring, 39–40.

Moore, R. (1975). *Racism and Black Resistance in Britain*. London, Pluto Press.

Moore, R. (1984). 'Schooling and the world of work', in I. Bates, L. J. Clarke, P. Cohen, D. Finn, R. Moore and P. Willis (eds.), *Schooling for the Dole?: The New Vocationalism*, pp. 65–103. London, Macmillan.

Mullard, C. (1980). 'Racism in society and schools: history, policy and practice'. Occasional paper no. 1, Centre for Multi-cultural Education. University of London, Institute of Education.

National Union of Teachers (1979). *In Black and White: Guidelines for Teachers on Racial Stereotyping in Textbooks and Learning Materials*. London, NUT.

Offe, C. (1984). *Contradictions of the Welfare State*. London, Hutchinson.

Parmar, P. (1982). 'Gender, race and class: Asian women in resistance', in Centre for Contemporary Cultural Studies (Race and Politics Group), *The Empire Strikes Back: Race and Racism in '70s Britain*, pp. 236–75. London, Hutchinson/CCCS, University of Birmingham.

Patterson, S. (1963). *Dark Strangers*. London, Tavistock.

Perkins, T. E. (1979). 'Rethinking stereotypes', in Barrett M., Corrigan, P., Kuhn, A., and Wolff, J. (eds.) *Ideology and Cultural Production*, pp. 135–59. London, Croom Helm.

Pollard, A. (1982). 'A model of classroom coping strategies'. *British Journal of Sociology of Education*, 3, 1.

Pollard, A. (1985). *The Social World of the Primary School*. London, Holt.

Race Today (1974). 'No longer sleeping rough', 6 (5), May, 140–1.

Race Today (1975). 'Who's afraid of ghetto schools?' 1 (1), January, 8–10.

Race Today (1976). 'A show of strength', 8 (6), June, 123.

Race Today (1979). 'Southall: what is to be done?', 11 (3), May/June, 52–4.

Race Today (1982). 'Reflecting on the trial of the decade: the Bradford 12', 14 (4), August/September, 124–32.

Rampton Report (1981). *West Indian Children in our Schools*. London, HMSO.

Reeves, F. and Chevannes, M. (1981). 'The underachievement of Rampton'. *Multi-racial Education*. 10 (1), 35–42. London, NAME.

Rex, J. (1973). *Race, Colonialism and the City*. London, Routledge and Kegan Paul.

Rex, J. and Tomlinson, S. (1979). *Colonial Immigrants in a British City: A Class Analysis*. London, Routledge and Kegan Paul.

Riley, K. (1985). 'Black girls speak for themselves', in G. Weiner (ed.), *Just a Bunch of Girls*, pp. 63–76. Milton Keynes, Open University Press.

Rist, R. (1977). 'On understanding the process of schooling: The contribution of labelling theory', in J. Karabel and A. H. Halsey (eds.), *Power and Ideology in Education*, pp. 292–305. New York, Oxford University Press.

Roberts, E. (1984). *A Woman's Place: An Oral History of Working-class Women 1980–1940*. Oxford, Blackwell.

Rose, E. J. B. in association with Deakin, N. and Abrams, M., Jackson, V., Peston, M., Vanags, A. H., Cohen, B., Gaitskell, J. and Ward, P. (1969). *Colour and Citizenship – A Report on Race Relations in Britain*. Oxford, Oxford University Press.

Rosenthal, R. and Jacobson, L. (1968). *Pygmalion in the Classroom*. Holt, Rinehart and Winston.

Sargeant, R. (1981). 'YOP washes whiter'. *Youth in Society*, November, National Youth Bureau, 16–17.

Select Committee on Race Relations and Immigration (1969). *The Problems of Coloured School Leavers*, Vols 1–4. London, HMSO.

Select Committee on Race Relations and Immigration (1973). *Education*, 1. London, HMSO.

Shakti (1983). 'Asian workers: emerging issues', January, 13–15.

Sharp, R. and Green, A. (1975). *Education and Social Control: A Study in Progressive Primary Education*. London, Routledge and Kegan Paul.

Sharpe, S. (1976). *Just Like a Girl*. Harmondsworth, Penguin.

Sivanandan, A. (1978). 'From immigration control to induced repatriation'. *Race and Class*, **XX**, 75–82 (1). London, Institute of Race Relations.

Sivanandan, A. (1982). *A Different Hunger*. London, Pluto Press.

Sivanandan, A. (1983). 'Challenging racism: strategies for the '80s'. *Race and Class* **XXV** (2), 1–11. London Institute of Race Relations.

Sivanandan, A. (1985a). 'RAT and the degradation of the black struggle'. *Race and Class*, **XXVI** (4), 1–33. London, Institute of Race Relations.

Sivanandan, A. (1985b). Talk to the Asian Teachers Association, 30 June, Birmingham.

Smith, D. (1980). 'Unemployment and racial minority groups'. *Department of Employment Gazette*, **88** (6), June, 604.

Solomos, J. (1983). 'Institutional racism: policies of marginalization in education and training'. Mimeo research on ethnic relations, University of Aston in Birmingham.

Solomos, J. (1986). 'Training for What?: Government Policies and the Politicisation of Black Youth Unemployment', in Z. Layton-Henry, and P. B. Rich, (eds.). *Race, Government and Politics in Britain*, pp. 204–26. London, Macmillan.

Spender, D. and Sarah, E. (eds) (1980). *Learning to Lose*. London, The Women's Press.

Stafford, A. (1981). 'Learning not to labour'. *Capital and Labour*, **51**, Autumn, 55–77.

Stanworth, M. (1981). *Gender and Schooling*. London, Women's Research and Resources Centre.

Stares, R., Imberg, D. and McRobbie, J. (1980). 'Ethnic minorities and MSC special programmes', cited in R. Sargeant, *Youth in Society*, November, National Youth Bureau.

Stebbins, R. A. (1980). 'The role of humour in teaching: strategy and self-expression', in P. Woods (ed.), *Teacher Strategies: Explorations in the Sociology of the School*, pp. 84–97. London, Croom Helm.

Stone, M. (1981). *The Education of the Black Child in Britain: The Myth of Multi-cultural Education*. London, Fontana.

Street-Porter, R. (1978). *Race, Children and Cities*. The Open University, Unit E361. Milton Keynes, Open University Press.

Swann Report (1985). *Education for All*. The Report of the Committee of Enquiry into the Education of Children from Ethnic Minority Groups. Cmnd 9543. London, HMSO.

Taylor, M. I. (1981). *Caught Between: A Review of Research into the Education of Pupils of West Indian Origin*. Windsor, NFER/Nelson.

Thomas, W. I. (1928). *The Child in America*. New York, Knorf.

Tomlinson, S. (1981). 'The educational performance of ethnic minority children', in

A. James and R. Jeffcoate (eds.), *The School in the Multi-Cultural Society*, pp. 119–46. London, Harper and Row.

Troyna, B. and Williams, J. (1986). *Racism, Education and the State*. London, Croom Helm.

Walker, S. and Barton, L. (eds.) (1983). *Gender, Class and Education*. Lewes, Falmer Press.

Waller, W. (1967). *The Sociology of Teaching*. New York, Wiley. (First published in 1932.)

Watson, J. L. (ed.) (1977). *Between Two Cultures*. Oxford, Blackwell.

Weber, M. (1948). 'Bureaucracy', in H. Gerth and C. W. Mills (eds.), *From Max Weber: Essays in Sociology* pp. 196–244. London, Routledge and Kegan Paul.

Weis, L. (1985). *Between Two Worlds: Black Students in an Urban Community College*. London, Routledge and Kegan Paul.

Whitty, G. (1985). *Sociology and School Knowledge*. London, Methuen.

Widgery, D. (1986). *Beating Time*. London, Chatto and Windus.

Willey, R. (1982). *Teacher Education in a Multi-Cultural Society*. London, CRE.

Williams, J. (1967). 'The younger generation', in J. Rex and R. Moore (eds.), *Race, Community and Conflict*, pp. 230–57. London, Oxford University Press and Institute of Race Relations.

Williams, J. (1986). 'Education and race: The racialization of class inequalities?' *British Journal of Sociology of Education*, 7 (2), 135–54.

Williams, R. (1961). *The Long Revolution*. Harmondsworth, Penguin.

Willis, P. (1977). *Learning to Labour: How Working-class Kids Get Working-class Jobs*. Hants, Saxon House.

Wilson, A. (1978). *Finding a Voice: Asian Women in Britain*. London, Virago.

Wolpe, A. M. (1977). *Some Processes in Sexist Education*. London, Women's Research and Resources Centre.

Wood, J. (1984). 'Groping towards sexism: boys' sex talk', in A. McRobbie and M. Nava (eds.), *Gender and Generation*, pp. 54–84. London, MacMillan.

Woods, P. (1977). 'Teaching for survival', in P. Woods and M. Hammersley (eds.), *School Experience: Explorations in the Sociology of Education*, pp. 271–93. London, Croom Helm.

Woods, P. and Pollard, A. (eds.) (1988). *Sociology And Teaching: A New Challenge for the Sociology of Education*. London, Croom Helm.

Wright, C. (1985). 'School processes: an ethnographic study', in S. J. Eggleston, D. K. Dunn and M. Anjali (with C. Wright), *The Educational and Vocational Experiences of 15–18 Year Old Young People of Ethnic Minority Groups*. A Report to the Department of Education and Science. Warwick, University of Warwick.

Young, M. and Whitty, G. (eds.) (1977). *Society, State and Schooling*. Lewes, Falmer Press.

Name Index

Subject Index